NATIONAL COMMUNISM

Also of Interest

† Available in hardcover and paperback.

About the Book and Author

NATIONAL COMMUNISM
Peter Zwick

According to the generally accepted view that nationalism is alien to communism and that internationalism disallows divisions based on nations, the existence of national communism is often interpreted as a sign of the breakup of the world communist movement. This book reexamines the evidence on the role of nations and national variations, beginning with Marx and moving through Leninism and Stalinism to Titoism, Maoism, Castroism, and current national liberation movements (e.g., in Nicaragua). Professor Zwick concludes that nationalism has always been an inherent element of communism. He demonstrates with numerous concrete cases that, rather than signaling the decline of communism, national adaptation is the source of its strength. The limits of national variation as defined by the Brezhnev Doctrine are precisely defined and examined in the cases of Hungary, Czechoslovakia, and Poland.

The book bridges the gap between Marxist theory and communist practice with respect to the central role that nationalism will continue to play in the contemporary world. No other study presents this material in a cross-national, comparative perspective.

Peter Zwick is an associate professor and acting chairman of the Department of Political Science and a member of the Russian area studies faculty at Louisiana State University. His research focuses on biographical studies of the Soviet political elite and analyses of administrative reorganization in the USSR, Soviet nationality policies, and Soviet socioeconomic development.

NATIONAL COMMUNISM

Peter Zwick

Westview Press • Boulder, Colorado

Published in 1983 in the United States of America by
  Westview Press, Inc.
  5500 Central Avenue
  Boulder, Colorado 80301
  Frederick A. Praeger, President and Publisher

Library of Congress Cataloging in Publication Data
Zwick, Peter, 1942–
  National communism.
  Includes bibliographical references and index.
  1. Nationalism and socialism. I. Title.
HX550.N3Z88 1983   335.43'5   82-17642
ISBN 0-86531-427-6
ISBN 0-86531-428-4 (pbk.)

Printed and bound in the United States of America

To Shelly

Contents

1
The Nationalist and Communist Roots of National Communism

In his classic critique of contemporary communism, *The New Class,* the Yugoslavian Marxist Milovan Djilas argued: "Today, national Communism is a general phenomenon in Communism. To varying degrees all Communist movements . . . are gripped by national Communism."[1] Djilas contended that "in order to maintain itself" any communist regime "must become national."[2] These observations, made in the 1950s, have unquestionably been confirmed by subsequent developments within the communist movement.

In the past few decades China and the Soviet Union have taken markedly different courses and the two nations have been in serious conflict. The communist leaderships of Yugoslavia, Hungary, Czechoslovakia, and, most recently, Poland have openly challenged the Soviet hegemony in East Europe. A war between Vietnam and Kampuchea over national territorial issues has drawn China into an invasion of Vietnam. Cuba has developed its own communist model, which has had some influence in Latin America, most notably in Nicaragua. The nonruling parties in some Western nations have embarked on a separate, Eurocommunist road. In short, wherever there are communist movements there are national variations. The right of each communist party to determine its own future in the context of unique national conditions has become the universal theme of Marxists.

This contemporary marriage of communism and nationalism, movements that have historically been at opposite ends of the ideological spectrum, raises some difficult questions. How can "international" communism become "national" communism without losing its ideological identity as a global movement that transcends national boundaries? After all, wasn't Karl Marx an internationalist who abhorred nationalism and called on the workers of all countries to unite? Didn't Engels, Marx's collaborator, predict that the nation-state would "wither away" under communism? Isn't nationalism historically a right-wing political movement that has been universally condemned by communists?

The apparent contradictions between what is seen as Marxist theory and contemporary communist practice have raised some doubts as to the future of communism. For those who view national and communist commitments as antithetical, such as Djilas, "national Communism is Communism in decline."[3] An alternate but less orthodox interpretation would be that there is no inherent contra-diction between national and communist sentiments. This latter view, which will be the underlying theme of this book, holds that whatever vitality persists in contemporary communism actually derives from its national orientations. Rather than being a source of weakness, nationalism is communism's major source of strength, and rather than being communism in decline, national communism is the only form capable of survival in the contemporary world.

As a first step toward understanding the relationship between nationalism and communism and the phenomenon of national com-munism, we must give these concepts some meaning. Often, however, they are defined in vague terms that contribute little, if anything, to our understanding of them. For example, one scholar has defined national communism as "the explicit assignment of priority to internal considerations even if openly challenged by those who consider themselves the essential spokesmen of international communism."[4] And another has characterized national communism in terms of what he believed were its two essential features. "First, national communism means putting the interests of one's state above the interests of any other country. . . . Second, it implies that Marxism can and should be adapted to local conditions, as interpreted by the local leader."[5] The problem with these definitions is that they depend, in turn, on related concepts such as "Marxism" and "international communism" that are not specifically defined.

It is possible, of course, that the ideas of nationalism, communism, and national communism are void of content. They may merely be the ideological inventions of social scientists and politicians who wish either to classify political movements artificially or to control those movements. In order to counter the view that nationalism and communism may mean anything and everything or mean nothing at all, we must begin with a brief review of how these concepts developed and have merged into the phenomenon we call national communism.

NATIONALISM AND COMMUNISM—MYTHS OR REALITIES

Nationalism

In the past two centuries many political leaders have appealed to national emotions in order to promote their causes. The goal of these nationalists has been to convince their followers that a shared national identity exists and that this national community constitutes a viable political system. But what is a nation? What common characteristic is strong enough to provide a permanent political bond for an otherwise atomized population?

The element most often suggested as the critical source of a nationality is language. Opinion on this matter is by no means unanimous, and although few students of the subject would argue that language is the *sole* element of a nationality, it is generally conceded that a nation is a linguistic collectivity. "Nationality," in the words of one scholar, "denotes a group of people . . . who are distinguishable from all others by speaking the same language, sharing in some of those cultural values that are tied to the use of a particular language. . . ."[6]

The objection most often raised against this linguistic definition of nationality is that there are numerous historical and contemporary instances of multilingual nations, and that there are also many linguistic groups that are divided among several nations.[7] If speaking a common language sets a group apart and establishes within it a communication linkage through which social relations are transmitted, how can the exceptions be explained? The answer provided by those who conceive of nationality as a linguistic unit is that to "speak the same language" does not necessarily mean to use a single language. In *Nationalism,* K. R. Minogue observed that "a language may be taken not merely as a set of words and rules of syntax, not merely as a kind of emotional reciprocity, but also as a certain conceptualization of the world."[8] Presumably, then, Switzerland is a nation despite the fact that four languages are spoken within its borders, because the Swiss "speak the same language" in the sense that they share a world view different from that of other nationalities.

Language, no matter how it is defined, is undoubtedly an important element of group identification, but as Minogue also noted, "The nationalist belief that a language expresses the soul of a nation is a piece of mysticism difficult to construe rationally."[9] A language is indeed capable of transmitting the spirit of a culture, but it does not follow that nationalism is the unavoidable consequence of this commonality of language. Nationalities do "speak the same language," but not every group that speaks the same language is necessarily a nationality.

Similarly, other commonly mentioned sources of national identity, such as race, religion, custom, and geography, are usually integral elements of nationality; but like language, none can be isolated as the sole criterion of nationhood. The fact is that nations are determined not by specific internal sociocultural criteria that provide a sense of community, but by the existence of others who may be identified as strangers or foreigners. The nation is a conceptualization of "us" defined by the presence of "them." Nationalism is therefore a means of mobilizing a people in defense of their political community, which, in modern times, has taken the form of the nation-state. When the medieval principle of allegiance on the part of a few noblemen to the defense of the king's person and property became antiquated in the wake of the industrial revolution and its accompanying technological complexity, it was replaced by a new principle of allegiance on the part of the entire population to the defense of the institutions and property of the state.[10]

Nationalism, then, must be viewed in its historical perspective as an idea that emerged in direct response to a particular set of political and economic conditions existing within western Europe. Although it may sound curious to those who have become accustomed to identifying nationalism with the horrible excesses of Hitler's Third Reich, the fact remains that the principle of rule by the governed, which is modern democracy, and the principle of popular allegiance to the nation-state first emerged at the time of the American and French revolutions as mutually supportive tenets of modern government.[11] When, at the end of the eighteenth century, popular support replaced heredity and divine right as the legitimator of political authority, the people had to be provided with a new source of group identity that could transcend purely local, parochial interests. Allegiance to the political system had to be broadened in order to ensure that enough people with diverse enough interests were included to make the modern state self-sustaining and competitive in the Western industrial world. This new spirit of the people was nationalism. As Hans Kohn observed: "The growth of nationalism is the process of integration of the masses of the people into a common political form. Nationalism presupposes the existence, in fact or as an ideal, of a centralized form of government over a large and distinct territory."[12]

In other words, nationalism was a liberal idea at its inception and has always been an integral part of democracy. It was John Stuart Mill, a liberal spokesman, who "identified the principle of nationality as a clause of liberalism itself" because the right of a people or a nation to govern itself and be free of foreign control was, according to democratic theory, natural and inalienable.[13] In *Nationalism: A Religion,* Carlton Hayes has noted that one of the characteristics of nationalism is that it assumes different forms as it is adopted by different groups. Hayes labeled the nationalism of the utilitarians like Mill "liberal" as opposed to the "traditional" nationalism of the Burkean conservatives that preceded it. According to Hayes, liberal nationalism was converted by the twentieth-century imperialists into "integral" nationalism, which is characterized by totalitarianism.[14]

The benign liberal version of nationalism eventually developed into more pathological forms because the nationalist cause can be invoked by any group with a national grievance. The *reductio ad absurdum* (or in this case the *reductio ad Hitlerum*) of the nationalist position is that the right of national self-determination can justify aggression as easily as defense. The liberal faith in the rationality and essential goodness of humanity has not been borne out by history, and the lesson of the twentieth century has been that nationalism in the hands of an evil master will have evil results.

According to Hans Kohn:

> Nationalism is a state of mind, permeating the large majority of a people and claiming to permeate all its members; it recognizes the nation-state as an ideal form or organization and the nationality as the source of all creative cultural energy and economic well-being. The supreme loyalty of man is therefore due to his nationality. . . .[15]

As a "state of mind" nationalism is neither a left-wing nor a right-wing movement. What makes nationalism illiberal is what makes any movement absolutist—the substitution of a single goal (such as racial mastery or class domination) for the diverse needs of a population.[16]

In *The Meaning of Nationalism,* Louis Snyder contended that "nation" and "nationalism" are abstractions that have no inherent content. "Nationalism," Snyder thought, "may mean whatever a given people, on the basis of their own historical experience, decide it to mean."[17] He contrasted nationality, which he viewed as a social science term, with race, which he conceived of as a fact of natural science: Whereas race is natural, or a physical reality, nationality exists only in people's minds.[18] Snyder's definition of a nation as "a community formed by the will to be a nation" is, therefore, very similar to the explanation offered by Hans Kohn that "in modern times, it has been the power of an idea, not the call of blood, that has constituted and molded nationalities."[19] Kohn's thesis, with which Snyder would no doubt have agreed, was that "a living and active corporate will"[20] transforms a collectivity into a nation. Leaders with political goals to achieve shape this corporate will to suit their own purposes and give nationalism its content. Thus, as form in search of substance, nationalism has taken many shapes, each molded by the circumstances of time and place. The fact that nationalism is essentially contentless and defies universal definition does not, however, devaluate it as a political force. On the contrary, it is just this malleability that explains nationalism's survival and contemporary vitality.

If it is true that a nation is simply a collectivity of individuals who conceive of themselves as a nation and that nationalism is whatever nationalists say it is, must we therefore conclude that the ideas of nation and nationalism are empty of substantive meaning? Despite the vagueness of the notion, one fixed principle does appear to characterize nationalist movements. This single contentual element is the belief that the "state" is the ideal form of political organization. The constituent elements of the state are multidimensional and may include religion, ethnicity, geography, and any other appropriate sources of identification; and all of these are combined into a unified conception of the "nation." Nationalism stands in sharp contrast to principles such as Christian humanism, technological cosmopolitanism, and even proletarian internationalism, all of which contend in their own way that the bonds of humanity transcend politico-administrative boundaries. Because it makes the political entity, the state, the fundamental social institution, nationalism is truly a "political," as opposed to an economic, or religious, theory. Class and sect are replaced by nationality, and it is the politics of the state, rather than the will of God or the force of class conflict, that shapes humanity's future. What distinguishes nationalism, then, is that it is a theory of "political determinism."

Nationalism has been described as a modern, secular religion that has replaced traditional religion as the source of human inspiration. The similarities between nationalism and religion are numerous, but they do not make of nationalism a religion. As one student of nationalism pointed out, the facts that nationalism emerged at the same time that religion was on the decline as a moral force in the West and "that once men worshipped God and now they seem to worship the nation" do not explain, "Why the nation?"[21] The reason nationalism appears to have replaced religion is that humanity, if it has any need to worship at all, worships *power*. Although the nation was not the only form of political organization to emerge, it was the one that, in combination with technological developments in Europe and America, produced the most powerful and politically successful systems in the world. European nationalism was the organic product of European social and economic developments. When industrial wealth and technology replaced God as the source of political power, the state inexorably replaced the church as the repository of that power; and nationalism replaced religion as the dominant form of worship of that power. The power wielded by the leaders of the industrialized nation-states of nineteenth- and twentieth-century Europe was historically unprecedented and coveted by all political authorities. The common denominator of nationalism is not love for an abstraction called the state; rather it is worship of the power that may be derived from the state.

Anyone who would challenge the authenticity of nationalism and the power of the nation-state must challenge not only the reality of its power but the myths that underpin it as well. In the nineteenth century it was the communists who began to question the idea of the nation as the vehicle of human progress and the principle of nationalism as the highest expression of social allegiance. The communist challenge was based primarily on the contentions that Western political organization had resulted in economic exploitation and injustice rather than progress, and that nationalism was a false source of identification for everyone but the elites of society. Communism was not a reaction to nationalism per se, but it did offer a different ideal form of human organization.

Communism

The picture of nationalism that has emerged thus far is that of a mobilization myth comprising some fundamental ideological principles that have manifested themselves in an infinite variety of forms. Is the same true of communism or does this ideology, owing to the influence of its founders and the strength of its organization, have a content that dictates specific forms? Throughout this book we shall consider many aspects of contemporary communism, including its ideological content and its political structure, but what concerns us at this juncture is neither how communism has developed nor how it currently operates but the far more basic question: Does communism exist?

Many would no doubt suggest that one need go no further than the events in Hungary in 1956 or in Czechoslovakia in 1968, the Cuban missile crisis, the Vietnam War, or the confrontations in the Middle East to know that communism is real. Yet there are those who continue to argue that there is no such thing as a communist movement and that communism is nothing more than a myth.

The issue of whether or not communism exists has been treated as essentially a taxonomic one. For a category to be meaningful, two conditions must hold true: (1) all items belonging to the group must possess certain common characteristics; and (2) these group characteristics must be unique to that category and distinguish it from all others. Thus, in order to accurately label some of the world's political systems "communist" one must demonstrate that the category "communism" satisfies both these conditions. To be a scientific analytic category, communism must be more than a name applied arbitrarily to any political system that chooses to call itself "communist."

But is it possible to define communism specifically or must we be satisfied with a loosely circumscribed, amorphous, and subjectively determined notion with no real substance? John Kautsky is one of those who have argued most persuasively that communism is a myth without content.[22] Kautsky's central thesis is that

> the concept of Communism, like that of totalitarianism, is little more than a surrogate for the proper name of particular historical social systems. . . . It remains generally indefinable except in terms of particular historical regimes, parties, institutions and ideologies. . . . There is no way to identify an institution or idea as Communist apart from a particular social system so labeled.[23]

If Kautsky's contention that a political institution is only communist because it is so labeled is correct, what is it about these systems that makes us believe they belong to a single category?

Kautsky's answer is that "the appearance of uniformity" is "due to the fact that they are (or were) mobilization regimes."[24] By "mobilization regimes" he means governments whose overriding concern is socioeconomic modernization. Thus all the characteristics commonly identified as communist are, according to Kautsky, neither exclusively nor universally communist but are shared by many other modernizing regimes.

Contrary to Kautsky's view is the idea that communist systems are distinguishable from others, and that although there may be striking similarities among all modernizing systems, the communist *ideology* sets communist systems apart. Richard Lowenthal, for example, has isolated at least four unique features of communist ideology.[25] According to Lowenthal, communist ideology (1) requires a "long-term program of economic and social transformation" that includes nationalization of industry and collectivization of agriculture; (2) requires repeated revolutions from above to destroy the new class stratifications that result from the developmental process and that constantly regenerate the "utopian myth"; (3) because it is a secular religion, provides a justification for "cultural revolution" attacking all traditional social institutions and practices; and (4) demands that its followers assume a hostile attitude toward capitalist systems, which results in less aid from the developed West, more emphasis on defense, and, as a consequence, a more costly developmental process. The total effect of these ideological factors is that "only regimes inspired by communist ideology tend to acquire totalitarian powers in the full sense of an institutional monopoly over policy decision, organization, and information by the ruling party, and the freeing of the state from all legal limitations in the exercise of its task."[26]

Similarly, Emile Ader identified seventeen communist character-istics,[27] Chalmers Johnson isolated six,[28] and Richard C. Gripp suggested that there are at least five characteristics of the communist model.[29] Without delving into the details of each of these attempts to identify communism's essential features, it may be generally stated that these efforts (and numerous similar ones) have been concerned with determining what the communist ideology prescribes in the way of attitudes and what it demands of communists in the way of action.

The problem is more complex than simply to determine whether communism actually exists—it surely does, even if only in people's minds. Similarly, the issue is more complicated than to decide whether communist ideology is myth or reality. The essential task is to determine whether being (or believing one is) a communist results in any distinctive behavioral consequences, such as uniquely Marxist-Leninist policies. Even if communism were a myth, it would have to be considered "real" if the ideology had real consequences. Even a symbolic ideology (as opposed to a guide to action) can establish the existence of a communist type if the effects of that ideology are common to the group.

Kautsky's position is that the so-called essential elements of communism either are not shared by *all* communist systems or are also present in some noncommunist systems. He therefore rejects communism as a meaningful analytic category and concludes that it would "be simpler to resolve the problem by abandoning the category 'Communist' altogether."[30] It may be simpler and more scientifically correct to discard a category because its uniqueness and exclusivity cannot be demonstrated; but by so doing, one risks ignoring the behavioral consequences that may result from self- and other identification. If an actor believes that he is communist, this belief will affect his attitudes and behavior. If others believe that an actor is communist, that will affect their perceptions of and reactions to his behavior.

The point is that communism may not be an analytical category, but it is a system of self- and other identification. Systems are not specified in terms of the exclusivity and uniqueness of their constituent elements. The boundaries of a system are determined by degrees of interaction and patterns of interdependence. A collectivity becomes a system when the units that compose it interact with one another more interdependently than with any other units. The units of the communist system identify themselves as such, and are so identified by others who also identify as communists. In addition, those outside the system identify it as communist and interact with the system accordingly.

Irrespective of the fact that communism, like nationalism, remains void of specific content until it realizes itself in a national context, the label "communist" remains an appropriate one because it results in patterns of interaction in pursuit of common goals and in common perceptions about threats to survival. The result is a behavioral syndrome distinguished by the belief that people are in essence economic beings, and that solutions to human problems must be economic rather than political.

The importance of the distinction between communism as a definitional category and communism as a system of self- and other identification is that the limits of the system are determined by interactive behavior rather than a priori assumptions. The strength— and weakness—of the system approach to communism is that its limits are often vaguely circumscribed. Whether a particular actor identifies itself as communist, for example, may be conditioned as much by the international consequences of such a declaration as by belief. Whether other nations identify a movement as communist may be the product as much of internal power struggles as of ideology. Clearly, the criteria applied in any such self- or other assessment will vary widely and are virtually infinite. In some instances reliable indicators of system interaction, such as trade agreements, military alliances, and treaties, suggest the limits of the communist system. However, the product of communist practice must never be confused with ideological absolutes.

Throughout this book reference will be made to communism, and judgments will be made as to whether particular movements are communist, but those references and judgments will be based on an evaluation of patterns of behavior relative to a self- and other designated system of actors, rather than an arbitrarily defined set of absolute principles.

THE COMMON FEATURES OF NATIONALISM AND COMMUNISM

Nationalism and communism are historically distinct movements. In fact, as we have seen, communism was a reaction against the excesses of nineteenth-century nationalist policies produced by capitalism. Yet it is also clear that there are numerous important similarities between nationalism and communism that, if we wish to fully comprehend the meaning of national communism, must be made explicit.

Both nationalism and communism are world views (*Weltanschauungs*), not methods of governing. The exponents of either the nationalist or communist cosmology may be democrats or dictators, depending upon the political culture from which they arise (and also depending upon how one defines these terms). There was no historical inevitability about the fact that nationalism and communism sank to their twentieth-century nadirs as totalitarian regimes. What K. R. Minogue has observed about nationalism is equally true of communism: "The good it does could all be done in other ways; but equally, it has contributed little more than a new vocabulary to the history of political evil."[31]

Nationalism and communism are not themselves religions, but they do have quasi-religious characteristics. They are millenarian world views in that they promise secular deliverance and salvation in the form of a perfect world order. Therefore, the followers of these "faiths" tend to be messianic, and they are willing to justify virtually anything in the name of their millenarian goals. What begins as a commitment to improve the political or economic institutions of society is transformed by these ideologies into a "religious" obligation to perfect those institutions and deliver humanity from all evil. When this occurs the means employed become far less important than the ends to be achieved.

As do all millenarians, communists and nationalists appeal to the most depressed elements of society. "Millenarians," observed Frances Hill, "show the relatively wretched how to build a new world."[32] Both ideologies are expressions of collective social grievances, the difference being that in the case of nationalism, foreigners are depicted as the enemy, whereas in the case of communism, the villain is an economic class. It is this common reaction to exploitation that gives nationalism and communism their messianic, religious quality. Although their devils are different, nationalist and communist revolutions are both essentially rites of social exorcism.

Another feature that nationalism and communism share is that they are antiindividualistic ideologies. The success of these mass-oriented social movements depends upon collective action. Although nationalism stresses the common interest of a geographically defined group and communism emphasizes the common interest of an economic class, both are "socialist" cosmologies in that they put the good of the community above that of the individual. The individualist position is that a community is merely a collectivity of individuals and social happiness is the product of the satisfaction of individual needs. Contrariwise, the socialist argument is that individuals have meaning only in a social context, and only when the needs of a community are satisfied can an individual be truly happy. Whether the group consists of the nation or the proletariat, the community comes before the individual in both nationalism and communism.

One important outgrowth of the fact that nationalism and communism are mass movements expressing communal grievances is that both have been very susceptible to charismatic leadership. Strictly speaking, charisma refers to a supernatural characteristic transcending human qualities (the term is often inappropriately used to mean simply a strong personality) that followers ascribe to their leader. In the absence of any real cultural, political, or economic unity, the personality of the charismatic leader substitutes as the focus of community identification. Nationalism and communism are open to charismatic control because they are mobilizing movements that generally emerge in transitional societies, where strong traditional influences shape the mentality of the population. Concepts such as the proletariat or the nation are too complex for people whose social identity is derived from extremely parochial associations to integrate into their pattern of beliefs and behavior. The charismatic leader bridges this intellectual gap. As these transitional societies continue to mature, and more complex political symbols such as national interest, parliaments, or five-year plans begin to take hold, the need for charisma as a unifying force diminishes, and both nationalist and communist systems begin to depersonalize their leadership. In the end, personalized symbols of charismatic leadership are replaced by institutional symbols of authority.

Communism and nationalism are modern responses to the social upheavals engendered by industrialization. In the universal search for the meaning of human history, "nationalism," as Minogue has cogently noted, "provides an escape from triviality."[33] Similarly, communism provides meaningful answers to the questions posed by people in the throes of modernization who wonder what it all means and, most importantly, where they are going. The nature of the appeal of both nationalism and communism is that they are not "trivial" responses, in that they provide hope for infinite progress to people who have had the traditional meaning of their lives destroyed by forces they can neither comprehend nor control.

Are nationalism and communism altogether different solutions to the same problem? We have seen that the *Weltanschauungs* of nationalism and communism are similar: They are both messianic solutions to the difficulties of modernization that promote the rebellion of the masses against exploitation. The significant difference between them is that they arose as reactions to different enemies. The bête noir of nationalism was foreign domination by multinational empires and that of communism was the domestic domination of the bourgeoisie over the proletariat. When, as we shall see in Chapter 3, the two views of the enemy were merged by Lenin into the villain of economic imperialism, the outcome was national communism.

From the moment of communism's inception as a viable political movement following the Bolshevik Revolution of 1917, the vehicle of communist progress has been the nation-state, not the international proletariat. National communism is a twentieth-century millenarian attempt to achieve economic, political, and social justice within a national framework. Consequently, communism has assumed many forms, owing to the infinite variety of national experiences on which it has been superimposed. *The fundamental theme of this analysis is that from its very conception communism has been national and that the term "international communism" has been badly misinterpreted by communists and noncommunists alike.*

It will be demonstrated in Chapter 2 that the notion of national communism is an implicit and integral part of Marx's conception of internationalism. And in Chapter 3, we will see that it was Stalin's insistence on institutional and programmatic uniformity throughout the communist movement that was inconsistent with Marxist-Leninist thinking. Chapter 4 will recount how the Stalinist approach resulted in an iron-fisted ideological rigidity that cracked under pressure for the reestablishment of principles of national integrity within the communist movement. Chapter 5 will analyze the relationship between national communism and national liberation, with special attention to the major variations that have developed in China, in Cuba, and elsewhere in the non-European world. Finally, Chapter 6 will explore some of the possibilities for the future of national communism.

SUGGESTIONS FOR FURTHER READING

Daniels, Robert. *The Nature of Communism.* New York: Vintage Books, 1963.

Demaitre, Edmund. "The Origins of National Communism." *Studies in Comparative Communism* 2 (1969):1–20.

Gripp, Richard. *The Political System of Communism.* New York: Dodd, Mead and Company, 1973.

Hammond, Thomas. "The Origins of National Communism." *The Virginia Quarterly Review* 34 (1958):277–91.

Kautsky, John. *Communism and the Politics of Development.* New York: John Wiley, 1968.

Kohn, Hans. *The Idea of Nationalism: A Study of Its Origins and Background.* New York: Macmillan Company, 1944.

Minogue, K. R. *Nationalism.* Baltimore: Penguin Books, 1967.

Seton-Watson, Hugh. *Nations and States: An Enquiry into the Origin of Nations and the Politics of Nationalism.* Boulder, Colo.: Westview Press, 1977.

Snyder, Louis. *The Meaning of Nationalism.* New Brunswick, N.J.: Rutgers University Press, 1954.

Wesson, Robert. *Communism and Communist Systems.* Englewood Cliffs, N.J.: Prentice-Hall, Inc., 1978.

2
Marxism and
National Communism

Any analysis of the development of national communism must begin with an examination of the ideas of Karl Marx
and Friedrich Engels. As the forefathers of contemporary communism,
Marx and Engels are presumably the source of all ideological "truth"
concerning the role of nations and nationalism in the revolutionary
process. Unfortunately, however, the writings of Marx and Engels
on these subjects tend to be ambiguous. In large measure this lack
of theoretical clarity is the product of Marx's attitude toward the
influence of any noneconomic factor on human behavior. Although
he generally conceded the existence of such noneconomic elements,
he firmly denied their permanence or historical importance. Instead,
he insisted that they were merely transitory manifestations of economic
conditions. Because there is no precise measure of the extent to
which nationalism actually motivates human action, criticisms of
Marx on this subject have been contradictory. Djilas, as we have
seen, asserted that "national Communism is Communism in decline."[1]
Djilas's judgment was that the national form of communism constituted a serious departure from Marxist thinking. The reasoning
underlying this argument was that since national communism is
inspired by nationalism, and since Marx clearly repudiated nationalism, national communism is un-Marxist, or worse, anti-Marxist.

Marx himself has been both reproached for underestimating the
historical importance of national forces[2] and accused of being a
"German nationalist" and "great power chauvinist."[3] The truth of
any of the contradictory judgments depends, of course, on how the
terms nationalism and national communism are defined. Unfortunately, Marx generally failed to distinguish among such ideas as
nation, state, national sentiment, and nationalism,[4] and his own
inconsistencies have been responsible for the confusion that has arisen

as to his true position. Therefore, while it may not be possible to reconcile entirely the conflicting interpretations of Marx's attitude toward nationalism, at least some of the apparent ambivalence may be dispelled by carefully narrowing the focus of this analysis and taking into consideration those factors that have made the writings of Marx and Engels so difficult to decipher.

There are many ways in which questions relating to Marx's attitude toward nationalism might be phrased. Was he a nationalist? Did he condone nationalism? Did he comprehend the historical importance of nationalism? However, the purpose of this study is to review the phenomenon known as national communism; consequently, only two questions need concern us: Can the roots of contemporary national communism be traced to the theories of Marx and Engels? And how would Marx and Engels react to national communism if they were alive today? If these two questions can be answered, we will not only know whether Marx was a nationalist, but, more importantly, be able to place national communism in a theoretical and historical perspective.

PROBLEMS IN INTERPRETING THE MARXIST VIEW OF NATIONALISM

The first step toward unraveling Marx's position on the role of nations in the revolutionary process is to consider the problem of how Marx is to be interpreted. Marx was not a dogmatic ideologue, but neither was he a detached, objective social scientist. He was not attracted by the problems of practical politics or intraparty power struggles, but neither did he shun these activities when he believed that the future of the socialist movement was at stake. Marx's rigorous empiricism was balanced by a certain tactical flexibility that permitted him to make allowances for developments he had not correctly diagnosed. For example, consider how Marx's opinion of Russia's revolutionary potential changed.

The first edition of the *Manifesto of the Communist Party,* published in 1848, contained no mention of Russia. In 1848, England, France, and Germany were the focus of Marx's attention, and as far as he was concerned Russia was "the last great reserve of the reaction of all of Europe."[5] Yet, in 1882, when the Russian edition of the *Manifesto* was published, Marx wrote in the preface, "If the Russian revolution becomes the signal for a proletarian revolution in the West, so that both complement each other, the present Russian common ownership of land may serve as a starting-point for communist development."[6] Unquestionably, this guarded admission that

Russia, an economically backward country, could provide the spark for a European socialist revolution constituted an important concession by Marx to changing political conditions.

The argument could be made that as a scientific observer of society, Marx had no vested interest in the promotion of a particular ideological viewpoint in the face of contradictory historical currents—that his theoretical modifications were the product of scientific reevaluation rather than political opportunism. However, his role in forming the International Workingmen's Association (IWMA), the First International, casts considerable doubt on this interpretation.[7]

The IWMA was conceived more or less spontaneously by representatives of British and French trade councils for the purpose of promoting cooperation among European socialists. Seeking to avoid the distractions of political activity while working on *Capital,* Marx had nothing to do with its formation, but he was invited to attend the first meeting at St. Martin's Hall in London on 28 September 1864. Owing to his previous experience with the Communist League, Marx was appointed to the committee charged with writing the IWMA statutes. However, because of poor health and the pressure of his writing, Marx was unable to attend the first meetings of this committee. In his absence, the Italian socialists, under the influence of the nationalist Mazzini, as well as some reform-minded Owenites and Proudhonists, drafted the IWMA rules and principles, which Marx later was to describe to Engels as "an appallingly wordy, badly written and utterly undigested preamble, pretending to be a declaration of principles, in which Mazzini could be detected everywhere, the whole thing crusted over with the vaguest tags of French socialism."[8]

Obviously disgusted with the proposed ideological position of the IWMA, Marx filibustered the drafting committee and maneuvered to have all the papers "left behind," as he put it, "for my opinion." He then wrote his own *Address to the Working Classes,* and "on the pretext that everything material was included in this Address," Marx "altered the whole preamble [and] threw out the declaration of principles."[9] Candidly, he confided to Engels, "It was very difficult to frame the thing [the *Address*] so that our view should appear in a form acceptable from the present standpoint of the worker's movement. . . . It will take time before the reawakened movement allows the old boldness of speech. It will be necessary to be *fortiter in re, suaviter in modo* [bold in matter, mild in manner]."[10]

In that *Address,* Marx hailed the English Ten Hours Bill as a "marvelous success" and praised the development of the cooperative movement as a "still greater victory."[11] Were these the appraisals of a scientific socialist who had reevaluated the historical evidence, or were they the opportunistic capitulations of a politician who was attempting to preserve his influence and power within the socialist movement? In his letter to Engels, Marx revealed himself in this episode to have been a practitioner of the art of the possible, and a man well aware of the political exigencies of time and place.

The readiness with which Marx was prepared to jettison ideological principles as a tactical political necessity was prompted by his need to maintain the Marxist character of the movement. The German Lassalle, the Frenchman Proudhon, and the Russian Bakunin each posed a serious challenge to Marx's attempts to guide the socialist movement, and, as the case of the IWMA illustrates, many of Marx's statements were strategic rather than theoretical. Being able to distinguish between these two is the key to deciphering Marx correctly.

The candor that Marx exhibited in his correspondence with Engels further compounds the problem of determining his true attitude on any issue. "I was obliged," he wrote Engels, "to insert two phrases about 'duty' and 'right' into the Preamble to the Statutes, ditto 'truth, morality and justice,' but these are placed in such a way that they can do no harm."[12] This is particularly true with regard to Marx's opinions on nationalities and the role of nations. Many of the critics who have suggested that beneath a thin public veneer of internationalism Marx was, in truth, a common German nationalist ground their allegations on the fact that he and Engels frequently employed derogatory racial and ethnic slurs when they referred to their political opponents.[13]

One of these critics, James Guillaume, who, along with Bakunin, was expelled from the First International by Marx, described Marx and Engels as "German patriots above all else," who cheered the German victories over France in 1870 because they ensured "the domination of the German proletariat over the French proletariat" and would "transfer from France to Germany the center of gravity of the European workers' movement."[14] How can Guillaume's view that Marx saw the Franco-Prussian War as an opportunity for the German workers to supplant the French, and Marx's and Engels's use of derogatory racial epithets, be reconciled with the statements in the 1848 *Manifesto* to the effect that "national differences and antagonisms between peoples are daily disappearing" and "the supremacy of the proletariat will cause them to vanish still faster"?[15]

In order to arrive at a satisfactory answer, we must consider Marx's personality as well as his ideology. Marx was often a bitter and violent political opponent who found it difficult to control his emotions in the heat of battle. Solomon Bloom, the author of the only full-length analysis of the national implications in Marx's works, contended that "most of his occasional nationalist utterances were the *obiter dicta* of an opinionated and choleric personality," and that Marx was a jealous, frustrated emigré who not only employed invectives to attack his political opponents, but made "unjust partisan accusations and misrepresentations against them."[16] In spite of the many nationalist-sounding comments in Marx's writings, Bloom concluded that "Marx simply was not a nationalist."[17] On balance, from the perspective of the total body of Marx's work, Bloom believed that "the note of internationalism, humanitarianism, and tolerance is found to be unquestionably dominant."[18] Bertrand Russell, on the other hand, like Guillaume, rejected what he considered to be Marx's internationalist facade and described him as nationalist and racist.[19]

One important point that may help reconcile this apparent (or at least perceived) inconsistency in Marx is that Marx was always conscious of the character and mental disposition of those to whom he directed his appeals. Marx wrote many types of works for various audiences, and the style and content of each was strongly influenced by the nature of the medium employed as well as the intended target. The *Manifesto's* polemical style stands in sharp contrast to the scholarly approach of *Capital* or *The German Ideology*. Similarly, the articles that appeared in the *New York Daily Tribune* from 1851 to 1862 were written for an American liberal rather than a European socialist readership. When we analyze Marx's works it must be with a keen awareness that we will not derive the same level of meaning from each source. The *Manifesto* was a call to arms, largely bluff and rhetoric. In terms of its intended impact it was "full of sound and fury, signifying nothing," for it simply had no effect whatsoever on the revolutions of 1848. On the other hand, Marx labored for years on *Capital* and only managed to publish the first of its three lengthy volumes during his lifetime (Engels published the remaining two). The standards of judgment we apply to the *Manifesto* cannot be the same as those we might apply to *Capital*. The difficulty is to determine which of his works more truly reflect Marx's views.

Marx's infrequent though caustic remarks on nationality must, therefore, be understood with a view to the audience for which they were intended. As with all persons, there was a private and a public Marx. There were also the man Marx and the theories of Marx. He may indeed have been a nationalist in the particular and an internationalist in the abstract. But whatever the merits of the arguments of those who have appraised Marx the man as a nationalist, the term as it has been defined here—worship of the nation-state as the ultimate political form—is patently inappropriate as a description of Marx's formal ideology. Thus, by focusing their arguments on the nationalist tendencies in Marx's personality, neither his critics nor his supporters have shed any light on Marx's views on national communism. In fact, they have clouded this issue. What remains is to explore the alternatives to the idea of Marx as a nationalist, with the knowledge that neither the scientific nor the political aspect of his personality ever totally dominated the other.

THE NATION AND THE REVOLUTIONARY PROCESS

"Internationalist" is the word most frequently employed to describe Marx's thought. This designation has been taken to mean that Marx believed that nations had no role to play in the revolutionary process. In point of fact, a theory that totally rejects the nation as a positive political force and dismisses nationality as a source of social identification cannot be properly labeled "internationalist." This extreme antinational viewpoint, of which Marx and his contemporaries were aware, is cosmopolitanism.

Had Marx been a cosmopolitan, he undoubtedly would have disclaimed national communism, which rests on the notion that the means employed to attain socialist goals may be tempered by historically unique national conditions. As a cosmopolitan, Marx could not have accepted the logic of "national roads" to communism or the pluralism of the polycentric communist world. Had Marx, on the other hand, been an internationalist—in the sense that the word "international" means between or among nations—then his view of the world both before and after the revolution would have made allowances for distinct national units, each guided toward communism by its national proletariat within the context of disparate historical traditions. The critical problem, therefore, is whether Marx was an internationalist or a cosmopolitan, and substantial scholarly controversy has been generated by attempts to solve it.

The antipodal positions on the internationalist versus the cosmopolitan character of Marxism have been expounded most clearly by Solomon Bloom and Joseph Petrus. Bloom's contention was that Marx's

> positive attitude toward nationality was in itself sufficient to set him apart from many another radical thinker and leader. His approach was distinguished . . . by an acceptance of the nation as a substantial historical entity, by an attempted reconciliation of national and class factors in politics, and by an *internationalist rather than a cosmopolitan view of the organization of the world* [emphasis supplied].[20]

Even more explicitly, Bloom continued, "The socialist world of his imagination consisted of a limited number of advanced nations."[21]
Quite to the contrary, Petrus asserted:

> Thus, with the advent of communism on a world scale, the "national proletariat" would dissolve the existing states, and the modern nations, or countries, would merge into cosmopolitanism.
>
> In summary, *Marx envisioned "internationalism" transforming itself, as the negation of negation, into "cosmopolitanism"* when the Industrial Revolution completed its historical mission on a global scale [emphasis supplied].[22]

Despite his disagreement with Bloom on Marx's vision of the postrevolutionary socialist world, Petrus did concede Bloom's contention that as Marx matured he increasingly recognized the depth of national emotions among all economic classes, including the proletariat. And, more importantly, Petrus recognized that Marx was aware of "the diversity of differences in the historical, ecological and behavioral patterns of nations" with similar economic systems.[23] Thus, whether or not Marx pictured the final socialist world as cosmopolitan, there appears to be agreement that his idea of the interim stages did include nation-states as an integral part of the world political order, and that meant proletarian nation-states as well.

Even when they assumed their most strident voices and espoused their most extreme positions, Marx and Engels did not reject national paths to the revolutionary goals of the movement. In the *Manifesto* they declared: "Though not in substance, yet in form, the struggle of the proletariat with the bourgeoisie is at first a national struggle. The proletariat of each country must, of course, first of all settle matters with its own bourgeoisie."[24] And in his *Critique of the Gotha Program* Marx reminded the working class that "its own country is the immediate arena of its struggle."[25]

Clearly, whatever the ultimate fate of nations was to be, Marx "admitted considerable local variations, even within the same system of production,"[26] and believed that a nationally identified proletariat had a positive role to play in the revolutionary process. Critically important is the fact that Marx was not postulating a theory of nationalist revolution. The source of revolutionary identity was unquestionably the class. What Marx did recognize was that because of numerous historical circumstances the working class of each nation would have to employ distinctive strategies in order to liberate itself. National variation was, therefore, the *sine qua non* of successful Marxist revolution.

But how much variation would Marx have been willing to tolerate within a communist system? This is a difficult question to answer because Marx did not have to face the Hungarian situation in 1956, cope with Czechoslovakia in 1968, or deal with the Polish problem in 1981. Nevertheless, the limits of his toleration were at least tested by the conflicts that accompanied the dissolutions of the Communist League and the First International, and these instances are, perhaps, illustrative of the Marx-Engels reaction to challenges to established Marxist lines.

When the European revolutions of 1848 had failed, Marx and other communist emigrés retreated to England, the only country that continued to tolerate them. But by the end of 1850, Marx and Engels, as heads of the London Committee of the Communist League, were being challenged by those of their colleagues who wished to see the League assume a more revolutionary stance. Rather than lose control to these radicals, Marx and Engels maneuvered successfully to re-locate the headquarters of the League in Cologne (where it was illegal and forced to operate underground), thereby placing it out of the reach of the London leftists. By 1852 the Cologne group was in prison for its revolutionary activities, the rump groups that had remained in London had dissolved, and Marx and Engels had returned to their scholarly isolation to await the formation of an organization that would be more amenable to their leadership style and programs.[27]

We have seen how in 1864 Marx maneuvered to make the IWMA just such a group; however, when the Paris Commune collapsed in 1871, Marx again realized "that for the time being the revolutionary game was up" and took measures remarkably similar to those of 1850.[28] When faced with challenges from the anarchistic Bakunin faction, the French Proudhonists, and the social democratic Lassalleans of the First International, Marx first consolidated his position on the General Council and "excommunicated" all factions not willing to subordinate their sectarian interests to the international movement (i.e., all those who opposed his leadership). Then, after "packing" the Hague Congress of 1872, he had the headquarters of the International moved away from London—this time out of Europe altogether to New York. The First International faded into oblivion in Philadelphia a few years afterwards. Again Marx had subverted an international workers' organization rather than have it fall into the hands of his political opponents.

The issues which destroyed the IWMA were not national, but many of the cleavages occurred along national lines. When the First International collapsed in 1874, Engels told the general secretary it was "well" that the "*old* International is entirely wound up and at an end," because the Paris Commune had exploded "this naive conjunction of all fractions," among which were the "leaders of the English Trade Unions," "German Communists," "Belgian Proudhonists," and "Bakuninist adventurers."[29] Engels concluded that the International "in its old form has outlived itself." "I think," he averred, "that the next International—after Marx's writings have had some years of influence—will be directly communist and will openly proclaim our principles."[30]

There had been serious divisions within the International before the failure of the Paris Commune, some of them nationally inspired, that the IWMA leadership was willing to tolerate;[31] however, when the demise of the Commune brought forth a wave of Bakuninist and Proudhonist criticism of Marx and the General Council of the IWMA for not actively supporting the Communards, Marx finally decided that the First International could not fulfill its revolutionary role, and maneuvered to kill it.

When the Communist League and the First International broke down into national blocs over critical revolutionary issues, Marx did not immediately abandon them. Only when he became convinced that these national forces could no longer be directed toward revolutionary goals as he defined them did he condemn these national variations as reactionary. This Marxist distinction between legitimate and illegitimate *national* forces was, in turn, based upon the relationship that Marx postulated between economics and nationalism.

ECONOMIC DEVELOPMENT AND EUROPEAN NATIONALISM

Marx believed that nation-states are revolutionary vehicles because they are the organizations through which the bourgeoisie exercises political power. Thus, nationalism, which promotes the development of the state, is a progressive force in an economically advanced bourgeois system because it brings that system closer to the revolutionary stage. On the other hand, nationalism inspired by the yearnings of an economically backward national minority to liberate itself from imperial exploitation was condemned by Marx as reactionary. "Progressive nationalism" was possible only in the "leading civilized countries" (as Marx and Engels referred to them in the *Manifesto*), which included Germany, France, England, and, at times, Poland and Hungary. Nationalism in the Austrian Hapsburg Empire, Turkey, and the South Slavic regions was, from the Marxist standpoint, nonprogressive. Writing about Panslavism in 1849, Marx summarized his thinking on the nonprogressive nationalities as follows:

> There is no country in Europe which does not contain in one corner
> one or several ruins of peoples, left-overs . . . made subject to the
> nation which later became the carrier of historical development. These
> remains of nations . . . this ethnic trash always becomes and remains
> until its complete extermination or denationalization, the most fanatic
> carrier of counterrevolution, since its entire existence is nothing more
> than a protest against a great historical revolution.[32]

By "left-overs" Marx meant groups such as the Gaels of Scotland,
the Bretons of France, the Basques of Spain, and the South Slavs
of Austria, all of whom were, in his words, "nothing more than the
waste products of a highly confused development."[33] In contrast, the
"Germans and Magyars took the historical initiative in 1848. . . .
They represent the Revolution," while the South Slavs, Romanians,
and Saxons "represent the counterrevolution."[34] Poland was a special
case that Marx considered crucial to the very preservation of European
society. "There is but one alternative for Europe," Marx warned.
"Either Asiatic barbarism, under Muscovite direction, will burst
around its head like an avalanche, or else it must re-establish Poland,
thus putting twenty million heroes between itself and Asia and gaining
a breathing spell for the accomplishment of its social regeneration."[35]
Obviously Marx did not regard the Russians very highly.

The critical point is that when Marx wrote in support of national
self-determination for the Poles or the Magyars, he did not view it
as an absolute right or as a principle of humanity. Marx dismissed
national self-determination as a legitimate political goal because he
believed that the problems of the enslaved peoples of eastern Europe
and Asia were the product of economic exploitation; once this evil
was eliminated there would be no necessity for national self-determination. Marx did not believe that every national group had the
right to statehood after the revolution. There would be no need of
that since the national proletariats of the major civilized countries
would not seek to exploit national minorities. Whether one or another
of these smaller nationalities deserved independence *before* the revolution was to be determined solely by its potential contribution to
the weakening of capitalism.

This situationalist attitude toward the right of self-determination
for small national groups may be illustrated by Marx's analysis of
English-Irish relations. As long as Marx had faith in the imminent
success of the proletarian revolution in England, he thought that
support for Irish separatism was not in the best interests of the
development of communism. Thus in the 1840s Marx contended
that Irish claims for national self-determination were retrogressive.

However, when in the 1850s it became increasingly clear to Marx that an English proletarian revolution was still far in the future, he revised his position. Marx now believed that Ireland's separation would drastically weaken the economic base of the English power structure and thereby hasten the revolution.[36] Bloom aptly summarized the Marxist view of the relationship between national aspirations and economic conditions when he observed that, for Marx, "neither blood, numbers, geography, consciousness of common traditions nor common culture, could by themselves create or validate the right to separate statehood. To have practical significance, that right must be implemented by an advanced economy."[37]

The right of national self-determination was selectively granted by Marx to those systems that had exhibited revolutionary potential, or to those nations whose independence would contribute to the decline of an advanced capitalist state. Marx may not have been a German nationalist, but it is clear that he granted the advanced European nationalities certain rights that, if exercised by less developed national groups, would have been judged counterrevolutionary.

The details of Marx's vision are now more clearly in focus. Before the revolutions in the advanced societies of Europe, nationalism among the bourgeoisie was to be tolerated, indeed promoted, because it fostered revolutionary conditions by bringing capitalism closer to its eventual collapse. Both during and after the revolutions, communists were to be permitted to experiment on a national basis as long as they remained true to the essential Marxist scheme and did not become lost in some Proudhonist, Lassallean, or Bakuninist heresy.

The problem that continues to cloud the issue of the Marxist roots of contemporary national communism is that in today's world, prerevolutionary nationalism has generally taken the form of anticolonial national liberation struggles outside Europe, and communist regimes have been established in many economically backward nations. Hence, in order to get a total picture, it is necessary to consider Marx's attitude toward the role of nations in the revolutionary process throughout the world, not merely in Europe. Specifically, the question must be put: Is anticapitalist nationalism in precapitalist society progressive, or did Marx repudiate this form of national communism in non-European regions?

ANTICOLONIALISM AND NON-EUROPEAN NATIONALISM

The simple fact is that Marx had a different set of historical rules for the "uncivilized" people of the world. What we today call the

"Third World," or the "developing" world, was, at the time Marx lived and wrote, the colonial world. By the second half of the nineteenth century the colonial empires of England, France, Germany, and the other European powers had been well consolidated, and it is not surprising that Marx characterized colonialism as a manifestation of bourgeois capitalism intended solely to secure markets and raw materials for European industry. Marx dismissed as a bourgeois idea the justification of colonialism as a Christian civilizing mission and he stressed its exploitative aspects. In an article that appeared in the *New York Daily Tribune* on 25 June 1853, Marx described English activities in India as "scientific barbarism," "plunder by means of murder," "diffusive horror," and a means to "subjugate" the East Indian Empire.[38]

Yet despite these negative appraisals of colonialism, Marx did not categorically condemn the actions of the colonial powers, nor did he judge colonialism by the standards of humanitarianism, Christian brotherhood, or the universal rights of mankind. Abstract considerations of justice were always secondary to the tactics of revolutionary practice. Marx's analysis of colonialism led him to the conclusion that it, like nationalism, could be condoned if it generated revolutionary conditions. Colonialism, according to Marx, accomplished this end by economically modernizing previously uncivilized societies.

The British presence in India, for example, had certain positive aspects despite its exploitative cruelty. Marx shed no tears over the destruction of the Indian social system. On the contrary, he believed that this backward social system provided the "foundation of Oriental Despotism," by which he meant an "undignified, stagnatory, and vegetative life" that resulted in "wild, aimless, unbounded forces of destruction, and rendered murder itself a religious rite in Hindostan."[39] Marx was of the opinion that this stagnant, ahistorical quality of Asiatic life derived from the fact that there was no system of private ownership of land in Asia.[40] Consequently, Asia, left to itself, did not develop according to the rules of history outlined by Marx and Engels in the *Manifesto*. In fact, it was not until 1859 that Marx made any mention of the Asiatic mode of production,[41] and even then it was clear that "Asiatic" was a geographical designation that remained outside of the dialectical stages of historical development, previously identified as ancient, medieval, and bourgeois.[42] In short, Marx's original Europocentric description of historical processes could not explain the economic stagnation of an area that contained the vast majority of the world's population.

Given this view of an immutable Asiatic system incapable of instigating its own economic development, it is understandable that

Marx would have discovered a progressive aspect in colonialism. Writing of the English effect in India, Marx reported, "English interference . . . dissolved these small semi-barbarian, semi-civilized communities, by blowing up their economical bases, and thus produced the greatest, and, to speak the truth, the only *social* revolution ever heard of in Asia."[43] Naturally the British colonials had not intended to restart the wheels of progress in Asia. "England," wrote Marx, "in causing a social revolution in Hindostan, was activated only by the vilest interests. . . . But that is not the question."[44] The significant question was: Can the destiny of mankind be realized without a "fundamental revolution" in Asia? Marx replied that "whatever may have been the crimes of England she was the unconscious tool of history in bringing about the revolution."[45]

Marx's line of reasoning leads to the conclusion that struggles for national liberation from colonial exploitation are counterrevolutions if they occur before the creation of a bourgeois economic base. For example, he deplored the Indian Sepoy Rebellion in 1857. He ventured that the sepoys had little chance against the superior British, and in the long run they would be defeated because they were not ready for revolution. The fact that the Sepoy Rebellion was an anticolonial uprising was of little consequence to Marx.

This last point is critical, for it suggests that although Marx was ready to accept various approaches to revolution within Europe, he could not accept any form of Asian revolution that was not predicated on European economic principles of development. Revolution in India or China could come only after English-type bourgeois capitalism had been introduced. "Skipping" stages of economic development or adapting the revolutionary movement to Asian or African experiences was, in Marx's opinion, unscientific socialism.[46] Premature national liberation efforts could only forestall the real revolution and were therefore reactionary. Marx states this most succinctly and forcefully in the conclusion to his *Tribune* article, "The Future Results of British Rule in India."

> The bourgeois period of history was to create the material basis of the new world. . . . Bourgeois industry and commerce create these material conditions of a new world in the same way as geological revolutions have created the surface of the earth. When a great social revolution shall have mastered the results of the bourgeois epoch, . . . and subjected them to the control of the most advanced peoples, *then only* will human progress cease to resemble that hideous pagan idol, who would not drink the nectar but from the skulls of the slain [emphasis supplied].[47]

The patent implication of this conclusion is that Marx did not believe that communist revolutions would occur simultaneously or even in rapid succession throughout the world. When Marx called on the workers of "all countries" to unite, he meant those of the civilized world of western Europe and not the colonial peoples. More importantly, particularly with respect to the question of national liberation, Marx apparently did not believe that colonialism would, or necessarily should, end even after the revolution succeeded in the most advanced systems. In a letter to the German Social Democrat Karl Kautsky written in 1882, Engels summarized the Marxist position on the relationship between a successful revolutionary proletariat and the colonial peoples.

> The countries inhabited by a native population, which are simply subjugated, India, Algiers, the Dutch, Portuguese and Spanish possessions, must be taken over for the time being by the proletariat and led as rapidly as possible towards independence. . . . But as to what social and political phases these countries will then have to pass through before they likewise arrive at socialist organization, we today can only advance rather idle hypotheses, I think.[48]

The "semi-civilized" countries, as Engels referred to them, were undoubtedly a unique case, and not even the scientific methodology of the historical dialectic could contribute to a knowledge of what path of development they would pursue. Engels wrote, "One thing alone is certain: the victorious proletariat can force no blessings of any kind upon any foreign nation without undermining its own victory by doing so. Which of course by no means excludes defensive wars of various kinds."[49]

As cryptic as this last statement is with regard to the limits of colonial interference by a successful proletariat, it leaves no doubt that even at the end of their lives Marx and Engels had not developed a doctrine of national liberation for countries inhabited by non-European populations. In fact, they foresaw the indefinite continuation of colonial control after the proletariat was successful in Europe.

THE MARXIST VIEW OF NATIONAL COMMUNISM

Marx's views on nationalism may be simply summarized. Nationalism, as a political movement that depicts the state as the ideal vehicle for human progress, he rejected as bourgeois ideology. This rejection did not preclude, however, the use of nationalist movements in the most advanced European systems to promote the revolutionary consciousness of the proletariat.

Marx's position on national communism was somewhat more complex. National communism, in the sense of proletarian coop- eration across international boundaries as opposed to a cosmopolitan merging of peoples, was a cornerstone of Marx's conception of internationalism. This was not an internationalism consisting of a general feeling of compassion or brotherhood in the name of humanity; Marx repudiated these ideals as meaningless and without revolutionary content. Marx's version of internationalism called for the disap- pearance of antagonistic national differences and the transcendence of purely national concerns by proletarian interests, but he did not ignore the historical and cultural factors that create a nation's problems and thereby necessitate nationally unique solutions.

Marx's acknowledgment of national idiosyncrasies must not be confused with "socialism in one country." Marx and Engels repudiated this idea when it was proposed by certain German Social Democrats such as Ferdinand Lassalle and George Vollmar.[50] In fact, the limits of Marx's tolerance of national differences among the international proletariat were quite narrow. Whether national feelings were to be bolstered or quashed, whether colonialism was to be endured or condemned, and whether nations were to be sustained or dissolved were invariably to be determined by what one analyst described as the "dictates of administrative efficiency,"[51] or in more Marxist phraseology, the requirements of proletarian revolution.

Contemporary national communism has taken two forms: that of the antihegemonic (essentially anti-Soviet) ruling parties in Eastern Europe; and the antiimperialist, Marxist national liberation move- ments of nonruling groups throughout Asia (and to a lesser extent in Latin America). Can the roots of both types of national communism be traced to the ideas of Marx and Engels? Would they have condoned such developments? Marx and Engels repudiated cosmopolitan uni- formity. They endorsed the national aspirations of economically advanced peoples, and condemned those of uncivilized populations. They never dogmatically insisted on a specific pre- or postrevolu- tionary course of development for the industrially advanced nations of Europe. Neither did they prescribe a specific path of development for the uncivilized world, although they were convinced that its path would be similar to the European pattern once the proper course was set by the activities of the colonial powers.

On the other hand, Marx neither accepted nor sanctioned the principles of national self-determination or national liberation that have become an integral element of the second form of contemporary national communism. In Marx's opinion, national claims made by uncivilized populations with no economic base were premature and patently bourgeois. He certainly preferred Western guidance of colonially oppressed peoples until such time as they were economically prepared for their own proletarian revolutions (i.e., until they had become industrialized and had both capitalist and working classes). Must we, then, conclude that the brand of national communism practiced by most, if not all, of the non-European communist parties (including that of the USSR) is untraceable to Marx and would surely have been denounced by him as counterrevolutionary?

The answer to this question is wholly speculative and depends largely on one's view of the importance of ideological consistency in Marx's thought. An underlying assumption of this analysis has been that Marx's ideological positions were frequently tempered by a remarkable degree of tactical flexibility. Above all else, Marx was consumed by a passion for revolution, and whether or not the Bolshevik, Chinese, or Vietnamese revolution was consistent with "Marxist" theory would probably have been far less important to Marx than the fact that it actually occurred.

At the same time, Marx exhibited a manifestly authoritarian attitude when it came to judging the rectitude of any revolutionary idea, an attitude that contributed to the destruction of two internationalist efforts during his lifetime.[52] Marx demonstrated that he could grant a certain degree of latitude to factionalists but he could as easily withhold it. Perhaps this propensity of Marx left a permanent impression on the movement in that each of his contemporary successors who has asserted ideological leadership has similarly claimed the authority to determine whether the actions of the other members are in conformity with the requirements of revolutionary progress.

National variety within the limits of proletarian internationalism was, indeed, part of Marx's vision. Those who have contended that proletarian nations had no role to play in Marx's internationalist scheme, and those who have asserted that Marx made no allowances for national variations within the communist movement, are mistaken. Marx declared in the *Manifesto* that with the coming of the revolution, "the hostility of one nation to another will come to an end,"[53] not the system of nations itself. The "state" as a mechanism of exploitation might, in Marx's scenario, "wither away"; yet administration of community affairs would continue indefinitely. In this process of social administration (which might also be called the "political process"), the possibilities for national differences are as infinite as the historical, geographical, and ecological variations that created them.

Whatever Marx would or would not have condoned, and whatever he actually said or did not say, the communist movement continued and developed long after he had passed from the scene. While many strains of Marxism have emerged, Lenin, Stalin, and the Bolshevik movement in Russia unquestionably had the greatest historical impact on communism. By virtue of their revolutionary success in 1917, they made communism a "national" movement for the first time. This initial nationalization of communism was inspired by Marx, but it also represented a new model that substantially modified the relationship between international communism and national development. It is to these modifications that we must now turn our attention.

SUGGESTIONS FOR FURTHER READING

Avineri, Shlomo, ed. *Karl Marx on Colonialism and Modernization.* New York: Doubleday and Company, Inc., 1968.

Bloom, Solomon. *The World of Nations: A Study of the National Implications in the Work of Karl Marx.* New York: Columbia University Press, 1941.

Drachkovitch, Milorad. *The Revolutionary Internationals.* Stanford: Stanford University Press, 1966.

Goodman, Elliot. *The Soviet Design for a World State.* New York: Columbia University Press, 1960.

Herod, Charles. *The Nation in the History of Marxian Thought: The Concept of Nations With History and Nations Without History.* The Hague: Martinus Nijhoff, 1976.

McLellan, David, ed. *Karl Marx: Selected Writings.* Oxford: Oxford University Press, 1977.

Petrus, Joseph. "Marx and Engels on the National Question." *Journal of Politics* 33 (August 1971):797–825.

Wolfe, Bertram. *Marxism: One Hundred Years in the Life of a Doctrine.* New York: Dial Press, 1965.

3
The Soviet Hegemony

In 1889, eight years after Marx died, the Second International was organized to promote the revolutionary interests of the working class. By that time, however, the lack of progress toward socialist revolution had generated some new questions among Marxists. In this atmosphere of growing frustration and disappointment, it was inevitable that disagreements over what had gone wrong would emerge, and that opinions would diverge on the question of what corrective actions might get the Socialist International back on the revolutionary track. Given Marx's ambiguity on the national question, and the fact that nationalism had become an increasingly important force in European affairs in the latter part of the nineteenth century, much of the internal wrangling centered on the "national problem."

The socialists faced two related questions. First, what was to be the relationship between working-class movements and national movements in the prerevolutionary era of capitalism? Second, what was to be the policy of socialism toward national impulses *within* the international movement? These were not just theoretical questions of purely intellectual interest. Upon the answer to the first question depended the entire revolutionary strategy of the working class in Europe and throughout the world. The very success of the revolution depended on the correct answer. Upon the answer to the second question rested the future of socialism once the revolution was successful—in short, the survival of the international movement. These two questions constitute the dual themes of this chapter, because it was in the process of coming to terms with these issues that twentieth-century national communism took shape. Contrary to the opinions of those who contend that "the question of national communism only emerged after World War II,"[1] this examination of the post-Marx period will show that the ambivalence in Marx's thoughts on national problems persisted and plagued the socialist movement throughout the histories of both the Second and the Third Internationals. National communism, rooted in Marx, was not, as we shall see, a postwar aberration in Eastern Europe, but an inherent characteristic of proletarianism. In fact, the real aberration consisted of Stalin's unfortunate and ultimately unsuccessful attempt to quash national variation by brute force. But even this attempt, as will be made clear, took the form of national communism at its most extreme.

It was patent to Marx's followers that he was not a nationalist and that nationalism had no place in Marxism. What was at issue among the post-Marx socialists was the significance of national movements in Europe and in the "Eastern" world for the proletarian revolution to come. Do national movements, they wondered, either for autonomy within empires or for independence from them, contribute to or retard the socialist revolutionary process? The answer to this question would, of course, dictate the attitude that Marxists should assume toward national movements.

Until the success of the Russian revolution in 1917, the debate over the role of national movements was concerned almost exclusively with the problem of creating conditions conducive to working-class revolution, not with developing hypotheses about the role of nations in the postrevolutionary phase. This emphasis was consistent with Marx's own approach to the problem. As the preceding chapter has demonstrated, national variations in revolutionary strategy were not inconsistent with Marx's strategy. In fact, cosmopolitans like Proudhon had registered their disagreement with Marx's views on the national question, and the split between the internationalists and the cosmopolitans was already well established before Marx's death. But the post-Marx debates on the national question involved a far more complex set of issues.

Before the content of the disagreements is considered, two general characteristics of the national disputes must be noted. First, the unity of thought and purpose imposed on the international socialist movement during the Stalin era was atypical of the preceding period of socialism. On this national question, and virtually all others, conflict had been the norm. Neither Marx nor Lenin had yet been elevated to the pantheon of socialist gods—untouchable and omniscient. That myth was created by Stalin, a man in search of absolute power, which required access to absolute truth. The point is that a wide diversity of opinion had existed on this issue and no single national policy had emerged from these debates. Therefore, it is a mistake to refer to "a socialist national policy" before the Bolshevik seizure of power.

Second, and more noteworthy, is the fact that throughout the post-Marx era (as during Marx's lifetime) the socialist movement was plagued by national divisions. Because membership in the Internationals was by national sections, it was inevitable that some national distinctions would emerge. What was not inevitable, but occurred with disturbing regularity, was that positions on national issues coincided very strongly with national problems extant in the states from which the policies derived. In short, the national settings from which socialists came appear to have strongly influenced their attitudes on national questions. A half century or more before the Pole Gomulka challenged the Russian Khrushchev, or the Frenchman Marchais stood up to the Russian Brezhnev, Poles, Frenchmen, and Russians were disagreeing with each other over national issues, and their nationalities were not coincidental to these disputes.

Should socialists support national movements or not? Is the drive for national independence or autonomy in conflict with the goals of socialist revolution? The answer provided by Marx and Engels to such questions was, Support all progressive movements, which meant, Support any idea or movement that will hasten the coming of the revolution. But this raises a second question: Are national movements progressive? As we have seen, Marx's answer was, It depends. Time and place are critical considerations in Marxist thought. Things are not good or bad (except the revolution itself), true or untrue, they are historical or nonhistorical. At first, when Marx believed that the revolution in Great Britain was imminent, he opposed the Irish national movement on the ground that it would retard the development of British capitalism and thus retard proletarian progress. Later, when it became clear that the British capitalists had consolidated their position, Marx switched his support in favor of Irish independence on the grounds that it would contribute to the deconcentration of bourgeois power and wealth, thereby stimulating the English working-class movement. The same was true of his relativist position on the future of eastern European national movements. So the Marxist solution to the national problem was to support national movements if they somehow contributed to the objective historical process leading to proletarian revolution. Supporting national movements did not make one a nationalist.

For Marx's successors the question was the same: Was support for national movements still a progressive act around the year 1900 and later or had time changed the situation? Hence, the debate was actually not over support for national movements, but over whether these movements were in any way progressive in the era of mature capitalism. Eventually, the national question became the national *and colonial* question as the scope of the debate widened to include the new movements that were rapidly emerging in the colonial world.

At the risk of oversimplification, the post-Marx socialists can be classified into three schools of thought on the national question. The Proudhonist, cosmopolitan position of antinationalism was expounded most persuasively by the Polish socialist Rosa Luxemburg and became identified as the Left. (It was also supported by Trotsky.) The so-called Right or pronational viewpoint found its keenest expression in the ideas of the Austrian Social Democrats Carl Renner and Otto Bauer. Between these two extremes a Center position developed, expressed most coherently in the work of the Russian Lenin.

In the view of the cosmopolitan, antinationalist Left, the success of the proletarian movement depended exclusively on the unity of the working class and the development of its class consciousness. Anything that impeded the progress of that unity and consciousness was counterrevolutionary. Rosa Luxemburg, despite being both Polish and Jewish, argued that socialist support for national movements would force each proletariat to identify its interests with those of its bourgeoisie, since it would be the bourgeoisie that would be at the forefront of any national movement. If, for example, Polish proletarians, living under tsarist domination, were taught to think of Russians as their enemies, they would inevitably perceive the Russian proletariat as their enemy as well. And, if the Polish proletariat could pursue common interests with the Polish bourgeoisie for national independence, what, wondered Luxemburg, would be left of its class-consciousness when that independence was achieved?

Luxemburg and the leftists contended that the formation of fewer but larger states was an indication that capitalism was entering its final phase. To break up these empires was to retard capitalist development (because it inhibited concentration of capital), thereby delaying the inevitable revolution. Luxemburg's analysis led her to the conclusion that the internationalization of capital (through export to colonies and the formation of transnational enterprises) rendered national proletarian movements ineffective. Because the enemy had become internationalized since Marx had analyzed the situation, it was imperative that the proletariat also remain internationalized.

As if these ideological and economic reasons were not enough, Luxemburg had a practical political reason for not supporting the Polish national movement—it had no chance of success against the powerful Russian Empire. If the proletarian party supported Polish independence, it would be destroyed in defending a lost cause that had never been in its real interests. Despite Marx's optimism about the possibility of Polish independence and his appraisal of the beneficial effects it might have on the proletarian movement, Luxemburg categorically opposed socialist support for all national movements, including the Polish one.

The leftist position was not, however, a deviation from Marxism. Although she was accused by Lenin of Proudhonist, cosmopolitan "economism" (the belief that *only* economic forces could affect history), Luxemburg was arguing not against Marx, but beyond Marx. However progressive these national movements might have been in the past, the maturation of capitalism into a system of competitive empires demanded a new policy. The responsibility of the working-class movement was to contribute to the ultimate collapse of capitalism by doing everything possible to help it develop. When, and only when, the economic conditions were ripe, Luxemburg believed, the revolution would come and the proletariat would seize power, not in a single country, but throughout the world.

The critical weakness of Luxemburg's analysis, which her opponents were quick to attack, was that while she argued that times had changed with respect to the character of capitalism, she refused to recognize the growing importance of nationalism as a political force in Europe. Clinging to the single point of Marxist identification—class—Luxemburg and the leftists refused to recognize nationality as a source of legitimate societal cleavage.

The Right, on the other hand, was quite ready to concede the importance of nationalism in post-Marx Europe. It is no coincidence that the major proponents of the rightist position were the Austrians Carl Renner and Otto Bauer. The Hapsburg Empire was a multi-national amalgam of Austrians, Czechs, Poles, Hungarians, Ruthenians, Serbs, etc., which, unlike its Romanov counterpart in Russia, had begun to make some concessions to national autonomy and parliamentarianism by the latter part of the nineteenth century. Thus, for the Social Democrats of Austria the question was the same as elsewhere: how to bring about the working-class revolution as quickly as possible. But the answer was quite different under the Hapsburgs.

The Austrian socialists agreed that socialism could only follow capitalism, and that during the capitalist phase the obligation of the proletariat is to promote those policies that propel capitalism along its inevitable course. What had become apparent to virtually everyone by the end of the nineteenth century was that capitalism had taken a decidedly democratic turn. The consensus was that the democratization of bourgeois society was good for socialism because socialist parties would be freer to operate among the workers than in an autocracy such as Russia. Therefore, a good socialist had to be a good democrat in bourgeois society.

Unquestionably, one of the fundamental democratic principles was national equality, with its corollary that each nation had the right to rule itself and determine its own future. Renner and Bauer recognized that the dissatisfaction of national minorities in the Hapsburg Empire could be mobilized by the socialists through an appeal for national autonomy. Socialism being a movement of those alienated from the established social order, the principle of national self-determination had special appeal for Social Democrats in Austria, because it would at one and the same time promote democratic values and disaggregate the Empire. Support for national movements in Austria, and elsewhere in Europe where national minorities were oppressed, was, in short, perceived by Renner and Bauer as progressive.

The principle underpinning the Renner-Bauer thesis was that of national cultural autonomy. Defining "nation" as a "community of fate," Bauer called for a plan whereby each national group would have complete control over its cultural life (i.e., education, family life) on an "extraterritorial" basis. Rather than restricting national autonomy to specific geographical regions, the plan permitted members of each national group to participate in the cultural affairs of the nation regardless of their places of residence.

By treating nationality like religion, in allowing anyone who identified with a particular group to participate in formulating its doctrine and practice, Bauer hoped to avoid the problems of governing regions inhabited by many nationalities and the inevitable oppression of minorities living in an area dominated by a powerful nationality. The Austrian plan of extraterritorial national autonomy was ideal for a multinational empire composed of widely dispersed national groups.

On the question of what national cultural autonomy could contribute to proletarian revolution, Renner and Bauer diverged from Marx. It was their view that Marx had underestimated the vitality of nationalism, particularly the effect it had on class formation. Bauer believed that national culture in precapitalist societies was carried by the upper classes, but that capitalism had awakened the masses, permitting them to contribute to national cultural development (i.e., in art, literature, and education). The problem, as Bauer saw it, was that in a multinational state like Austria, economic oppression was based on nationality. Whether one was a member of the proletariat or the bourgeoisie depended in large measure on one's nationality.

Hence, in the capitalist stage of development, national oppression was transformed class oppression and "national hate was transformed class hate."[2] Capitalism, therefore, would create a nationalistic, class conscious proletariat rather than, as Marx had predicted, an internationally oriented proletariat.[3] Renner and Bauer concluded that when, in a multinational empire, national and class oppression combine, it is possible to be a nationalist and a socialist simultaneously.

Renner and Bauer presented their plan for extraterritorial national autonomy through the South Slav delegation to the Congress of the Austrian Social-Democratic Party held in Bruenn (Brno) in 1899. Owing primarily to the difficulties inherent in the administration of such a plan, the Bruenn Congress adopted a modified version of the Renner-Bauer proposal that was based on territorial national autonomy. The Bruenn Plan called for the division of the Hapsburg Empire into provinces that coincided as closely as possible with the territorial distribution of the nationalities, and the granting of full autonomy over cultural and educational affairs to each national region.[4]

Despite the failure of the extraterritorial element of the Renner-Bauer proposal, the Bruenn Plan was an attempt on the part of the right wing of the socialist movement to integrate the enduring phenomenon of nationalism into the revolutionary program. The Austrian socialists realized that nationalism would not disappear, before or after the revolution, and that national identification would persist indefinitely. As a first step toward coping with this problem, the Bruenn Congress reorganized the Austrian Social-Democratic Party along national lines and called for a similar division of the Empire.

The logic of the Austrian plan demanded that socialists support all movements for national autonomy. Since only mature capitalism could bring forth socialism, and since national self-determination had become an integral element of democratic capitalism (its most advanced stage), a socialist who refused to support national autonomy movements was, in effect, refusing to support socialist revolution. Obviously, socialists in systems inhabited by a single nationality would not face this choice, but the conclusion for socialists in multinational empires was inescapable: They must support national movements (although clearly bourgeois) because such movements ultimately led to socialism. This would be as true for Russian as for Austrian socialists. Dialectically, the Russians were less developed than the Austrians, but the only way to bring Russia to the final goal had to be to promote capitalist development by support for bourgeois democracy, and this, in turn, required support for the principle of national self-determination.

The Left and the Right began with the same premise—that socialists must aid all progressive movements and combat all counterrevolutionary ones—and arrived at antipodal conclusions as to the socialist obligation to support national movements. Luxemburg concluded with an absolute no, and Bauer with an absolute yes. It remained for Lenin to provide a third, more practical and, indeed, more Marxist answer: yes and no.

Although the idea of extraterritorial national autonomy failed at the 1899 Bruenn Congress of Austrian socialists, it had immediate impact on the affairs of the Russian Social Democratic Labor Party (RSDLP), which had been founded just a year earlier. One group in particular, the Jewish Bund,[5] which had associated itself with the RSDLP in 1898, found the Renner-Bauer proposal especially attractive. Given their history of oppression in an empire dominated by Russians, the Jews were understandably anxious to guarantee the autonomy of Jewish socialists within a Russian socialist party. Before the Austrian Plan, however, the Jews, lacking a territory of their own, had been unable to justify such autonomy on either national or socialist grounds. The Bund leaped at the extraterritorial national autonomy thesis as the ideal justification for the right of a nationality without territory to exist as a national section within the RSDLP.[6]

The Bund made its request for autonomy at the Second Congress of the RSDLP in 1903. Wary of any attempt to decentralize control over the party, Lenin successfully urged the defeat of the Bund proposal. Instead, the RSDLP, borrowing from the 1896 program of the Second International, adopted Article 9 of its own program, which demanded "the right of all nations in the state to self-determination."[7] The immediate effect of this action was the temporary disassociation of the Bund from the Russian party; more importantly, it focused the attention of the leadership of the RSDLP on the national problem. Yet owing to more pressing problems, including the Revolution of 1905, the principle of national self-determination was to remain vague for at least another decade.

Indicative of Lenin's early appraisal of the importance of national movements in the flow of revolutionary events is the fact that he did not address himself to the problem in any significant way until 1913, when he published a series of articles entitled "Critical Remarks on the National Question."[8] As a Russian, Lenin was fully aware of national oppression under tsardom, but as a Marxist he discounted the influence of national identity compared to class consciousness. It was during his residence in Crakow, situated between the Hapsburg and Russian empires, that Lenin formulated his initial theories on the relationship between national minorities and socialist parties.

In part because he developed his national policy rather late and in part because of his otherwise seemingly unshakable commitment to centralized revolutionary organization, Lenin has been accused of having been an opportunist who merely sought to use nationalism to further his revolutionary cause. Richard Pipes has concluded that "once he realized the value of the national movement as a weapon for fighting the established order, he stopped at nothing to employ it for his own ends."[9] Another critic asserted that Lenin's national policy only served the purpose of "corralling all the malcontents" in the tsarist empire.[10] What is certainly true is that Lenin had no sympathy for national movements *per se,* and that for him nationalism was, at best, an instrumental value rather than an end in itself.

Among his contemporaries, Lenin's critics wondered how he could support national self-determination, yet reject the Bundist request for autonomy. There is undoubtedly a certain ambiguity in a policy that rejects nationalism as an authentic value, but can support national movements. It was by way of resolving this apparent dilemma and answering his socialist critics that Lenin wrote his "Critical Remarks on the National Question." At the same time, he recruited a young Georgian member of the party to write a supplementary essay that outlined the Bolshevik position on nationalism in Russia. That essay, also written in 1913, was entitled "Marxism and the National Question." The author was Joseph Stalin. Lenin and Stalin attempted to make explicit what had only remained implicit in Marx's and Engels's writings, and in so doing, firmly established the legitimacy of national communism.

NATIONALITY POLICY IN THEORY

Nowhere did Lenin define the term "nation." Instead, he relied on Stalin's formulation of 1913: "A nation is a historically evolved, stable community of language, territory, economic life and psychological make-up manifested in a community of culture."[11] No single element was sufficient to make a group a nation, and a group that lacked even one of the required characteristics did not qualify. All German-speaking people did not, in Stalin's view, compose a German nation because they did not inhabit a single territory, and, more importantly from Lenin's perspective at the time, the Jews were not a nation by this definition because they shared neither a territory nor a language. Thus the Bundist claim for a national section within the RSDLP was negated.

The heart of Lenin's nationality policy was self-determination. He rejected the Renner-Bauer position on national cultural autonomy on the ground that any system of national autonomy, including federalism, in a multinational state would divide the proletariat and inhibit revolutionary progress. For Lenin, nations had but one right, that of self-determination, which meant the right of an oppressed national minority to political independence. "The right of nations to self-determination," Lenin declared, "implies exclusively the right to independence in the political sense, the right to free political separation from the oppressor nation. . . . It implies only a consistent expression of struggle against all national oppression."[12] In other words, oppressed nations in Russia were free to choose between political independence and national assimilation. There was no middle ground. "While, and insofar as, different nations constitute a single state," wrote Lenin, "Marxists will never, under any circumstances advocate either the federal principle or decentralization."[13]

Whence did this "right" of national self-determination derive? As with all such imperatives in Marxism, its source was history. Capitalism, according to Lenin, emerges in two successive stages. In the first, nations develop and boundaries harden. Only after capitalism fully matures do national frontiers give way to international cooperation. Thus, the nation-state is the normal form of political organization under capitalism, and capitalist development mandates in each instance "the political separation of these nations from alien national bodies, and the formation of an independent national state."[14] Once capitalism fully develops in these states, however, nationalism becomes counterprogressive; therefore, national groups must sublimate their national to their class interests.

In Lenin's opinion, Luxemburg's failure was that she did not understand that "the best conditions for the development of capitalism are undoubtedly provided by the national state."[15] And, on the other hand, the Bund's failure (as with all European Jewish movements) was that it did not recognize that national assimilation was inevitable under mature capitalism, and that to oppose assimilation into civilized societies was antiprogressive.[16] Lenin warned the socialists of the Left and the Right: "To throw off . . . all national oppression, and all privileges enjoyed by any particular nation or language, is the imperative duty of the proletariat. . . . But to go *beyond* these strictly limited and definite historical limits in helping bourgeois nationalism means betraying the proletariat. . . ."[17]

The danger inherent in a working-class movement's supporting nationalist aspirations was that the proletariat could lose sight of its true enemy. If, for example, in their justifiable opposition to Russian domination, Ukrainian Marxists permitted their hate of Russian bourgeois culture to transfer to the Russian proletariat, the Ukrainian socialist movement would "get bogged down in bourgeois nationalism."[18] Therefore, Lenin reminded his fellow socialists that "there are two nations in every modern nation," one proletarian and the other bourgeois.[19] To be *against* the oppression of one nation by another was not to be *for* the national goals of those being oppressed. The working class of an oppressed nation was obliged to support all forces that opposed independence, without losing itself in nationalist values. Similarly, the proletariat of oppressor nations must support the national self-determination claims of those people dominated by their nations, and not permit themselves to fall victim to the appeals of bourgeois nationalism. Implicit in Lenin's view is a clear distinction between great power nationalism, or what he called chauvinism, which could never be supported, and minority nationalism, which had to be supported if it was directed against the bourgeoisie of an oppressing nation.

The nations inhabiting tsarist Russia had the right of national self-determination because Russia was then entering the first stage of capitalist development, which required nation-state formation. Article 9 of the 1903 RSDLP program was a statement of principle, not of policy. Luxemburg's error in attacking national self-determination in Russia was, in Lenin's words, that *"she does not make the least* attempt to determine *what* historical stage in the development of capitalism Russia is passing through . . . , or what the *specific features* of the national question in this country are."[20] Lenin regarded this sort of leftist thinking as "abstract internationalism"[21] because it lacked Marxist historical concreteness. Lenin did not believe that support for the principle of national self-determination obliged him to support *all* national movements in practice.

Lenin's advocacy of national self-determination was indeed instrumental in that he believed it would serve a higher purpose. In this, however, Lenin was no different from the liberal democrats who supported national self-determination because they believed that the individual had the best opportunity for advancement within the nation-state system. Liberal democrats uphold the principles of national self-determination, national sovereignty, and noninterference in the internal affairs of other nations if, and only if, the purposes of individualism are served. If the national mechanism is employed to manipulate and enslave individuals (e.g., in Nazi Germany) the higher principles of liberal democracy demand an abrogation of these national rights. So it was with Lenin, who, in perfect consistency, supported all democratic values, including national self-determination, not because he believed in their universal validity, but because it was the obligation of a socialist to be a democrat in the era of capitalism.

More important, Lenin did not advocate national self-determination because he wanted to promote the proliferation of independent nations. His ultimate goal was just the reverse, but he believed that the goal of international cooperation lay at the end of the path of national independence. To the question, Why does nationalism exist? Lenin had a simple (perhaps too simple) answer: Because there is political inequality and oppression among nations. The nationalism of small, weak nations is an expression of their desire for just treatment and equal status. They are nationalistic because they are exploited. The nationalism of large, powerful nations is, on the other hand, an expression of collective egotism. It is a feeling of cultural superiority that is perceived as natural and as entitling a nation to dominate those less fortunate and less civilized. It is what Lenin called chauvinism.

Only the elimination of national inequality would, in Lenin's opinion, eliminate nationalism of both types. Because equality was a principal component of socialism, socialists could not be chauvinists. Hence, there could be no national exploitation under socialism. If there were no national exploitation, there would be no nationalism emanating from small nations. Because history had shown that large political units were economically superior to small ones, the small nations, in the absence of chauvinism, would voluntarily join together with larger nations for their own economic good. The element of compulsion having been eliminated by socialism, the proletariat of all nations would willingly abandon their irredentist claims and work together to build communism.

Lenin believed that the simple act of granting small nations the *right* to political independence would remove the cause of the demand and lead these small nations to reject the offer, preferring instead a voluntary association of equal nations under socialism. Because nationalism was merely a manifestation of the imperialist, capitalist order, both would vanish simultaneously. In short, Lenin never intended that any nation should actually exercise the right of national self-determination because, once granted, it lost its meaning. Rather than resulting in the disintegration of the Russian Empire, Lenin's right of national self-determination was intended to provide the foundation for its renaissance in a spirit of equality and cooperation.

Lenin did not, however, imagine that all this would occur overnight. He was prepared to accept the persistence of nations, even after the revolution, but not their permanence. Lenin's blueprint for the future of nations was vaguely utopian.

> By transforming capitalism into socialism the proletariat creates the *possibility* of abolishing national oppression; the possibility becomes *reality* "only"—"only"!—with the establishment of full democracy in all spheres, including the delineation of state frontiers in accordance the "sympathies" of the population, including freedom to secede. And this, in turn, will serve as a basis for developing the practical elimination of even the slightest national friction and the least national mistrust, for an accelerated drawing together and fusion of nations that will be completed when the state *withers away.*[22]

Nations would disappear—some day. Lenin, like Marx, did not contend that the revolution would wash away all preexisting institutions in a tidal wave of proletarian transformation. The seizure of state power by the proletariat (or its vanguard, the party) would be only the opening scene of what promised to be a drama of epic length. Only the final act, the achievement of communism, would bring with it the elimination of states and nations. Also like Marx, Lenin was a man consumed by revolution, not government, and his postrevolutionary images were as out of focus as his revolutionary tactics were in. Patently, however, both within Russia and around the globe, the postrevolutionary Leninist world was to be one of nations. Having to live with that fact was to cause Lenin and his successors some of their greatest problems.

NATIONALITY POLICY IN PRACTICE

Poised on the brink of power, the Bolsheviks of Petrograd awaited the shot from the gun of the cruiser Aurora on the river Neva that was to signal the beginning of the revolution. That round, fired on 7 November 1917, proved to be only the first in what was to be a prolonged civil war to decide Russia's fate. The tsar was gone, but the tsarists were not. The Bolsheviks were in power, but not in control. While the struggle unfolded the empire disintegrated as, one by one, the minority nationalities, taking Lenin at his word, seceded. It was Lenin who had insisted that national self-determination equalled political independence, but he had meant independence from an oppressive, bourgeois state. Before he had the opportunity to convince these nationalities that not all Russians were chauvinists, they exercised the right he had promised them.[23] To a regime struggling for its very survival in a civil war, however, political secession became an act against the government and the party.

Lenin was forced by the press of circumstances to focus his immediate attention on the political and economic transformation of Russian society under Bolshevism. Coordination of the new regime's military efforts against the counterrevolutionaries was placed in the hands of Leon Trotsky, a former Menshevik and critic of Lenin, whose views on the national problem were similar to those of Rosa Luxemburg. Direct responsibility for the national problem was placed under the jurisdiction of the new Commissar of Nationalities, Joseph Stalin, who had been Lenin's virtual echo on the national question up to that time. Some years would pass before these three would find themselves at deadly odds with one another over national issues. For the time being they shared a single goal toward which all policy was directed—consolidation of the Bolshevik regime's power over Russia.

Lenin faced an ideological dilemma. His prerevolutionary analysis of the national problem had led to the conclusions that national self-determination would be an important weapon *against* nationalism, and that the right to secede, once granted, would not be exercised. For Lenin to recant in the face of massive national secession would have been an admission that he was wrong (perhaps about other things as well), but to do nothing as the country disintegrated meant certain defeat for his regime. This was to be a crucial turning point, not only for Russia, but for national communism. Lenin had conceded much to national movements, but he had naively underestimated the forces of nationalism. The dismemberment of the multinational empire was the price of that miscalculation.

It was Stalin who first publicly suggested a way out. Now, he argued, that the proletariat had seized power in Russia, the regime could not permit the doctrine of national self-determination to become a counterrevolutionary weapon. Contrary to Lenin's earlier thesis that the right to self-determination was to be exercised by a nation as a whole and that the decision to secede was one to be made by all classes in an oppressed nation, Stalin contended that "it is necessary to limit the principle of free self-determination of nations, by granting it to the toilers and refusing it to the bourgeoisie."[24] In short, the Bolsheviks should grant independence to a nation only if it was requested by the proletariat (or its spokesman, the party) of that nation. This was, in effect, a "Catch-22." Since no true working-class representative would seek independence from the world's first socialist system, all secessionist movements would, by definition, be controlled by bourgeois, counterrevolutionary elements. Regardless of how many people supported national independence, the Bolsheviks would be obliged to honor only the wishes of the workers.

Lenin was unwilling to accept the new interpretation of self-determination in its entirety because it harked back to the leftist position, which he had rejected, that only proletarian movements could be progressive. Yet at the Eighth Party Congress in March 1919, Lenin proposed a program that included the statement: "As to the question who is the carrier of the nation's will to separation, the Russian Communist Party stands on the historico-class point of view. . . ."[25] Lenin was forced to concede that in postrevolutionary Russia Stalin was correct. Only the proletariat had the right to declare national independence. So proletarian self-determination replaced national self-determination, and the Bolsheviks were free "to mobilize national movements where they sought to come to power and put down national movements where they resisted communist control."[26] Trotsky summarized the new communist regime's position perfectly:

> We do not only recognize, but we also give full support to the principle of national self-determination, wherever it is directed against feudal, capitalist and imperialist states. But whenever the fiction of national self-determination, in the hands of the bourgeoisie, becomes a weapon directed against the proletarian revolution, we have no occasion to treat this fiction differently from the other "principles" of democracy perverted by capitalism.[27]

This shift on national self-determination only foreshadowed a more important concession to follow. Lenin came to the conclusion that given the level of national feeling in Russia, some form of federal association that conceded national autonomy was the only possible way to hold the system together. In preparation for the drafting of the new Soviet Constitution, Lenin wrote: "The Soviet Russian Republic is established on the basis of a free union of free nations, as a federation of Soviet republics."[28] Lenin, who had insisted that a socialist could never be a federalist, was writing a federal constitution. The real irony of this situation, as Richard Pipes has observed, was that despite Lenin's abhorrence of both nationalism and federalism, the Soviet Union "became the first modern state to place the national principle at the base of its federal structure."[29] (Russia officially became the USSR on 30 December 1922.)

How can Lenin's turnabout on federalism and national autonomy be explained? First, Lenin considered federalism a transitional form of political organization, appropriate under the conditions of the civil war period, but not a system to be maintained permanently. The fact that it has persisted to the present day is added testimony to Lenin's underestimation of nationalist forces under socialism.

Second, Lenin had little choice in the matter. As Stalin later explained, minority nationalism was much stronger than Lenin had expected, and at the time, federation represented a step closer to unity than the total disintegration that followed the revolution.[30] Finally, Lenin's concession to federalism may have been more apparent than real. For one thing, his rejection of federalism was with reference to a bourgeois state where, he believed, the interests of the proletariat were best served by either unity or separation. After the collapse of the Russian bourgeois state, the Bolsheviks needed time to convince the minority nationalities that socialists were not Great Russian chauvinists, and federalism could hold the system together until then. But more importantly, Lenin realized that federalization of the Soviet government would be counterbalanced by centralization of the party. The Program of the Russian Communist Party adopted in 1919 stated: "There must exist a *single* centralized Communist Party with a single Central Committee leading all the party work in all sections of the RSFSR [Russian Soviet Federated Socialist Republic]. All decisions of the RKP [Russian Communist Party] and its directing organs are unconditionally binding on all branches of the party, regardless of its national composition."[31] Clearly, no amount of governmental federalism could reduce the party's control over its national sections, and it was the party, in the final analysis, that possessed the real political power. As long as the party-state relationship was maintained, federalism would be a symbolic concession to national feelings.

Whatever Lenin's reasons, these concessions, which he accepted as tactical necessities, were fundamental principles to Stalin. Almost imperceptibly at first, Stalin began departing from Lenin's nationality policy. Yet a critical change had occurred. By labeling all secessionist national movements "counterrevolutionary," Stalin was, in effect, declaring that Bolshevism would henceforward be *Russian* Bolshevism. The effects of this shift were to be profound, not only on Soviet development but on that of the international movement in general.

Lenin's nationality policy was not, however, limited to domestic considerations. After all, the Marxist revolution was to be a world revolution, and it was to a world of nations that Lenin addressed himself. At the same time that he struggled with the problems of nationalism in Soviet Russia, he could not ignore the problems that it posed on a world-wide scale. In fact, the two were not unrelated in that Lenin's nationality policy was part of his general analysis of capitalism in the age of imperialism. While Lenin's approach to the problem of nationalism in the Soviet Union is a crucial element of the development of contemporary national communism, the real problem for Lenin lay outside his country because that was where he believed the ultimate socialist revolution would occur.

LENIN AND THE INTERNATIONAL MOVEMENT

The most profound crisis suffered by international socialism was precipitated by the assassination of the Archduke Ferdinand at Sarajevo in August 1914. The Second International had been the focal point of the European working-class movement. Although divided into national sections, the socialists of Europe (including the Russians) agreed that the revolution would begin in an advanced country (probably Germany) and then spread inexorably across the continent. Even those who were willing to concede the possibility of the revolution beginning elsewhere insisted that it would have to spread rapidly in order to survive. The responsibility of each national section of the International was to destroy its own bourgeoisie and join with all other socialist parties in the march toward communism. All that died with the Archduke Ferdinand.

The immediate issue confronting all European socialist parties was the same. Should they vote in favor of war credits in their respective parliaments when to do so was to come to the aid of their bourgeois governments against other nations, including the workers of those nations? The German Social Democratic Party, acknowledged as the leading party of the International, was the first to answer. Partly because the German government provided mis-information to the effect that a Russian attack was imminent, and in no small measure as a spontaneous outburst of patriotism, the German socialists voted for war credits. With domino-like inevitability the Austrian, French, Belgian, and British socialists reacted in defense of their own countries.

What alternative did any of the parties have? If they had refused to vote for war credits to pay for their nations' defenses, they would have been accused of supporting their people's enemies. By voting for war credits they were seriously jeopardizing the unity of the international movement. Clearly, the former was more politically suicidal than the latter. Besides, there was some ideological justification for their actions in that Marx himself had advocated support for national wars in cases where a progressive nationality was doing battle with a reactionary one.[32] The German socialists could argue that they were voting not in support of the German bourgeoisie, but against the world's most reactionary system, tsarist Russia. Similarly, the British, French, Belgians, etc. could assure themselves that by

voting to resist the reactionary Huns they were fulfilling their revolutionary obligations. The fact was, however, that the Second International, indeed socialism itself, was swept away in a tidal wave
of patriotic nationalism.

Lenin stood virtually alone in his opposition to socialist support
for national war efforts. He did not deny that Marx had made
allowances for national wars; rather he argued that since Marx,
capitalism had entered a new stage of development that had eliminated
the possibility of legitimate national wars. This new imperialist stage,
Lenin explained, was characterized by the internationalization of
capital. Having exhausted domestic markets, the capitalists of each
nation had begun to export their capital to the colonial world and
to join together in an international capitalist network that transcended
national boundaries. Lenin contended that since the capitalist world
was no longer merely a collection of individual bourgeois states, as
it had been when Marx was alive, it was no longer possible to support
national wars. The war that began in 1914 was the first imperialist
struggle for world control in which no nation could be labelled
"progressive." Under these new circumstances, Lenin argued, the
obligation of the socialist parties was to withhold support for all
bourgeois governments, and at the same time to mobilize the working
class against imperialism. Only by fomenting civil war in each
imperialist country could the proletariat hope to destroy capitalism.

Lenin's critics on the Left were quick to point out a glaring
inconsistency in his national policy. If imperialism had transformed
capitalism with the result that no national cause could be progressive,
what justification could there be for socialist support for national
self-determination? Wasn't the latter policy premised on the notion
of progressive national movements? If times had changed since Marx
and national wars were no longer possible, did not those same changes
make proletarian support for national movements impossible as well?
Lenin never addressed himself to these questions.

Some attempts were made to reconvene the Socialist International,
if only to discuss the issues that divided the national sections. The
problem was that the socialist parties of the Alliance countries
categorically refused to sit at the same table with the German socialists
who had voted to support German aggression. Lenin was convinced
that the Second International was finished and began to call for the
formation of a Third International to comprise genuinely proletarian
parties, not opportunists. In view of the massive defections from
the International at the outbreak of the war, the small leftist faction
opposed to cooperation agreed to hold a conference to work out a
new socialist program. Lenin hoped that this conference, which

convened at Zimmerwald, Switzerland, on 5 September 1915, would mark the beginning of a new International founded on his principles of resistance to the war and civil disobedience throughout Europe. It was not to be so. Only seven of the thirty-eight Zimmerwald delegates would support Lenin's plan to turn the war to socialist advantage.

Lenin had become convinced that the new International was necessary in order to combat what had become the greatest impediment to revolutionary progress: not capitalist imperialism, but socialist chauvinism. "Social patriotism," Lenin declared at Zimmerwald, "which in Germany represents the view of the openly patriotic majority of the former Social Democratic leaders . . . is a more dangerous enemy of the proletariat than the bourgeois apostles of imperialism. . . ."[33] But it was Trotsky's draft program that was adopted at Zimmerwald, and it simply called for a socialist campaign to pressure all governments to end the war. "Not one of Lenin's ideas," wrote one historian of the International, "the struggle against the 'social patriotic' labor leaders, the organizing of revolutionary action, the transforming of the imperialist war into a civil war, or the splitting of the Second International—found any echo in the manifesto."[34]

Even as the war progressed, socialist support for Lenin's position remained weak. The Zimmerwald leftists turned to what Lenin called "social pacifism," going as far, in some cases, as to withdraw their original support for war credits. But only one faction, the German Spartakists under Rosa Luxemburg, came around to the view that revolutionary struggle, not peace, was the proper socialist response to imperialist war. The Second International, like the First, had divided over many issues, but in its final disintegration the cleavages were strictly along national lines.

The war would come to its bloody conclusion and the Bolsheviks would come to power in Russia before that Third International would be born in Moscow in March 1919. Lenin was determined that it should not suffer the fate of its predecessors.

The Third International was Leninist in form and Russian in content. Dominated by Russians from the beginning, with its headquarters in Moscow, the structure of the Third International was highly centralized in order to guarantee support for Lenin's international program. Indicative of its character was the fact that while this was the Third International, Lenin insisted that only "communists" could join his International. Point 17 of the famous "Twenty-One Points" that set forth conditions for membership required that "all parties which wish to join the Communist International must change their names. Every party . . . must be called *Communist* party of such and such country. . . ."[35] This was not just symbolism. Lenin wanted it to be known that he had "declared war" not only on the bourgeoisie, but on the socialist parties that had "betrayed the banner of the working class."[36] Now that Lenin had his own national political base from which to operate, he would decide which parties were legitimate members of the international movement. Lenin did not deny the right of national communist parties to determine their own revolutionary methods, but Lenin's imprimatur was required before any party could be labeled "Communist." The Third Communist International (Comintern) was not, therefore, a mechanism to outlaw national variations among Marxists; rather it was an instrument to ensure that such variations fell within Marxist parameters, as delineated by Moscow. Through Comintern, Lenin appropriated the rubric "Communist" and gave it meaning.

Despite the movement of the International's headquarters to Moscow, most communist eyes remained fixed on western Europe for signs of the gathering clouds of proletarian revolution. His unexpected success in Russia notwithstanding, Lenin continued to believe, at least until 1920, that the revolution would spread rapidly throughout Europe, probably beginning in Germany. The failure of the European working class to fulfill its historically mandated role was, in retrospect, the most significant nonevent in the development of contemporary communism. Even before Comintern came into existence, however, signs of doom had already appeared on the horizon. In January 1919, Rosa Luxemburg and Karl Liebknecht, the leaders of the German Spartakist movement, were arrested and murdered by the authorities without a trial.

Two months later, when Comintern convened for the first time, the shifting orientation of the movement was apparent in the composition of the delegates. Thirty-nine *parties* were invited to Moscow; thirty-four *people* attended. Only four of those delegates (two Scandinavians, a German, and an Austrian) resided outside Soviet Russia.[37] Eleven of the delegates who claimed to represent their native countries were, in fact, members of the Russian party and attended the Eighth Congress of the Bolshevik Party that convened the day after the Comintern session. Officially, Russia sent seven delegates.

As an international organization, Comintern was a hastily conceived fraud. It was thoroughly Russian. Lenin insisted on its formation because he needed an organization capable of coordinating the activities of the parties of the advanced countries of Europe in the event of revolution. That he was willing to "slap together" the Third International is testimony to his belief in the imminence of that revolution. Zinoviev, the first chairman of Comintern, wrote enthusiastically in the premier issue of its journal: "Europe is hurrying toward the proletarian revolution at a break-neck pace. . . . The victory of Communism throughout Germany is now inevitable. . . . In a year's time . . . all Europe will be Communist."[38]

This euphoria was as short-lived as the events that stimulated it. Soviet republics were established in Hungary and Bavaria, but quickly overthrown. There were similar abortive attempts at Soviet-style governments in Vienna, Berlin, and Finland. Thus, by the opening of the Second Comintern Congress in July 1920, the high spirits of the previous year had been dampened by Europe's reactionary trend. Soviet Russia under Lenin had to adjust to the isolation of a communist outpost in a hostile capitalist world. Lenin began to look elsewhere for allies in the revolutionary struggle.

In the search for new revolutionary frontiers it was Lenin's theory of imperialism that molded the emerging Bolshevik perspective on international events. In this one brilliant theoretical stroke Lenin was able to explain not only what had gone wrong but what to do about it. As we have seen, Lenin employed the theory of imperialism as the foundation for his attack against the European socialists who had supported national wars. His position was based on the notion that capitalism had broken out of its national boundaries and had become an imperial phenomenon.

Marx had predicted that capitalist systems would collapse when domestic markets became exhausted as the exploited proletariat did not have the income to support production. At that point capital growth would slow to a halt as there would be no place in the economy to invest. What Marx had not foreseen was the ability to adjust rapidly to this impending problem by expanding investment and markets beyond national borders through the acquisition of colonies. The implications of this transformation of capitalism were enormous for the revolutionary movement. Lenin used it to justify the revolution in precapitalist Russia, explaining that since the capitalist empires of the West had successfully adjusted to imperialism, the revolution was most likely in the country that had been least successful in acquiring world-wide colonial territories—what he referred to as the "weakest link in the chain of imperialism." The weakest link, according to Lenin, was Russia, despite the fact that it had a very immature capitalist system and a weak proletariat. The theory of imperialism converted these revolutionary liabilities into the greatest of assets.

After the Bolshevik revolution and the subsequent failure of the proletarian movement in the West to materialize, Lenin gradually pinned his hopes on the efforts of the colonial peoples of the East. Imperialism had victimized the populations of Africa, the Middle East, and Asia as capitalism rapaciously expanded in search of new markets and cheap labor. The capitalists had shifted the burden of the system off the shoulders of the industrial proletariat and on to those of the colonial poor; therefore, the future of the colonies was intimately bound to those who were struggling for liberation from capitalist exploitation.

By changing the enemy from capitalists to imperialists, Lenin had changed the potential allies of Bolshevism. When bourgeois capitalists were the target, the focal point of the revolution had to be the working class of each industrial nation, who were expected to overthrow their respective exploiters and join together in an international association of industrial workers. Under imperialism the revolutionary struggle itself had been internationalized and Lenin sought to enlist all of the oppressed people of the world—peasants, bourgeois, and workers—in the antiimperialist campaign. The obligation of the industrial proletariats in the West was to force their respective governments to dissolve their colonial empires and lend support to revolutions for national liberation. The obligation of communists within the colonies, where they existed, was to support national movements, even if led by bourgeois elements, because this was the only way to destroy imperialism. The obligation of the antiimperialist nationalists was to permit the communists to function within their movements.

Despite the obvious change in revolutionary direction introduced by Lenin (of whose ramifications he was not fully aware), one critical point remained constant in his design. The purpose of these national liberation movements was to destroy the imperialist structure so that the proletariat of the West could seize power in the industrialized nations. For Lenin at least, the goal of these colonial revolutions was *not* the communization of the East. Lenin had not shifted the communist revolution eastward; he continued to believe that communism was an outgrowth of capitalism. Lenin was simply saying that if communism was to succeed, the colonial foundations of capitalism had to be destroyed, and the best way to accomplish this was to join together in an antiimperialist movement.

Not fully convinced that the revolutionary prospects in the West were hopeless, Lenin presented to the Second Congress of Comintern in July 1920 alternative Western and Eastern strategies. If the Western communist movements revived, there was no question in Lenin's mind but that Comintern must throw its full weight behind European proletarian revolution. If, however, the Western parties continued to lose the initiative, Comintern had to devote its efforts to the support of national liberation movements in the East.

In *The Bolsheviks and the National and Colonial Question* Demetrio Boersner argued that Marx had arrived at this very same strategic conclusion by 1870. According to Boersner, the later "Eastern Marx" lost faith in the feasibility of proletarian revolution and concluded that "national democratic revolution of the underdeveloped agricultural areas would have to precede socialist transformation of the ruling and colonizing countries."[39] Lenin (and Stalin), he contended, followed the "Eastern Marx" of 1870, whereas Luxemburg and Trotsky remained faithful to the earlier "Western Marx." Whether or not Marx himself actually made this shift, there is no doubt that Lenin did, and Boersner has made a critical observation about the effect of this change on the future of the movement. "The failure of the first offensive against the advanced capitalist West had the effect of giving the revolution national forms."[40] Having declared that the future of communism was dependent upon the fate of nations, Lenin irrevocably placed communism on its national course.

There was no turning back, but this new Eastern strategy was to be a cause of concern not only to the "Westerners" who continued to have faith in the European proletariat, but to many Easterners as well. The latter had misgivings that the Bolsheviks (i.e., Lenin) did not understand the colonial world and were merely using national liberation movements until they could return to their primary concern, the European proletariat. They were fully justified in these fears.

Two Easterners in particular challenged Lenin's notions on colonialism. One, Sultan-Galiev, a Tatar residing in Russia, was an official in the Soviet Commissariat of Nationalities, and the other, M. N. Roy, an Indian, was a delegate to Comintern. They were willing to make explicit what was implicit in Lenin's program—that the revolution in the West was dead and the East would, henceforward, be the center of the movement. Lenin was not wrong, but he, being a European, was not willing to go far enough. Sultan-Galiev, who was witnessing first-hand the reemergence of Great Russian chauvinism in the "new" Russia, quickly concluded that a proletarian state was just as likely to repress national minorities as was a bourgeois one. Observing that even the Easterner Stalin was willing to sacrifice national minority interests to those that he believed were communist, but that were in actuality nationalist, Sultan-Galiev issued a call for the formation of a Colonial International to promote the interests of colonial people.[41] Sultan-Galiev's thesis was radical to Western ears.

We maintain that the formula which offers the replacement of world-wide dictatorship of one class of European society (its bourgeoisie) by its antipode (the proletariat) . . . will not bring about a major change in the social life of the oppressed segment of humanity. . . . In contradistinction to this we advance another thesis: the idea that the material premises for a social transformation of humanity can be treated only through the establishment of the dictatorship of the colonies and semi-colonies over the metropolitan areas.[42]

In 1921 Sultan-Galiev established the *Intercolonial Union,* with headquarters in Paris. The first chairman of this organization based on the principle of Eastern dominance was a young Vietnamese then residing in Paris who, some years later, was to adopt the revolutionary name Ho Chi-Minh.[43] Sultan-Galiev, a Soviet citizen, was arrested in May 1923 and expelled from the party on Stalin's order.[44] In 1929 he was rearrested and never seen again. The message was clear. The Bolsheviks would support national movements only insofar as they furthered proletarian (now synonymous with Soviet) interests.

M. N. Roy's views were similar to those of Sultan-Galiev, but not being a Soviet citizen he was no threat to the political position of the Bolshevik government. His quarrel with Lenin, therefore, was over not national but colonial issues, with which Lenin was less familiar. Roy's point of departure from Lenin was over the revolutionary potential of the nationalist bourgeoisie in colonial countries. "I disagreed," Roy wrote, "with his view that the nationalist bourgeoisie played a historically revolutionary role and therefore should be supported by the Communists."[45] Roy believed that the communists should establish independent movements rather than aid the bourgeoisie. He understood Lenin's thesis that a national liberation movement in a colony under imperialism was the equivalent of a bourgeois democratic revolution in a Western system, but, he warned, the nationalist bourgeoisie would not be sympathetic to the communists once in power. The communist would support the nationalist, but would the nationalist support the communist? Roy recommended selective support for national movements when communist interests were guaranteed.

Conceding Roy's superior knowledge of the colonial situation, Lenin invited Roy to submit a set of supplementary theses to his own theses on the colonial question at the Second Comintern Congress in July 1920. Roy did just that, but his draft was strictly edited by Lenin before the Congress convened, so Roy brought his challenge to the floor of the meeting. An open debate on support for national liberation movements ensued. Roy contended that because the Western imperialist system depended on the colonies for its survival, "it is therefore essential to rule the revolutionary movement in the East, and adopt as a fundamental thesis that the fate of world communism depends on the victory of communism in the East."[46] Lenin replied just as directly, "The Hindu Communists must support the bourgeois democratic movement. . . . Comrade Roy goes too far when he says that the fate of the West depends entirely on the development and strength of the revolutionary movement in the Eastern countries."[47] The Congress rejected Roy's position (only 25 of the 218 delegates were from the East) and for the sake of unity Roy gave the appearance of being in essential agreement with Lenin's thesis that support for nationalism was the path to communism. Although far less sanguine about the ability of communists and nationalist bourgeois to cooperate, Roy permitted Lenin to strike the following words from his report: "This alliance of the Communist International and the revolutionary movement in the oppressed countries does not signify support for the doctrine of nationalism."[48] The Lenin-Roy thesis on the colonial question was, in reality, the Lenin thesis.

Suddenly, however, one voice threatened to shatter the facade of unity on the national and colonial questions that Lenin had constructed at the Second Congress. G. M. Serrati, an Italian delegate and Comintern official, declared that he would not vote for the joint Lenin-Roy thesis on communist support for national bourgeois movements in backward countries. Serrati pointed out that the thesis could be used by "chauvinist pseudo-revolutionaries" in the backward countries of Europe, and declared that "only by means of a proletarian revolution and through the Soviet regime can the subjected nations obtain their freedom. This cannot be done by temporary alliances of the Communists with the bourgeois parties called national-revolutionaries."[49] Roy was furious. "The one who regards it reactionary to aid these people in their national struggle," he shot back, "is himself a reactionary and sides with imperialism."[50] Equally displeased with Serrati, Zinoviev, speaking for Lenin, responded, "We have experiences from many countries and have found that we as communists must give support to every revolutionary movement."[51] The point that Serrati was making, which Roy and Zinoviev appear to have missed completely, was that there were political forces emerging in Italy and claiming to be revolutionary nationalists whom the Italian communists would never support—the Fascists.

Once again, the international movement, this time Lenin's Communist International, was split over the issue of the best road to proletarian revolution. Once again, each faction in the debate argued from its own national perspective. And once again, Lenin was in

the center on the question. The Westerners, such as Serrati, cleaved
to the principle of proletarian revolution in the industrialized states
of Europe as the only sure path to communism. The Easterners, like
Roy, Sultan-Galiev, and Ho Chi-Minh, declared the Western movement dead and asserted that communism would emerge and prosper
in the colonial world and be delivered to the West at some later
date. Lenin, a Westerner who had adopted an Eastern strategy, sought
to bring about the proletarian revolution in Europe by destroying
the imperial base of capitalism in the colonial world through struggle
for national liberation. Both Lenin and Russia straddled East and
West.

The Comintern debate was not new in the history of the international movement. What was unique in 1920, however, was that
one national faction was in power, and this fact gave the Bolsheviks
the self-proclaimed legitimacy to decide which was the "correct"
path to pursue. In 1914 Lenin had opined that "only absolute
ignoramuses . . . are capable of 'comparing' the Russian Marxist
agrarian programme with the programmes of Western Europe,"[52]
thereby asserting that each nation would have to decide on its own
how best to procede toward socialism. Point 16 of the Twenty-One
Points adopted at the Second Comintern Congress stated: "All the
decisions . . . of the Communist International . . . are binding on
all parties belonging to the Communist International." And Point
14 provided that "every party which wishes to join the Communist
International is obliged to give unconditional support to any Soviet
republic in its struggle against counter-revolutionary forces."[53] At
this time there was one Soviet republic—Russia.

Although, despite Serrati's objection, the Comintern Congress
decided to support all revolutionary nationalist movements, the East-
West breach remained real, if hidden. The issue did not reemerge
until after Lenin's death in 1924. Then, with Stalin maneuvering for
power in the USSR, this issue took on new importance as his major
antagonist, Trotsky, was identified with the Western view. Roy, who
had compromised with Lenin, began to pressure Stalin for a more
selective policy of support for national liberation in the East. It was
at the Fifth Comintern Congress in July 1925 that Roy again insisted
on the need to focus on the colonial issue. Roy had become convinced
that the interests of the national bourgeoisie in the colonies actually
coincided with those of the imperialists in all but the most backward
nations. Lenin, he argued, supported only progressive movements,
but the Fifth Congress had before it a resolution calling for communist
support for *all* national movements, which Roy opposed. Roy realized
that the Soviets were developing friendly relations with bourgeois

governments in the East (because they were shunned in the West), such as Turkey, Persia, and South China, and Stalin was beginning to equate the benefits of these ties for the Soviet Union with benefits for the international movement. Roy understood full well that these Eastern nationalists were using this "friendship" with the USSR to further their own political goals (often against local communists), and that in the minds of the nationalists, friendship with the Soviet Union was not synonymous with friendship toward communism. That equation of interests could occur only in the minds of those who believed that the USSR and communism were synonymous, i.e., Stalin. Communists, Roy warned his comrades, would be betrayed by the bourgeois nationalists, even if those nationalists remained friendly with the USSR. The Fifth Congress rejected Roy's arguments.

Stalin, as the emerging leader of the Soviet Union, was to put his own unique stamp on the development of international communism. Before that change can be identified, however, it will be necesary to return to the Soviet domestic situation to see how the national issue developed in the critical period of transition from Lenin to Stalin.

FROM LENIN TO STALIN

Within the USSR, the longer the Western revolutions were delayed, the more imperative it became to secure the position of the Bolshevik party against all opposition forces—ideological and national. Despite the wholesale postrevolutionary secessions, Lenin continued to believe that minority nationalism could eventually be overcome by a policy of proletarian equality, and that the persistent enemy of internationalism was Great Russian chauvinism. Ironically, Stalin, the Georgian, was convinced that the enemy of Bolshevik control was not Russian chauvinism but minority nationalism. Perhaps because he was Commissar of Nationalities and a minority national himself (the Georgians were the most fiercely nationalistic minority in the USSR), Stalin was more sensitive to the threat to Soviet power posed by non-Russian groups. In any case, the Soviet system having been established, Stalin warned that the nations of the USSR "cannot, as long as imperialism prevails, carry on a separate existence and successfully maintain themselves without the economic and military support of neighboring Soviet republics."[54] When reminded by one of his colleagues in March 1921 of the party's long-standing commitment to national self-determination, Stalin retorted:

We discarded this slogan two years ago. Our programme no longer contains this slogan. Our program speaks not of national self-deter-mination—an absolutely vague slogan—but of a better minted and more clearly defined slogan—the right of nations to political secession. . . . Inasmuch as the Soviet states join in federation voluntarily, the right to secession remains unavailed of because the peoples that form the R.S.F.S.R. have themselves so willed.[55]

One might quarrel with Stalin's assessment of the Soviet federation as a "voluntary" one, but his point was that the system was united and would remain so. Henceforth, the phrase "national self-deter-mination" could not be employed as a legitimating doctrine against the Bolsheviks. Stalin believed that the Russians were the most advanced nationality—in effect, the working class of the system. He developed the thesis that the nationality problem was, in reality, one of proletariat versus peasants—the advanced proletarian Russians on the revolutionary side, and the smaller, backward peasant na-tionalities on the counterrevolutionary side. What was required was a resolution of the animosity "between the Russian proletariat and the peasantry of other nationalities."[56] By identifying the Russian nation with the working class, Stalin created an ideological justification for his negative attitude toward minority national rights. "Besides the right of nations to national self-determination," Stalin declared, "there is also the right of the working class to consolidate its power, and to this latter right the right of self-determination is subordinate. . . . The right to self-determination cannot and must not serve as an obstacle to the exercise by the working class of its right to dictatorship."[57] If, in the new Soviet federation, the Russians were the working class, they had the right to dictate to all other nationalities, which, by definition, were less progressive than the Russians.

Although Lenin had supported the federation plan and had insisted on the reincorporation of the secessionist republics on the grounds that they had been misled by bourgeois and socialist nationalists, he became increasingly uneasy over Stalin's diverging views on the national issue. Some historians have even suggested that Lenin's growing anger with Stalin over his handling of nationality policy contributed to his declining health and eventually to his untimely death in January 1924.[58]

When the last of the three Caucasian republics (Georgia, Armenia, and Azerbaidzhan) was reincorporated into Soviet Russia in 1921, it was decided that the three should enter the federation as a unit, and that they should be economically, if not governmentally, unified. The Georgian communists in particular resented the lower status of being twice federated, rather than joining the system as a republic.

The more Moscow pressed for unity, the more the Georgian communists resisted, and by the end of 1921 Lenin had apparently concluded that he had moved too quickly in this matter. In August 1922 a commission was established to formulate a plan that would normalize relations between Moscow and the Georgians. That plan, drafted by Stalin, was called the "autonomization" plan, because it granted each of the Caucasian republics autonomous status, which was constitutionally inferior to that of the union republics that composed the federation. Despite strong Georgian protest against this second-class status, the Stalin autonomization plan was pushed through the party Central Committee.

Lenin, who had become ill at the end of 1921, suffered a serious stroke in May 1922 and was convalescing during the party debates on the autonomization proposal. Only after its adoption by the Central Committee did Stalin send Lenin the commission reports. Point 1 of the plan struck Lenin as indicative of the creeping chauvinism in his party. It called for "the formal adhesion of the republics to the RSFSR" and Lenin demanded that this offensive wording be replaced by "formal union with the RSFSR." "I hope," Lenin wrote to his colleague Kamenev, "the significance of this concession is clear: we recognize that we are equals in law with the SSR [Soviet Socialist Republic] of the Ukraine, etc., and join it on an equal footing in a new union."[59]

At this juncture Stalin emerged from Lenin's shadow. In a letter to the party leadership in response to Lenin's criticism of the autonomization plan, Stalin openly defied Lenin. "I think," Stalin declared, "we should be firm with Lenin." He accepted Lenin's revision of his "adhesion" wording, but went on to say, "Lenin's correction to paragraph 2 . . . should not in my opinion, be adopted," and "Comrade Lenin's correction of paragraph 5 is, in my opinion, superfluous." Finally, he accused Lenin of "national liberalism," which encouraged separatist movements among the minorities.[60] The specific issues involved are not important. What is important is that Stalin blatantly challenged Lenin on the nationality issue and enlisted the support of the party leadership for his position.

Whether Lenin ever saw Stalin's comments is not known, but, unable to attend the debate on the plan, Lenin summarized his position to Kamenev: "I declare war to the death on dominant nation chauvinism."[61] Stalin was not then strong enough to block Lenin's revisions of the autonomization plan, but the lines of battle were clearly drawn. The incident that was to bring the issue to a head occurred, naturally, in Georgia.

Exasperated by Moscow's nationality policies, particularly the autonomization plan, the Central Committee of the Georgian Communist Party resigned *en masse* on 22 October 1922. In a heated confrontation over this action, Moscow's agent in Georgia, Ordzhonikidze, struck one of the Georgian Central Committee members, Mdivani, in the presence of one of Lenin's deputies to the conference. It is difficult to understand why, in the midst of economic chaos, international tension, and pressing political problems, this incident of one communist physically abusing another so deeply affected Lenin. The intensity of purpose with which he responded suggests that to Lenin, already partly paralyzed and aware of his limited future, this act symbolized a mutation of the goals, attitudes, and behavior of the regime he had worked so hard to create. Lenin clung to the principles he had enunciated before the revolution. If minority nationalism was ever going to disappear in Russia, it would disappear only in response to the end of chauvinism; it could not be administered out of existence by a decree from Moscow, and it certainly could not be beaten out of existence as Ordzhonikidze had attempted to do. Lenin believed in centralism because it advanced the revolution; for Stalin, centralism had become an end in itself.

Lenin was losing control and he knew it. But more than personal power was at stake. In Lenin's mind, Stalin's position on the nationality issue represented everything he had hoped to avoid. On 9 December 1922 Lenin received a report on the Mdivani beating that exonerated Ordzhonikidze and laid full responsibility on the Georgians. On 13 and 16 December Lenin suffered a series of attacks and on 22 December a stroke once again paralyzed him. In spite of the fact that he was subsequently restricted by the Politburo of the party (which appointed Stalin to "watch over" him) to a few minutes of dictation each day, Lenin continued to focus on the national problem. From notes dictated on 30 December 1922 the following excerpts are particularly pertinent:

What a bog we have slipped into. Evidently, this whole scheme of "autonomization" was fundamentally incorrect and inopportune.

I think the fatal rôle here was played by Stalin's hastiness and administrative predilections, and also by his irascibility towards the notorious 'social nationalism.'

It is well known that Russified non-Russians are always on the prodigal side when it is a matter of truly Russian attitudes.

The Georgian, who treats this side of the matter [the need for caution and indulgence] with disdain and disdainfully bandies about the accusation of 'social nationalism' (while he himself is an authentic and genuine not merely 'socialist nationalist' but crude Great Russian Derzhimorda [a Gogol character who personifies the brutality of local officials in tsarist Russia] also), this Georgian in essence violates the interests of proletarian class solidarity.[62]

Is it any wonder then, that on 4 January 1923 Lenin dictated the following note?

> Stalin is too rude, and this defect, though quite tolerable in our midst and in dealings among us Communists, becomes intolerable in a General Secretary. That is why I suggest that the comrades think about a way to remove Stalin from that post and appoint in his place another man who in all respects differs from Comrade Stalin in his superiority, that is, more tolerant, more loyal, more courteous and more considerate of the comrades, less capricious, etc.[63]

Consumed by the Georgian episode, Lenin demanded the records of the investigation commission. At first Stalin refused on the grounds that Lenin should not be bothered with "day to day matters," but Lenin persisted and received the report. Obvious gaps caused Lenin to suspect a cover-up, so he appointed his own private commission to look into the matter. Their report on 3 March apparently confirmed Lenin's suspicions (it has never been made public), because on 5 March he had this message telephoned to Trotsky: "I earnestly ask you to undertake the defense of the Georgian affair at the Central Committee of the Party. That affair is now under 'persecution' at the hands of Stalin and Dzherzhinsky and I cannot rely on their impartiality."[64] It remains unclear whether Trotsky ever undertook this mission.

On 6 March 1923 Lenin dictated two messages. Concerning an incident in which Stalin reportedly verbally "abused" Lenin's wife in a telephone conversation, Lenin wrote to Stalin: "I must ask you to consider whether you would be inclined to withdraw what you said and to apologize, or whether you prefer to break off relations between us."[65] And concerning the Georgian incident, Lenin declared to Mdivani, the victim of the attack: "I follow your affair with all my heart. I am outraged at the rudeness of Ordzhonikidze and the connivance of Stalin. . . ."[66] On 7 March, the day his letter was delivered to Stalin, Lenin suffered a massive paralyzing stroke. He never spoke again, although he did not die until eleven months later on 21 January 1924.

Rudeness—to his wife, Krupskaya; to the Georgian Mdivani; to himself—this is what Stalin stood for in Lenin's diseased (but not irrational) brain on the last day of his functional life. It was the nationality issue that made it evident to Lenin that the party had to rid itself of Stalin and Stalinism. Lenin, according to one of his private secretaries, was "preparing a 'bomb' against Stalin,"[67] because the latter was prepared to ride roughshod over anyone, including fellow communists, who resisted Russian control over the movement. Lenin never got his final chance.

Russia had become the centerpiece of the Bolshevik revolution, and the Great Russian nationality was transformed into the progressive class in whose name the party would rule. In *The Russian Dilemma,* Robert Wesson wrote, "In Russia, chauvinism was no narrow, selfish feeling but a holy cause and the height of virtue."[68] The Russians had traditionally conceived of themselves as a civilizing force in the Empire, and the Bolsheviks inherited this self-image. Russified non-Russians, like Stalin, intensified it. Lenin's goals had transcended the simple restoration of the Russian Empire and he believed that other nations were far more capable of leading the movement. Lenin's global vision did not permit the establishment of a new Russian Empire, but there was an inevitability about Stalinism. In Wesson's words, "The universalism of Marx, whereby nationalism was a backward manifestation destined to disappear in the economically integrated society of the future, was superlative for a multinational empire."[69] Lenin may have believed that he was liberating the minority nationalities when the Red Army overthrew the "bourgeois" secessionists, but Stalin seems to have understood from the beginning that the real goal was the restoration of a centralized, autocratic Russian Empire. From the idea that Russia was the heart of the Bolshevik Revolution it was only a short step to Stalin's exultant affirmation: "We, the Soviet federation, by the will of historical destiny now represent the vanguard of world revolution. . . . It has been our destiny to take precedence of all others."[70]

THE FINAL STEP: SOCIALISM IN ONE COUNTRY

The implications of the failure of the Western revolutions were no less profound for Soviet domestic development than they had been for the orientation of the International. Because the revolution had broken out in what everyone agreed was a precapitalist country, revolutionary formulae had to be recast to take into consideration this suprising turn of events. Inevitably, the question arose: What role will the Soviet Union play in the future development of the international working-class movement?

As Robert Tucker observed in his biography of Stalin,[71] the entire notion of "building socialism" was alien to Marxist thought because industrialized systems would have been capable of supporting socialism from the outset. If there had to be an industrial proletariat and an advanced capitalist economy before socialism could come to life, the USSR faced the enormous task of industrialization before it could be considered socialist. Could this be accomplished? More to the point, should it even be attempted? After all, how far could the USSR go without the aid of European proletarian forces?

In the immediate postrevolutionary period the answers to these questions seemed clear. A year after the Bolshevik seizure of power, Lenin advanced the generally accepted theory that "the complete victory of socialist revolution is unthinkable in one country. . . . It requires the most active *cooperation* of at least several advanced countries, *among which we cannot classify Russia.*"[72] In apparent agreement with this thesis, Stalin wrote in the introduction to the first edition of his *The Foundations of Leninism* (the passage was deleted from subsequent editions), "To overthrow the bourgeoisie the efforts of one country are sufficient; this is proved by the history of our revolution. For the final victory of socialism . . . the efforts of one country, particularly a peasant country like Russia, are insufficient; for that, the efforts of the proletarians of several advanced countries are required."[73]

Neither Lenin nor, for that matter, Marx required that the entire world become socialist before any individual country could. At a minimum, only a few of the most advanced countries would have to be revolutionized for socialism to become a reality. Yet the success of the Russian Revolution had proved in practice what most had denied in theory: that the proletarian revolution could begin in a precapitalist economy. If the theorists were wrong on where the revolution could start, might not they be wrong on how far it could progress in isolation?

Having survived both the world and civil wars (much to everyone's amazement), the Bolshevik regime faced a number of complex, long-range problems. The radical reorganization of the economy that Lenin had introduced under the label of "War Communism" was a disaster, and by 1920 the regime had settled into a more or less conciliatory relationship with the peasants and bourgeoisie. The so-called New Economic Policy (NEP) was the Bolshevik *modus vivendi* with Russian capitalism and private enterprise until a blueprint for long-term industrialization on more socialist lines could be devised. Hence, the conflict over what was to be known as "socialism in one country" began as a debate over Soviet Russia's immediate economic future. Specifically, it focused on the role of the peasants in Russia's industrialization and what the policies of the regime should be toward them. Owing largely to Stalin's maneuvering, however, what began as an economic debate ended in a bitter struggle for leadership of the USSR and the International and left an indelible mark on the development of national communism.

One group, the right wing (represented by Bukharin and at first by Stalin) argued that an indefinite continuation of the regime's conciliatory policy toward the peasantry was required if the USSR were to industrialize rapidly. Because food was an essential incentive for worker productivity and because agricultural products were virtually the only commodity that Soviet Russia could barter for machinery in the West, the right wing contended that the peasantry should be permitted to produce as much as possible without centralized controls. The independent peasant would provide the foundation for Soviet industrialization. The left wing (represented by Preobrazhensky and by Trotsky) maintained that industrialization would require massive capital accumulation in the hands of the government, but the rightist plan provided no direct means for the government to acquire that capital. The only way to achieve industrialization quickly, Preobrazhensky believed, was to tell the peasant what to produce and force him to deliver what the regime needed. In addition, the left wing was concerned that Bukharin's proposal would give the peasants too much power and that the regime would eventually be subject to economic blackmail by a strong private interest. Ideologically, the rightist position appeared to be a permanent sellout to capitalism in the Soviet Union.

Almost as an aside, Bukharin reminded his opponents in February 1924 that his plan to continue market conditions under NEP was suited to "one country in isolation," because it provided what the USSR needed until the world revolution came.[74] Stalin picked up this tangential point and through it made his greatest, if not original, contribution to Marxist-Leninist ideology. Stalin's reasons for making "socialism in one country" not only his slogan but his means to absolute power were multifold. Unquestionably, they had much to do with the fact that his two most powerful antagonists in the Lenin succession, Trotsky and Zinoviev, were on the Left. Stalin needed an issue to distinguish himself from his opponents and establish his own ideological identity independent from that of Lenin. But, beyond these very crucial power considerations, it is clear that from the outset Stalin had much more faith in the ability of the Russians to establish socialism than most of his comrades. His position on the disruptive effects of minority nationalism during the civil war period reflected Stalin's sincere belief that the Russians could "complete" the revolution.[75]

At first, since only he recognized "socialism in one country" as an issue, Stalin appeared to launch his offensive against no one in particular. Stalin claimed that it was Lenin who had first recognized the possibility of socialism in one country as early as 1915: "It was Lenin . . . who discovered the truth that the victory of socialism in one country is possible."[76] In one very important sense, Stalin was correct. What he was saying was that the fact that socialism would, at some future date, become an international phenomenon did not prevent the USSR from developing independently and indefinitely in the interim. After all, had not Lenin accepted the harsh terms of the Treaty of Brest-Litovsk in March 1918 for the sole purpose of preserving the Russian revolution? Had not Lenin immediately launched the radical program of War Communism in Russia, before any European revolutions had succeeded? Stalin's position was that because the Soviets were in no position to make the German revolution happen, they had no choice but to pursue their own national goals. Stalin's thesis was unique in emphasis, not content. Everyone, including Stalin, concurred in the desirability of the spread of revolution, but only Stalin hammered home the point that this did not mean that the Bolshevik revolution could not continue without the European revolutions.

Stalin launched his major campaign on the "socialism in one country" issue at the Fifteenth Party Conference in October 1926.[77] Both Trotsky and Zinoviev came out squarely against the doctrine, reminding Stalin that he and Lenin had denied its authenticity some years earlier. Zinoviev attacked "socialism in one country," labeling it "national narrow-mindedness," and stated categorically: "The final victory of socialism in one country is impossible. The theory of final victory in one country is wrong."[78] But it was Stalin who gained the verbal offensive.

What point was there, he wondered aloud, in moving toward socialism if one knew it could not be achieved? How could the people be mobilized to perform the immense and exhausting tasks that lay before them without the certainty of success to inspire them? Did not the very future of the international movement depend on the continued survival of the Soviet Union? To the conference, half of whose voting delegates had joined the party after the Revolution, Stalin exclaimed: "To hell with all the old formulas, long live the victorious Revolution in the USSR."[79] The doctrine of "socialism in one country" was the Soviet declaration of independence from an international movement that had failed. Stalin even pleaded guilty to Zinoviev's charge of "national narrow-mindedness," but what was wrong with optimism and pride in the Bolshevik revolution?

In a brilliant verbal attack, Stalin, using language his audience understood, identified his opponents on this issue as political eunuchs who lacked faith in their own people, preferring instead to pin their revolutionary hopes on foreigners. The appeal of "socialism in one country" was irresistible to those thousands of party cadres who were working day in and day out to transform their country into a socialist reality. They, like Stalin, had never been in the West and had no reason to believe that European socialists were superior to themselves. The fact that the objective conditions of history were theoretically inappropriate for socialism in the USSR meant either that the old ideology was wrong or that the Bolsheviks were wrong; they preferred to believe the former. One did not have to be a chauvinist to fall victim to the appeal of "socialism in one country," just a good Soviet communist who saw his national movement rising like a phoenix from the ashes of a hopelessly conservative Europe. No longer were the cadres being asked to sacrifice for the chimera of a revolutionary dream thousands of miles away; they were being offered a revolutionary reality within their grasp. Whether Stalin understood all this when he took up the banner of "socialism in one country" is problematic, but it was an idea whose time had come in the Soviet Union. In the final analysis "socialism in one country" was the ultimate manifestation of the national communism that had been implicit in the movement since Marx and Engels penned the *Communist Manifesto.*

In the beginning national communism was only a matter of each revolutionary party deciding for itself the most appropriate path toward socialism under its national conditions. Socialist Europe was to have been a Europe of socialist nations. As Lenin put it, "The way to the common goal—complete equality, the closest association and the eventual *amalgamation of all* nations—obviously runs along different routes in each concrete case, as let us say, the way to a point in the center of this page runs left from one edge and right, from the opposite edge."[80]

Stalin saw things differently. A Georgian, he knew and mistrusted minority nationalities; an Easterner, he lacked faith in the revolutionary potential of the West; and a centralizer, he did not believe in revolution from below. In his view the Bolsheviks needed centralized power to survive internally and the USSR needed to enlist the support of centralized, established authorities with bureaucratic control to survive internationally. The Russians were simply more reliable than the national minorities, and the bourgeois nationalist governments and movements of the East were more reliable than the revolutionary forces that called themselves communist. By identifying the movement with the anticolonial revolutions of the East, Stalin was undercutting the prestige of the communist establishment in Europe while avoiding dependence on the mass movements he so mistrusted. Stalin's policy toward the Chinese communists is the clearest evidence of this strategy (see Chapter 5).

Whereas Lenin and Roy sought to spread communist revolution in accordance with national conditions—each believing that his strategy would most effectively result in world communism—Stalin sought to consolidate the gains of the Russian Revolution and centralize control over the international movement in Moscow. Lenin had attempted to reconcile the conflicting trends of national revolutions according to local formulae on the one hand and centralization of power on the other. The problem was that with only a single party in power, the pull of centralism was inexorable. At one point, Lenin wrote:

> The Polish proletarian movement is taking the same course as ours, towards the dictatorship of the proletariat, but not in the same way as Russia. . . . Communism cannot be imposed by force. When I said to one of the best comrades among the Polish Communists, "You will do it in a different way," he replied: "No, we shall do the same thing, but better than you." To such an argument I have absolutely no objections. They must be given the opportunity of fulfilling a modest wish—to create a better Soviet power than ours.[81]

But Stalin did object, not only to the Poles, but to all national communist variations. The Soviets, through the party at home and Comintern abroad, would dictate revolutionary dogma. The Bolshevization of communism, begun by Lenin as a matter of necessity, was completed by Stalin as a matter of principle.

Was this transformation an avoidable choice or the product of historical circumstance? Individual judgments may vary, but some facts are plain. First, the reorientation of the movement eastward was a direct response to the failure of the proletarian parties in the West. Serrati resisted along with the other Europeans because they could not admit the truth to themselves. Trotsky resisted along with other Westerners in Russia on the ground that, in the long run, Bolshevism could not survive without European communism, and because they saw power slipping from their grasp. But the Soviet Union would have to survive in a hostile capitalist environment, and steps were taken, first by Lenin and then by Stalin, to ensure that survival. The shift away from Europe necessitated an adjustment to Eastern conditions, particularly the fact that the most effective revolutionary force was nationalist antiimperialism, not communism. Albeit to destroy imperialism by supporting all national movements, Comintern (Moscow) put the stamp of approval on leaders and movements that were non-Marxist, and in many instances anti-Marxist. Stalin recognized the flaw in the Marxist revolutionary blueprint, and this recognition enabled him to ride the tide of historical events as they shifted eastward away from Europe. At the same time, Stalin's willingness to pursue without limits Lenin's principle of centralization enabled him to consolidate control over the international movement.

The second unavoidable fact is that when Bolshevik revolutionaries were replaced by managerial bureaucrats, when the future was rendered remote by the pressing problems of the present, and when personal political ambition took precedence over international obligations, the legitimate aspirations of non-Soviet communists became counter-revolutionary. The national variations that had been characteristic of the movement became intolerable aberrations to Stalin. At this juncture, national communism within the USSR became communist nationalism—a cardinal virtue; and national communism elsewhere became bourgeois nationalism—a deadly sin. The irony, of course, is that Soviet communism was itself a national variation, which Stalin attempted to convert into a universal model.

So that nationalism should cease to exist in the USSR, Stalin employed nationalism. So that national communism should cease to exist in the world, Stalin employed national communism. Stalin sought to deny to everyone else the rights that he, by exercising them, had established as legitimate and effective revolutionary options.

It would not be until another party came to power by its own revolutionary efforts (in Yugoslavia and later China) that the inherent contradiction between Marxist-Leninist national communism and Stalinist communist nationalism would disintegrate the movement, perhaps permanently. In the interim the Soviet Union under Stalin pursued the unilateral course of survival and, later, national aggrandizement with single-minded purpose. Perhaps no single act epitomized more clearly the lengths that Stalin was willing to go to preserve his Soviet regime at the expense of the international movement than the Soviet-Nazi Nonaggression Pact of 1939. If there was any remaining doubt that communism and the USSR were one and the same in Stalin's mind, that agreement dispelled it.

On 15 May 1943, in the midst of what Stalin called "The Great Patriotic War" (it is still called that today), the Third International, the last remaining vestige of Lenin's internationalism, was disbanded. There has been no other.

Ostensibly Comintern was dissolved as an act of conciliation in recognition of Western assistance to the USSR. It was undoubtedly undiplomatic for Stalin to continue to sponsor an organization committed to the downfall of the capitalist system on which he so desperately depended. But Comintern's dissolution may also be read as a recognition of reality. Comintern, always suspect as a Soviet instrument, had been completely discredited by its slavish obedience to Stalin's nationalist policies. Whatever succeeded it, Stalin realized, the Third International had outlived its usefulness.

Ironically, it was the collapse of the Third Reich that foreclosed the possibility of a revival of the Third International. "Socialism in one country" could work only as long as there was only one socialist country. With the emergence of a truly international communist system at the end of World War II, the stage was set for an entirely new drama to unfold, one that might be called "national communism redux."

Suggestions for Further Reading

Boersner, Demetrio. *The Bolsheviks and the National and Colonial Question.* Geneva: Libraire E. Droz, 1957.

Lazitch, Branko, and Drachkovitch, Milorad. *Lenin and the Comintern.* 2 vols. Stanford: Hoover Institution Press, 1972.

Low, Alfred. *Lenin on the Question of Nationality.* New York: Bookman Associates, 1958.

Meyer, Alfred. *Leninism.* New York: Praeger Publishers, 1962.

Pipes, Richard. *The Formation of the Soviet Union: Communism and Nationalism, 1917–1923.* Cambridge: Harvard University Press, 1954.

Stalin, Joseph. *Marxism and the National and Colonial Question.* New York: International Publishers, 1935.

Ulam, Adam. *Stalin: The Man and His Era.* New York: Viking Press, 1973.

Wolfe, Bertram. *Three Who Made a Revolution.* Boston: Beacon Press, 1948.

4
National Communism Redux

Stalin's strategy to establish Soviet hegemony over the multinational communist system that emerged after World War II was strikingly similar to that he employed to establish Bolshevik control over the multinational Russian Empire after the Revolution. His policy recognized, in principle, the right of a nation to determine its own political future (Lenin's formula), but it reserved to the proletariat (or its representative, the party) the right to act in pursuit of self-determination (Stalin's formula). Accordingly, the Soviet party could condemn any national movement as "counterrevolutionary" if it did not serve proletarian interests as defined by Moscow.

There was, however, one crucial difference between Stalin's postrevolutionary nationality policy and his postwar international one. Since Moscow's authority to impose Soviet policy legally ended at the Soviet border, Stalin had to accomplish de facto in Eastern Europe, and later in China, what he had been able to accomplish de jure in the Ukraine, in Georgia, and throughout the USSR. In a mood of confidence born of the earlier success of his nationality policy and his recent victory over the Axis powers, Stalin was convinced that through ideological persuasion, economic pressure, Soviet military power, or some combination of these factors, the USSR could easily control the international communist movement and its new national leaders. Khrushchev once related that Stalin had boasted that he would get rid of Tito by merely "shaking his little finger." Regardless of whether Stalin actually used these words, he had eliminated his domestic enemies (real and imagined) with as little effort as shaking his little finger, and he approached the entirely new international communist movement with this proven but inappropriate strategy. But the difference between domestic and foreign policy, which Stalin refused to recognize, was to stimulate the emergence of postwar national communism as the continuation of a trend that Stalin had earlier managed to sedate, but not kill.

This is not the place to recount the history of the formation of the Soviet bloc. Suffice it to say that with Soviet troops in Poland, Hungary, Romania, and Bulgaria, it was relatively simple to establish Soviet-type governments in those countries once Stalin had concluded that this was the best policy to pursue in response to mounting American pressure in the form of the Marshall Plan. The creation of a Soviet-controlled communist government in Czechoslovakia was delayed by indigenous democratic forces, which finally succumbed to Soviet pressure in 1948. And the formal establishment of the communist German Democratic Republic was retarded by international political factors that were not resolved until 1949. Yugoslavia and Albania were different cases from the rest. Although Stalin was later to contend otherwise, these countries were taken over by native communist parties that had come to power largely on the basis of their own partisan efforts. While the fact that Soviet troops had driven the Germans back across Europe undoubtedly made it possible for the Yugoslavians and Albanians to defeat their own occupation armies, Soviet troops never played a direct role in those essentially guerrilla efforts. Thus, of all the East European parties, only the Yugoslavians and Albanians could make any claim at all to have defeated the Axis powers independently of Moscow. However, it would be a mistake to conclude that the independent seizure of power by the Yugoslavs was the cause of their eventual split with Stalin. As we shall see, the Yugoslavs never sought independence; it was thrust on them unwillingly. The independent wartime efforts of the Yugoslav communists provided them with a legitimating source of national support when the split came but were not the reason for it.

In any event, once the political fact of a bloc of communist states allied with the USSR was established, Stalin created an umbrella organization to coordinate its activities: the Communist Information Bureau (Cominform). Cominform, officially created in September 1947, was not a revived Comintern. Its original membership consisted only of the parties of the Soviet Union, Bulgaria, Czechoslovakia, France, Hungary, Italy, Poland, Romania, and Yugoslavia—those parties of Europe that either were in power at the time or stood a reasonable chance of coming to power. Cominform had no published rules of membership and was, in fact, not an international political party as had been the former Internationals.[1] Cominform was the Soviet party's official entrée into the domestic affairs of the bloc and was organized for the specific purpose of preventing the spread of

Western influence (Poland and Czechoslovakia had already planned to accept Marshall Plan aid). Cominform, whose headquarters were ironically in Belgrade, met only four times. The first two sessions were organizational and the third, key meeting was convened in Bucharest, the new headquarters, for the purpose of excluding Yugoslavia from the membership. The fourth, final meeting was held in Budapest in November 1949 and consisted of nothing more than a continued diatribe against "Titoism." It was this phenomenon of Titoism, which Stalin identified as bourgeois nationalism, that is most closely associated with the rebirth of postwar national communism. It is the events leading up to and following the "excommunication" of Tito by Stalin and his subsequent "absolution" by Khrushchev that explain the emergence and describe the character of contemporary national communism; thus it is to these events that we now turn.

TITOISM AS NATIONAL COMMUNISM

Of the available designees, Tito's Yugoslavia was among the least likely candidates for the dubious distinction that Stalin assigned it. Tito had been a loyal Stalinist who owed his political career to Stalin's patronage. He was a Comintern representative at the height of Russia's cynically self-serving exploitation of the organization in the late 1930s. Tito was, in fact, virtually the only Yugoslavian communist leader then residing in Moscow who survived the purges. The leaders of the Yugoslavian party were so decimated by the Soviet secret police that the organization was on the verge of being dissolved. Only as a last resort was the Yugoslavian party put under the direction of the remaining trustworthy (from Stalin's perspective) party leader—Tito. When he returned to Yugoslavia, Tito, under Comintern direction and sponsorship, managed to convert the tattered remains of the Yugoslavian Communist Party (CPY) into an efficiently organized, well-disciplined, centralized, cadre party, which, when the Axis powers invaded, served as the focal point of the partisan resistance movement.

Tito, like Stalin, pursued power with cunning ruthlessness complemented by pragmatism. Like Stalin, he identified his wartime struggle as a patriotic effort in the name of all nationalities inhabiting Yugoslavia. Ideological rhetoric gave way to nationalist slogans, and Tito labeled his organization "The National Liberation Movement of Yugoslavia."[2] In short, Tito and Stalin mobilized their populations against a foreign national enemy in the name of the Motherland, not against capitalism in the name of Marx. Tito had declared, "The

National Liberation Movement in Yugoslavia concerns itself with
the only and most important aim—the struggle against the invader
and his aides and creation of a democratic, federative Yugoslavia,
and not establishment of communism, as some of our enemies
claim."[3]

Yet Stalinist communism was indeed what Tito established in
Yugoslavia, and after the war, as before and during, Tito was among
the most outspoken Stalinists. As Dennison Rusinow observed in
The Yugoslav Experiment, there were a number of points of contention
between Moscow and Belgrade in the postwar years, including the
exploitative nature of joint stock companies (which Stalin admitted);
mistreatment of Yugoslavian citizens, especially women, by resident
Soviet troops; the superior attitude of Russian officials in Belgrade
who demanded free access to all Yugoslavian agencies and files; and
even the slow progress that the Yugoslavians were making in col-
lectivizing agriculture. But, on the whole, the Yugoslavian party and
government were carbon copies of their Soviet counterparts and these
differences, though they exacerbated the split, did not cause it.[4] In
brief, the Soviet-Yugoslav split cannot be understood in terms of
what the Yugoslavs were doing to alienate Moscow, although these
are the terms in which the disagreement was couched by Stalin;
rather it must be understood in terms of what Stalin was seeking
to accomplish and what Tito represented in Stalin's tortured but not
illogical mind.

It is not necessary to enter into the so-called "cold war debate"
(as to whether it was the United States or the Soviet Union that
took the offensive after Potsdam, thereby causing the other country
to "defend" itself against aggression) to recognize that Stalin decided
to create a physically and ideologically impenetrable barrier around
the Soviet Union. Whether the East European outposts were established to serve as launching pads for future aggression against Western
Europe, or whether they were the first line of defense against "fascist
revanchism" is irrelevant to the present discussion. What is relevant
is the fact that when Stalin decided to build this network, he realized
that its value to the Soviet Union was directly proportionate to
Moscow's ability to control the foreign and domestic actions of its
national regimes. Stalin understood the simple political truth that
the most trustworthy ally is one totally dependent upon you for his
own political power—a local agent of Soviet authority.

Whether inspired by offensive or defensive motives, this was Great
Russian chauvinism writ large; now that it affected sovereign nation-
states that were not to be incorporated directly into the Soviet
constitutional structure, it took the form of Soviet imperialism. To

borrow Lenin's phraseology, the "weak link" in this "chain of imperialism," the one leader who did not owe his political authority solely to Stalin, was Tito.[5] Thus, given Stalin's national goals, which still equated the success of communism with that of the USSR, Tito had to go; not because he was a bad Stalinist, but because he was a good one. Tito had claimed no right other than the one established by Stalin, that of a nation to create socialism within the confines of its own borders, under its own national leadership. It was not the content of Yugoslavian policy that was to divide Moscow and Belgrade. The issue was in which city that policy would be made.

On 18 March 1948 Soviet advisers stationed in Yugoslavia were withdrawn by Stalin without prior notice. The Yugoslavs were apparently taken completely by surprise and on 20 March Tito wrote Stalin for an explanation. The response was shattering. Stalin answered on 27 March that Tito's position was "incorrect and therefore completely unsatisfactory."[6] Specifically, Stalin made reference to three shortcomings.[7] First, high-ranking officials of the CPY had been publicly slandering the Communist Party of the Soviet Union (CPSU) by charging that "great-power chauvinism is rampant in the USSR" and that "the Cominform is a means for control of the other Parties by the CPSU."[8] While recognizing the right of any party to criticize the CPSU, Stalin drew the line at efforts to discredit the CPSU and warned ominously, "We think that the political career of Trotsky is quite instructive."[9] Second, Stalin criticized the CPY for not assuming a leading role in Yugoslavia as required by Marxism-Leninism. Although he was in complete political control of the country, Tito was aware of the need for cross-sectional support, and therefore maintained the structure of a People's Front government rather than eliminating all nonparty groups as the Soviets had done. On this point, the Yugoslavs were accused of employing Menshevik tactics in not asserting the total authority of the party, and Stalin reminded them that Lenin had viewed the Mensheviks as "liquidators of the party."[10] Finally, Stalin charged that the Yugoslavs permitted a known English spy to serve in the government. This, while acceptable for imperialist governments, was "entirely impermissible for Marxists."[11]

In sum, the charges against the Yugoslavian party leadership were that it was Trotskyite, Menshevik, and un-Marxist. The Yugoslavs had not merely created intolerable conditions for Soviet advisers that necessitated their withdrawal (reference was made to insults and abusive behavior); they had fallen into grave ideological transgressions. But as far as Tito was concerned, except for collectivization of agriculture, Yugoslavia had thus far emulated Stalin's policies faithfully. Tito understood from the outset that, although couched in

ideological terms, Stalin's grievances against Yugoslavia had nothing
to do with the correct interpretation of Marxism-Leninism.

On 12 April 1948, Tito explained to the CPY Central Committee:

> Comrades, remember that it is not a matter here of any theoretical
> discussions, it is not a question of errors committed by the Communist
> Party of Yugoslavia, of our ideological digression. . . . Comrades, the
> point here, first and foremost, is the relations between one state and
> another. It seems to me that they are using ideological questions in
> order to justify their pressure on us, on our state. That, comrades, is
> the issue.[12]

Tito's distinction between ideological and state interests is crucial.
The only theory that could justify such a distinction in the era
following the Bolshevik Revolution of 1917 was that the interests
of international communism and those of the Soviet Union were
not necessarily identical. The essence of the Titoist heresy was the
view that two states ruled by communist parties could have not only
different interests but antithetical ones. To suggest to Stalin that
there could be a difference between Soviet state interests and communist ideological goals was a direct challenge to the Soviet Union's
self-proclaimed position as the archetype of international communism.
Tito simply believed that Russians had no right to tell Yugoslavians
what to do and nothing in Marxism-Leninism gave them that right.
All of this, however, was completely contrary to Stalin's plans in
1947–48.

To justify their hegemony in East Europe, Soviet theoreticians
devised a new type of socialist system—the people's democracy.
People's democracies were agriculturally based systems with weak
proletarian movements, which had neither the resources nor the
political capacity to support a socialist revolution. Under these
circumstances, only the direct assistance of the USSR could overcome
the objective conditions that militated against socialism, and only
Soviet involvement could ensure the continued success of progressive
social forces. In the face of capitalist aggressiveness people's democracies required not only continued Soviet protection, but Soviet
presence as well. With Soviet troops in Poland, Hungary, Bulgaria,
Romania, and Germany the task of creating people's democracies
was relatively simple.

Although in loyal obedience to Moscow Yugoslavia was the first
to refer to itself as a people's democracy, the task of converting
Yugoslavia into a dependent system was formidable. One of Stalin's
tactics in this effort was to create Cominform and give Tito a leading

role in the organization. Tito had welcomed Cominform as a means to facilitate communication among the new socialist states of Eastern Europe, but Stalin's purpose was to integrate the interests of Yugoslavia with those of states that the USSR could directly control. This conflict of purpose did not become manifest until late 1947 when, at the same time that Stalin was moving to consolidate his control over the bloc, Tito began to initiate his own plans for a Balkan federation to include Bulgaria, Romania, and, possibly, Greece. This brought Soviet and Yugoslav policies into direct conflict, and Stalin could tolerate no further autonomous action from Tito.

According to Tito's confidant and biographer Vladimir Dedijer, Tito's sponsorship of a Balkan federation that did not include the USSR enraged Stalin. When the Soviet leader called delegations from Yugoslavia and Bulgaria to Moscow to discuss the federation proposal Tito refused to attend, sending instead his closest associates Djilas and Kardelj. Stalin was particularly angry with the Bulgarian party leader Dimitrov, who had announced the federation plan at a press conference before consulting Moscow. It soon became clear to those present at the meeting that Stalin objected not to the federation idea, but to the fact that he had "learned about it from the newspapers."[13] It appears that statements by Tito and Dimitrov had been interpreted by other communists to have been sanctioned by Stalin and he objected to having words put in his mouth. At one point, Stalin told those assembled: "The Poles were here. I asked them what they thought of Dimitrov's statement. They said, 'A wise thing,' and I told them it was not a wise thing. Then they countered that they also thought it was not a wise thing. . . ."[14] To Kardelj, who insisted that the Yugoslavs had always consulted with Moscow on all important foreign policy issues, Stalin shouted, "It isn't true. You do not consult with us at all on any question."[15] Quite understandably, the Yugoslavs left this meeting of 10 February 1948 deeply concerned about their country's political future. On 11 February, Kardelj was unexpectedly summoned by Molotov, the Soviet foreign minister. When he arrived, Molotov shoved a paper in front of Kardelj and demanded that he sign it immediately. It was an agreement by Yugoslavia to consult with the USSR on all foreign policy questions. Kardelj, "boiling with rage," signed.[16]

In light of Stalin's hostility, it should not have come as a surprise when one month after the Moscow meeting the Soviet leader moved to undermine Tito's leadership of Yugoslavia and his position in the international communist movement. In the belief that a single dissonant voice would disrupt the image of unanimity upon which the legitimacy of Soviet control in Europe was based, Stalin was willing to go to any length to remove the Titoist obstacle. What Stalin failed to realize was that the autochthonous and independent character of the Tito regime was what made it acceptable to the Yugoslavian people. Any suggestion that Tito was the agent of a foreign interest or even that he represented communist versus national interests would have deprived him of his most important source of political legitimacy.

Both Stalin and Tito perceived the conflict as one for political survival, a view that left little room for compromise. It is important to remember that throughout this preliminary period the issue was not one of a Yugoslavian "road to socialism" that varied from the Soviet model. In fact, throughout the conflict, Tito scrupulously avoided the implication that he was a national communist. What Tito did say was that "the road and incentive to socialism are not incorporation into the Soviet Union, but the development of each country separately. That is where we differ from the Soviet party."[17] Milovan Djilas, who was later to break with Tito over improving relations with the USSR, phrased the issue thus: "In my opinion the fundamental question is whether socialism is to develop freely or by the expansion of the Soviet Union."[18]

It was only after 28 June 1948, when Yugoslavia was officially expelled from Cominform, that the leaders of the CPY were forced to reappraise their position and search for a path of development uniquely suited to an isolated socialist system. Their search for a new polar star led the Yugoslavs back to Marx and Lenin, whom they read as if for the first time. Only then did they gradually come to the conclusion that the Russians had taken a wrong turn in the road toward communism, because of the Russian propensity for centralization, bureaucratization, and authoritarianism. Rusinow has observed that this was a particularly difficult period for the CPY leader because in order to defy Stalin they had to criticize the USSR and in the process they were forced to reject their own roots.[19]

Having been attacked for ideological shortcomings, the Yugoslavs' first reaction was to adopt policies that would prove that they were "more Catholic than the Pope." They responded to Stalin by pushing through agricultural collectivization and centralization of the economy, which alienated the Yugoslavian people. By 1950, however, faced with what Rusinow described as the "conflict between received dogma and reality,"[20] the CPY leadership was finally forced to concede that traditional Soviet-style methods were not merely inadequate but counterproductive. The initial Yugoslav reaction adds further credibility to the argument that it was not a Yugoslavian rejection of Soviet values that precipitated the 1948 crisis. At a loss to understand which way to turn, Djilas reread *Das Kapital* to see, in his words, "if I could find the answer to the riddle of why, to put it in simplest terms, Stalinism was bad, and Yugoslavia is good."[21] This statement hardly represents the thinking of an individual with a clearly conceived ideological challenge to Soviet hegemony. Tito expressed his answer to Djilas's question this way: "What happened? For one thing, the Bolshevik revolutionary mind, which Lenin exemplified, was supplanted by the bureaucratic and policy mind. . . . They've blundered into the rankest type of nationalism: into Great Russianism, which always had imperialist overtones."[22]

Djilas and his colleagues believed that they had rediscovered the essence of Marxist thought—that the worker should rule and the state wither away. Therefore, they based the new Yugoslav model on the principle of "workers' self-management," which was adopted as law on 27 June 1950. Stalin's decision to excommunicate Tito for ideological heresy was, therefore, self-fulfilling. Rather than capitulate and beg forgiveness for crimes they had not committed, the Yugoslavs committed the offense and established their own "higher form" of socialism, which they described as a return from the Stalin deviation to "true Leninism."

In reality, the adoption of the self-management principle did not have an immediate dramatic impact on the Yugoslavian political system. The fact is that the system remained about as centralized and authoritarian as it had been, and not substantially different from the Soviet model in that regard. Djilas was to discover this the hard way when he publicly suggested that the sooner the process began the better. For that direct assault on party authority Djilas was stripped of his political power and eventually imprisoned. But, as we have seen, the Soviet-Yugoslav conflict was never over what either side did but over who could decide to do it. In that sense contemporary national communism was not substantive but procedural in origin. It was form rather than content that divided Tito and Stalin. The irony of the situation is that had he been given the right to decide what course to pursue, Tito would undoubtedly have adhered to the essentials of the Soviet model and Yugoslavia would have remained a loyal ally of the USSR. However, when Stalin attempted to deprive the Yugoslavs of the right to determine their own future, they had no choice but to develop their own model. To have done otherwise would have meant certain political defeat within the country. Tito's choice was to confront his own people with Soviet support or to confront Stalin with his people's support. His decision established national communism as the permanent mode of socialist development and exposed Stalinist hegemonic pretensions as Soviet imperialism. In one of his early responses to Soviet criticism, Tito summarized his feelings thus: "No matter how much each of us loves the land of Socialism, the USSR, he can, in no case, love his own country less. . . ."[23]

On the surface, Tito's patriotic pronouncement conforms to the thesis that national communism has always been the dominant mode of socialist development; yet there was something new about this particular situation that provided Tito with added legitimacy. When, as we have seen, the socialists of Europe patriotically aligned themselves with their bourgeois governments at the outbreak of World War I, Lenin took them to task for abandoning their internationalist obligations. Lenin could do this because he had not as yet identified himself with a particular country, but was still tied to what remained of the Second International. In short, communism at that juncture was still synonymous with an international party organization, not a national party in power. When Stalin elected to equate the fate of the Communist International with that of the USSR he undoubtedly bolstered the legitimacy of the Soviet leadership, but at the same time he robbed the movement of its international orientation. Hence, when Tito declared independence for his party, no legitimate authority could accuse him of betraying the international movement. He was not forced to say that he loved Yugoslavia more than international communism, only that he loved Yugoslavia at least as well as the Soviet Union—"the land of Socialism." True, Tito had been officially excommunicated by Cominform, not by Stalin, but no one had any delusion that there was a real difference. The Cominform document merely reiterated the complaints registered by the CPSU Central Committee (Stalin) during the previous months. Yugoslavia's crime was specified at the beginning of the Cominform message. "The Information Bureau declares that the leadership of the Yugoslav Communist Party is pursuing an unfriendly policy toward the Soviet Union and the CPSU. An undignified policy . . . discrediting the Soviet Union, has been carried out in Yugoslavia."[24] The Soviet accusation that the cause of all this trouble was that "nationalist elements . . . managed . . . to reach a dominant position in the leadership of the Communist Party of Yugoslavia" and that the party had "taken the road to nationalism"[25] was essentially accurate, and would have been ideologically devastating had it not been leveled by a man who had walked that nationalist road himself.

In sum, the new element in the national communist formula was not that for the first time more than one communist nation existed, but that the moral superiority inherent in Lenin's internationalist position had been lost by Stalin, leaving the future development of national communism unrestrained by anything other than force.

Stalin's pattern of enforcement in Eastern Europe was predictably similar to the one he employed in the Soviet Union during the period of consolidation in the 1930s. Having rid himself (or so he believed) of his new "Trotsky" in Yugoslavia, Stalin rapidly proceeded to purge the "nationalist" elements in the bloc. Arrests, trials, and, in some cases, executions were the fate of top party officials who had shown any sympathy for Titoism. The victims included Pauker and Luka in Romania, Rajk and Kadar in Hungary, Slansky and Clementis in Czechoslovakia, Kostov in Bulgaria, and Gomulka in Poland. By mid-1949 Stalin was pulling all the strings and his marionettes—Rakosi (Hungary), Gheorghiu-Dej (Romania), Chervenkov (Bulgaria), Bierut (Poland), Gottwald (Czechoslovakia), and Ulbricht (East Germany)—danced. Of course, as with all such shows, the strings were invisible only to those who viewed the performance with eyes half closed or whose capacity for self-delusion permitted them to ignore the obvious.

Stalin expected Tito's regime to collapse without Soviet support. He had not anticipated Tito's political resiliency and ideological flexibility. Although Western leaders were initially surprised at and suspicious of the Soviet-Yugoslav rift, it was not long before Tito's excommunication was recognized as an opportunity for expanding Western influence in the Balkans. Slowly at first, and then with more resolve as the nature of the dispute became clear, the United States extended economic aid to Tito beginning in early 1949.[26] Whether Tito could have survived without American aid is problematic. Unquestionably, the American connection substantiated Stalin's contention that Tito was an agent of imperialism; but this presented no additional threat to his survival. Tito was determined to demonstrate by any means necessary that it was possible for a socialist system to exist independent of any external control. At no time during this period was it certain that he would succeed; however, from historical hindsight it is clear that once having succeeded, Tito made it impossible for the Soviet Union ever to reestablish the grip it had held during the Stalinist era. In Djilas's words: "Soviet Communism has become the mainstay of conservative Communist forces at home and abroad while Yugoslav Communism is a model of the weakness and disintegration of Communism, both in theory and practice, and at the same time is a model for national Communism and a hope for democratic transformation."[27]

Moreover, Yugoslavia was not the only system within the Soviet sphere in which national forces against Soviet hegemony had emerged.

Stalin's East European purges, though typically excessive, were not directed against imaginary opponents. Djilas believes that the emergence of these national forces is the inevitable by-product of communism. "Every Communist government, as soon as it reaches stability, strives to stand on its own feet and to subordinate all its objectives to national ideals and opportunities, while every Communist party, even if not in power, strives for political independence from the Communist great powers."[28] In other words, national sentiments were not a consequence of Tito's independent rise to political power and therefore cannot logically be presumed absent among those communists whose power was wholly dependent on the USSR. However, that dependence made it quite impossible to convert those national feelings into political reality. That was the essence of the difference between Yugoslavia and the rest of the Soviet bloc, and it persists to the present day.

NATIONAL COMMUNISM IN THE SOVIET BLOC

Despite the facts that, with the exception of Yugoslavia and Albania, the communist parties came to power as the result of Soviet support and that the leaders of these parties were, in most cases, wartime residents of Moscow who returned home with advancing Soviet troops, the so-called satellization process did not begin in earnest until after Cominform's creation. Although Tito was the first target of this campaign directed by Stalin's lieutenant Zhdanov, national sentiments were far more predominant among communists directly beholden to the USSR. The irony of Tito's eventual expulsion was that whereas he had welcomed Cominform, other East European communists such as Poland's Gomulka had greeted the prospect with trepidation. They were concerned that Cominform membership would make the newly established communist governments of Europe appear to be representatives of a Soviet-controlled organization. Given that the communists in Poland, Hungary, Bulgaria, and Romania continued to be embroiled in domestic political conflicts with major parties representing peasant interests, they could ill afford the negative image they would have as agents of Soviet interests. At one point Gomulka even suggested that even though Cominform was not a bad idea, perhaps it could be kept secret, thereby protecting the appearance of independence of the Eastern European parties.

Tito, on the other hand, expressed no such concern. With his independent, cross-sectional domestic political base of support, Tito could enter Cominform as a partner equal to any state, including the USSR, without tarnishing his image. In this matter of Cominform,

Djilas recalled that "the only two delegations that were decidedly for the Cominform were the Yugoslav and the Soviet. Gomulka was opposed, cautiously but unequivocally holding out for the 'Polish road to socialism.'"[29] Clearly, the Eastern European communist leaders understood that in order to retain power they would have to develop national support, and that required the development of economic and social policies that conformed to national conditions and fulfilled national needs. Stalin, not having formulated his blueprint for the bloc, did not, before Cominform, discourage this experimentation in socialist national development.

Symbolic of the mood of the period preceding the anti-Tito campaign was the publication in January 1947 of the new Polish party theoretical journal *Nowi Drogy (New Roads)*. On the heels of Soviet occupation forces, teams of Soviet managers and technicians permeated the Soviet zone for the specific purpose of exploiting the economic resources of the region to Soviet advantage. There was little anyone in these countries could do to prevent the blatant Soviet expropriation of remaining national wealth. The Soviet "advisors" administered newly organized joint-stock companies that gave the USSR legal interests in the East European economies, and, in some instances, they even advised against the nationalization of key industries because it might interfere with the flow of goods to the USSR.[30] What the East Europeans could, and did, do was resist (quietly at first) Soviet pressure to institute economic and social policies that they considered inappropriate, simply because those policies had been adopted in the Soviet Union. Stalin's attempt to initiate ideological conformity was, in other words, less successful than his infiltration of the administrative and military structures of the Soviet zone.

The explanation for this resistance to ideological conformity appears to be twofold. First, in many instances the native communist leaders were incapable of introducing the Soviet reforms either because they had not consolidated their own power or because they feared resistance they could not control. Second, on numerous points the European communists simply did not believe that the Soviet model was appropriate, and even if they could have initiated the measures they chose not to. In most cases, it was a combination of these two factors that led to the "national roads."

It was Gomulka who brought this disagreement into public view in his first article in *New Roads,* and to Gomulka belongs the credit for being the first Eastern European communist leader to defy Stalin. Before Cominform, the key issue was Gomulka's resistance to collectivization of agriculture in Poland. Standing virtually alone, even within his own party (most of whose members were unwilling to face the consequences of defying Stalin), Gomulka declared: "We have totally rejected the collectivization of farms."[31] Gomulka's explanation for this departure from the Soviet agricultural model was simple: "Our democracy is not similar to Soviet democracy, just as our society's structure is not the same as the Soviet structure."[32] Whether inspired by courage or naiveté, Gomulka was expressing a domestic political reality. Poland had a rural economic base, and the Polish peasant had a long history of fierce independence. Any sudden attempt to collectivize agriculture in Poland would, in Gomulka's view, have resulted in peasant resistance that would eventually have destroyed the Polish economy. There was nothing to recommend collectivization in Poland, except Stalin's insistence that it be carried out as quickly as possible.

Nevertheless, specific economic differences were not at the heart of Gomulka's defiance of Stalin. Gomulka's heresy was patriotism. He believed that the reason communism had never been strong in Poland was that it had failed to recognize the importance of the independence issue in the public mind. Indeed, he suggested that the Polish Socialist Party had been far more realistic than the communists on the independence issue, and that to be successful in Poland, a party had to be independence-minded.[33] That is why Gomulka resisted the formation of Cominform and why, when Stalin declared Tito a heretic, Gomulka became the inevitable victim of Stalin's desire to "unify" the Eastern European bloc.

In the wake of Cominform's declaration against Tito, the pressure mounted within the Polish party for Gomulka to relinquish leadership. On 19 August the Politburo presented Gomulka with a resolution entitled "The Rightist-Nationalist Deviation in the Party Leadership and the Means of Overcoming It," which enumerated his shortcomings: his failure to collectivize agriculture (this was a principal charge against Tito); his hesitance to purge the moderate socialists in the communist party; his equivocation on anti-Titoism; and even his capitulation to the Nazis during the occupation. Stalin had pulled out all the stops, and in view of the overwhelming strength marshalled against him, Gomulka agreed to the "Deviation" document, except that part concerning his dealings with the Nazis. Abjectly, he admitted to the Central Committee: "The mistakes I have mentioned arise from my strong nationalism, as well as from my unrestrained social-democratic conceptions. I am doing everything I can to liquidate both of these from my system of thought."[34] Ironically, Gomulka's recantations were reported to the public in the pages of *New Roads* in October 1948. This speech was followed on successive days by additional admissions, until Gomulka had "confessed" to everything demanded of him. He was relieved of his party leadership and his government position and, finally, was arrested but never stood trial. In September 1954, eighteen months after Stalin's death, Gomulka was quietly released from custody. He, and the Polish road, had survived.

Others in Eastern Europe were not so fortunate. In Hungary, the Foreign Minister and former Interior Minister Laszlo Rajk was executed for "Titoism" and treason. The same fate befell the Secretary General of the Czechoslovak Communist Party, Rudolf Slansky, who, along with numerous other Czech communists, was identified in the pages of the Cominform journal as one of "the traitors and enemies of the Czechoslovak people—Trotskyites, Titoists, Zionists,[35] bourgeois nationalists in the service of the American imperialists—[who] strive to . . . push the country on to the path of Titoist Yugoslavia."[36] The target in Bulgaria was Dimitrov's heir apparent Traycho Kostov. The irony of Kostov's execution was that he was a loyal Stalinist who had no connection with Titoism whatsoever. "Kostovism," wrote Nissan Oren, "was not Titoism; nor was it Bulgarian nationalism. . . ."[37] Oren believes that Kostov was purged because he was a Stalinist. "As in the Purge of the thirties, the blows were aimed not at deviationists as such but at prominent figures, who were to be put down as object lessons. . . . By choosing Kostov as his chief victim, Stalin intended to reveal the depth of the abyss to everyone under him. . . . If Kostov could become a traitor overnight, there was no immunity for anyone."[38] The fact that Dimitrov was eventually succeeded by his brother-in-law, Chervenkov, suggests that the domestic leaders may have cooperated with Stalin for their own personal reasons. This same, apparently irrational, fate awaited Anna Pauker and Vasile Luca in Romania. Both loyal Stalinists, they were also Jews, and Fejto suggests that Gheorghiu-Dej used the anti-Tito campaign to purge Jewish elements, a purpose with which Stalin sympathized. Walter Ulbricht apparently employed the same technique against Jews in his German party organization.

The truth is that the East European purges had numerous causes, but a single goal—the creation of a monolithic Soviet hegemony. Some of those who resisted were sincerely committed to national rights; others were eliminated for reasons unrelated to the Tito controversy. By that time, however, anyone who presented a real or potential threat to Stalin, or to those in East Europe upon whom he relied, could be eliminated with impunity in the name of proletarian internationalism. Ironically, those who survived the purge—Gomulka, Nagy, Tito, and, of course, Khrushchev within the Soviet system—

were to be the protagonists in the greatest exhibition of national communism yet witnessed.

DESTALINIZATION: NATIONAL COMMUNISM UNLEASHED

By excommunicating Tito, Stalin had intended to prove that it was impossible for a communist regime to survive without Soviet patronage. The persistence and prosperity of the Yugoslav system demonstrated the opposite. The plan failed because Stalin underestimated the importance of domestic support for a communist leader. Tito was living testimony to the fact that a socialist regime with national support could thrive without Soviet assistance and in the face of Soviet hostility. Stalin's failure to teach Tito a lesson in communism resulted in at least four separate but unintended lessons for the other participants.

First, Tito's success convinced Stalin and his loyalists in the Kremlin that the preservation of Soviet interests required a redoubling of efforts to eliminate national forces in the bloc in order to prevent the emergence of any new "Titos." Second, for some Soviet leaders (notably Khrushchev and Malenkov), the Tito debacle was confirmation of Stalin's inability to cope with new conditions and of the pressing need to develop intrabloc relationships based upon something other than brute force and blatant Soviet national interest. Third, Tito's success against Moscow confirmed the surviving national communists' belief that the "national roads" policy could generate sufficient domestic political support to enable socialism to develop in Eastern Europe independent of Soviet control. Finally, for the Stalinists in the bloc, Tito's survival was a warning that national communists could mobilize a population and that the only guarantee of their personal power was a continued Soviet presence. This realization reduced the necessity for Stalin to impose his will on those Eastern European party leaders who had no domestic power base and knew it.

In summary, for those in power the vitality of the Tito regime was a constant reminder of the danger that national movements could pose to Stalinism. On the other hand, for those out of power (in the Kremlin and throughout the bloc) Tito's survival was proof of the necessity to adjust socialist goals to national conditions. Tito palpably demonstrated the futility of continued attempts to repress national movements in the name of an internationalist policy that was merely a thinly disguised expression of Soviet great power chauvinism.

Yugoslavia was the focal point of these conflicting perceptions and interests, but they were rooted in national conditions that existed independent of Titoism. The national forces were held in check only by Stalin's overwhelming presence; therefore, it was only a matter of weeks after his death on 5 March 1953 that the first signs of the tensions generated by Stalinist repression of national sentiments exploded in the form of a spontaneous workers' uprising in East Berlin. Three and a half years later, in November 1956, Soviet tanks in the streets of Budapest were to signify more dramatically the persistence of national motivations in the socialist bloc and the utter futility of all previous attempts to separate national and communist goals. Stalin's death did not signal the beginning of the national communist revival. The road to Budapest began in Belgrade, not Berlin. But Stalin's passing was perceived by all involved as an opportunity to establish a new pattern of relations for the bloc, which was to be referred to as the "Socialist Commonwealth."

Analysis of bloc relations in the post-Stalin period requires care. The issue under investigation is national communism—the assertion of the right of communist parties to develop policies appropriate to national conditions as they perceive them. The problem is that this issue of national independence can be easily confused with such concurrent trends of the post-Stalin era as liberalization, economic reform, democratization, and destalinization. The essence of national communism, however, is not the content of a policy, but who made that policy. This point is crucial because one of the commonly accepted interpretations of events from the prelude to the Hungarian Revolution of 1956 through the Czechoslovakian invasion of 1968 is that the thrust of national communism has been liberalism and democratic reform and the Soviet response has been to check these tendencies. The difficulty with this view is that while it explains some developments, it does not adequately account for significant changes within the bloc between 1953 and 1956, nor does it satisfactorily explain the subsequent Albanian and Romanian heresies. In other terms, to identify national communism with a specific policy content, be it liberal or conservative, is to imbue it with a normative quality that it does not deserve. To assume that the national aspirations of the East European systems are necessarily more democratic than Soviet leaders are willing to tolerate is to tinge the analysis of national communism with an ideologically inspired bias that distorts the facts.

In point of fact, the initial reaction to post-Stalin Soviet policy among the East European leaders was motivated by their determination to maintain Stalinism, which conflicted with the so-called Soviet "new course." Suddenly, the tables were turned throughout the bloc as Rakosi in Hungary, Bierut in Poland, Novotny in Czechoslovakia, Hoxha in Albania, Ulbricht in Germany, and Gheorghiu-Dej in Romania, all of whom had ousted their national communist opponents, found themselves being challenged by a new Soviet leadership demanding a different form of political leadership in the bloc. As Francois Fejto has so acutely observed: "Paradoxically enough, it was the resistance of the ruling cliques to de-Stalinization that was to lead some European communist parties . . . to the brink of desatellization. Rather than let themselves be drawn into the quicksands of liberalism, these leaders would deck themselves out in national colours and come forward as anti-Soviet Stalinists."[39]

The initial post-Stalin split erupted over the pace at which political decompression should proceed and the character of the leadership that should direct the change. The Khrushchev-Malenkov "new course," which included depersonalization of leadership by separating the posts of party and government leader, deemphasis on heavy industrial production in favor of consumer goods, and reduction of terrorism as a method of political control, was viewed by most of the Eastern European Stalinists in power as dangerous "revisionism." In the case of Hungary's leader Rakosi, for example, the fact that Khrushchev and Malenkov had agreed to share power (at least for the time being) because of the problems generated by the Soviet succession struggle was no reason for him to share power with anyone, and particularly with someone like Imre Nagy, whose economic views, while similar to Malenkov's, were anathema to the Hungarian Stalinists.

Similarly, the Czech leader Antonin Novotny (ironically Clement Gottwald contracted pneumonia at Stalin's funeral and died shortly after) was forced to share power with Zapotocky, who, backed by Malenkov, shared Nagy's views on economic reform through decentralization. In Romania, the party leader Gheorghiu-Dej surrendered that post to his friend George Apostol while retaining his position as head of the Romanian government. The Bulgarian leader Chervenkov made the same decision and turned leadership of the party over to Todor Zhivkov, a choice he was later to regret when Zhivkov used his base of power in the party to oust Chervenkov. Even the radical Enver Hoxha in Albania gave up leadership of the government under Soviet pressure. Finally, Bierut in Poland surrendered control of the government to Cyrankiewicz while retaining leadership of the party.

Some of these leaders maintained control behind the scenes despite the apparent surrender of authority, and all clearly wished to consolidate their power if possible. They did not have to wait long.

When, in 1955, Khrushchev outmaneuvered and removed Malenkov from the Soviet hierarchy, the latter's protégés fell in quick succession. Khrushchev's consolidation of power was read by the European Stalinists as a signal to reconsolidate their own power, and Rakosi, Novotny, Gheorghiu-Dej, Hoxha, and Bierut reemerged as the *primi inter pares* of their respective hierarchies, with the tacit approval of Moscow once again.

Pursuit of the "new course" posed a serious dilemma for the new Soviet leaders. They altered Soviet policy because they were convinced that continuation along the Stalinist path of all-out heavy industrialization was exhausting the economic systems (including the work force) of the USSR and Eastern Europe. Purges had devastated the ranks of the competent elites, superindustrialization drives irrespective of local conditions and capacities were proving extremely costly and inefficient, and disregard for human needs for consumer goods was generating deep resentment among the workers and peasants. Unquestionably, reform was necessary. The problem was that in order to bring about those reforms in the Soviet bloc the new leaders had both to demand that the Stalinists conform to the new Soviet model and to admit, if only tacitly, that the old Stalinist model was defective. Put another way, the only means the Soviets could employ to ameliorate the problems engendered by Stalin's unilateral dictation of policy to East Europe was to unilaterally dictate a new policy to East Europe, which they knew the Stalinists would resist.

Thus the "new course" required old methods; the Stalinists were not given any choice about destalinizing their systems. Clearly, destalinization was perceived by the new Soviet leaders as a political necessity and it contained many "liberal" elements, but it ironically reaffirmed the very essence of Stalinist policy toward the bloc—the right of the USSR to impose conformity to its political will. From the perspective of the Stalinists in Eastern Europe the rule was the same: If you wished to remain in power, you had to take your orders from Moscow.

Yet the Stalinists presented a formidable obstacle to change within the bloc during the initial years of the post-Stalin succession struggle in the USSR. The new leaders, as we have seen, were not in a position to remove the East European Stalinists. But as subsequent developments revealed, the entire course of Khrushchev's rise to power and his struggle to remain there was intimately connected with, and dependent upon, successful destalinization. Khrushchev obviously decided very early that his political future depended upon his ability to tear Stalin down, not to build him up. This was a dangerous decision in view of the fact that he was surrounded by

Stalinists within his own party as well as throughout the international movement. In large measure then, the success of his strategy, particularly in the initial phase, depended upon his ability to withstand Stalinist pressure and to associate himself with policies and symbols antithetical to the Stalinist order. Convincing the European Stalinists to go along with the "new course" in domestic affairs was only half the problem; the other half consisted of leading the bloc into a Soviet-initiated rapprochement with the symbol of anti-Stalinism in the socialist movement—Tito.

Having consolidated his position in early 1955 with the resignation of Malenkov as prime minister, Khrushchev reversed his earlier position on the "new course" and reemphasized the need for heavy industrialization. It was at this point that the European Stalinists were able to reconsolidate their own power. From his position of increased political security, however, Khrushchev launched the next phase of his own, and decidedly non-Stalinist, program of intrasocialist relations. On 26 May 1955, Khrushchev led a Soviet delegation on a week-long visit to Yugoslavia. Significantly, it was Khrushchev who went to Tito, and despite some clumsy initial attempts by Khrushchev to lay the blame for the split on secondary Soviet leaders, the final joint statement represented a formal Soviet concession to Yugoslavian independence. Specifically, the document pledged "compliance with the principle of mutual respect for, and non-interference in, internal affairs for any reason whatsoever, whether of an economic, political or ideological nature, because questions of internal organization, or difference in social systems and of different forms of Socialist development, are solely the concern of the individual countries."[40]

For the first time since Stalin had come to power the USSR formally recognized the right of another socialist nation to pursue an independent course of action. Inevitably, the response of national communists like Nagy and Gomulka to the conditions of the Soviet-Yugoslav rapprochement was that rights granted to one socialist country should be granted to all. This was a concession that Khrushchev was willing to consider, but that the European Stalinists perceived as an open invitation to revisionism and reform in their systems. Khrushchev had placed his East European counterparts in the position of having to support the Tito reconciliation that they perceived as a direct challenge to their own policies and power. But that was to be only the opening round in their struggle for survival. In the first half of 1956, in rapid succession Khrushchev dealt three devastating blows to Stalinism.

First, in February, at the first post-Stalin CPSU Congress (the

Twentieth), Khrushchev formally launched his destalinization campaign when he delivered his so-called "Secret Speech" denouncing
Stalin and his crimes against the people and leaders of the Soviet
Union and the bloc. Without prior consultation or warning, Khrushchev attacked the man who was responsible for the installation of
all the leaders in Eastern Europe and revealed that they had come
to power by means of Machiavellian manipulation and, in some
instances, murder. It is reported that when the Secret Speech was
circulated in the Politburo of the Polish party some of the members
fainted in shock at the revelations. Whether it was the shock of
surprise or of having been exposed is unclear, but the speech re-
verberated throughout the bloc. Khrushchev's attack on Stalin was
an undisguised attack on those whom the poet Evtushenko was later
to label the "Heirs of Stalin."

Second, on 17 April 1956 Cominform, which Stalin had established
in 1947 as the institutional vehicle for Soviet political control in the
bloc, was dissolved. The final statement noted that conditions within
the international movement had changed, and took particular note
of the "extension of socialism beyond the boundaries of a single
country."[41] Significantly, no mention was made of a possible replacement for Cominform; rather, the concluding paragraph suggested
that "each party or group of parties will, in the course of developing
its work in conformity with the common aims and tasks of Marxist-
Leninist parties and the *specific national features and conditions of
their countries,* find new and useful forms of establishing links and
contacts among themselves" [Emphasis added].[42] Cominform represented the last Soviet attempt to maintain a permanent political
organization for the purpose of providing ideological unity within
the movement. In its place an irregular series of *ad hoc* meetings
have been convened in Moscow and elsewhere to hammer out points
of ideological agreement among the members of the movement. Even
these, however, have been characterized by national division, and
the last world-wide meeting was held in Moscow in 1969. Since then,
the only significant attempt to forge ideological unity occurred at
the 1976 Berlin meeting of European communist parties, which will
be discussed later in this chapter. The point is that the dissolution
of Cominform in 1956 marked the end of the "Internationals" and
all that remains are regional economic (Council for Mutual Economic
Assistance) and military (Warsaw Treaty Organization) organizations
dominated by the USSR.

The third blow to Stalin's socialist order was delivered on 20 June
1956, when Khrushchev and Tito completed the process begun a
year earlier. Having previously recognized the right of another *country*

to pursue an independent path, Khrushchev now finally capitulated on the right of *parties* to be independent of the CPSU. The joint statement is the quintessential recognition of national communism:

> Believing that the path of socialist development differs in various countries and conditions, that the multiplicity of forms of socialist development tends to strengthen socialism, and proceeding from the fact that any tendency of imposing one's opinion on the ways and forms of socialist development is alien to both—the two parties have agreed that their cooperation shall be based on complete voluntariness and equality, friendly criticism, and comradely exchange of opinions on controversial questions.[43]

In this turnabout Khrushchev first admitted that Stalin had made mistakes and then conceded that the CPSU was not infallible on all issues of politics, economics, and ideology. For more than thirty years, including the period of the establishment of the socialist bloc following World War II, the Stalinist assertion of Soviet infallibility had legitimated the repression of all non-Soviet national sentiment in the movement. Khrushchev's recognition of an alternate, Titoist model of socialist development opened the door to the prospect of competition among socialist powers for the loyalty of the bloc, and more importantly implied that if no single version of the socialist vision was appropriate for all, then there could be as many socialist forms as there were socialist nations.

Khrushchev was, if the interpretation presented in previous chapters is correct, abandoning the Stalinist aberration and returning to the traditional Marxist-Leninist nationality policy. But the years of Stalinist repression had created pressures for reform that would eventually prove uncontrollable. As Paul Zinner observed:

> Perhaps it was the very strength of national feeling in some East European countries that induced the Soviet Union to adopt wholesale, ruthless methods to lower national self-esteem and to demolish traditional patterns of national self-identification. But the practitioners of these policies could not have been unaware of the probable repercussions of their deeds. Nationalism became the last rallying point, the final refuge of solidarity of masses of people who were otherwise torn asunder by social, economic, and political differences.[44]

Ten days after the publication of the Soviet-Yugoslav recognition of national communism, the workers of Poznan, Poland, began a spontaneous demonstration against their Stalinist leadership. Khrushchev had opened a Pandora's box of national sentiment that Soviet leaders would never again be able to close.

Poland: 1956

The events that led to the crises in Poland and Hungary in the autumn of 1956 were much too complex to be analyzed in any detail here. Numerous accounts of these "revolutions" are available, and the briefest outlines of what transpired will suffice for the purpose of this analysis. It must be emphasized, however, that many of the actions of those involved remain clouded owing to a lack of verifiable information or to conflicting reports.

There is no question but that Khrushchev's actions in the first half of 1956 sparked the Polish and Hungarian crises. Ironically, the Polish party leader Bierut died on 12 March 1956 from an illness he contracted in Moscow while attending the Twentieth CPSU Congress. Bierut's death opened the way for a reshuffling of the Polish leadership at the same time that the destalinization campaign was commencing. The new party leader, Edward Ochab, began his tenure by admitting the excesses of the past. He recognized the "painful and bitter truths about the mistakes of Joseph Stalin" and under the label of "Beriaism" he decried the unjustified persecution of members who disagreed with the party line. But, on the issue of Gomulka's expulsion and arrest, Ochab refused to admit that the party had been completely wrong. Gomulka, he said, had "tried to infuse the concept of a Polish road to socialism—correctly used by the party—with a foreign content, which meant essentially the abandonment of the development of socialist construction in Poland." Having declared that Gomulka was ideologically incorrect, however, Ochab went on to concede that "it is worth declaring with great emphasis that Gomulka's arrest . . . was unjustified and without function." The dilemma for Ochab and his colleagues was to find a way to rehabilitate Gomulka without rehabilitating Gomulkaism. As Ochab said, "the correction of the injustice done to Wladyslaw Gomulka does not in any way change the correct content of the political and ideological struggle which the Party has conducted and continues to conduct against the ideological conceptions represented by Gomulka."[45]

Throughout the spring of 1956 the Polish leadership continued to insist that while problems existed in the economic and social sectors, pursuit of the traditional pro-Soviet course (without the excesses of Stalinism) remained the correct path. But the pressure for real reform among the people finally broke through when the workers of Poznan took to the streets to protest living conditions on 28 June. The initial

Soviet and Polish response was to ascribe the Poznan uprising to the provocations of "imperialist agents and the reactionary underground."[46] Nevertheless, the Poznan uprising succeeded in opening a rift within the Polish party as well as between Soviet and Polish interests. A resolution of the Seventh Plenary Session of the Central Committee, which met 18–28 July, admitted that the workers of Poland had good cause to be dissatisfied with their conditions and with the leaders who had permitted the situation to deteriorate.[47] However, Nikolai Bulganin, representing the USSR at that session, attributed the entire affair to the "enemies of socialism," and warned that "to be easygoing under these conditions would be an unforgivable sin." "We cannot," Bulganin warned, "idly bypass attempts that are aimed at weakening the international ties of the socialist camp under the slogan of so-called national peculiarities."[48]

These thinly veiled threats against a revival of Gomulkaism only served to make Gomulka the rallying point of those Poles who realized that meaningful reform would be possible only if the country could establish its own course. In his biography of Gomulka, Nicholas Bethell observed that now that Stalin was the victim, the logical conclusion for the Poles to draw was that Stalin's victim, Gomulka, must have been correct all along and that only Gomulka could lead Poland out of Stalinism.[49] The Seventh Plenary Session of the Polish party closed in the midst of promises of reform but the Gomulka issue was not resolved. Ochab struggled with two masters, the Soviets who mistrusted Gomulka and the Polish people who mistrusted anyone else. Finally, on 4 August 1956 it was announced that Gomulka had been readmitted to the party. The stage was set for the showdown, which was to occur 19–20 October at the Eighth Plenum of the Polish Central Committee.

The decision to readmit Gomulka was, in effect, a declaration by the Polish party that national communism was no longer a heresy— a declaration that generated deep concern within the Kremlin. Could Gomulka's influence carry the Polish party away from its commitment to the USSR? Would the Polish leadership be swept up in a wave of popular national sentiment and lose control of the political situation? Before the Soviet leaders would permit Gomulka's return to the leadership of the Polish party, which was inevitable at the Eighth Plenum, they would have to receive satisfactory assurances that Gomulkaism and the Polish road did not include a break from the Soviet alliance system. Of particular importance was an assurance that Poland, with its long German border (albeit East German) would not renege on its commitment to the newly formed Warsaw Treaty Organization (WTO).

It was a foregone conclusion that when the Eighth Plenum of the Central Committee convened on 19 October Gomulka would not only be returned to the Central Committee, but also be elected to the post of First Secretary. Yet, despite this open challenge to Soviet authority, it came as a total surprise when Khrushchev, Molotov, Mikoyan, and other top-ranking Soviet leaders arrived in Warsaw, unannounced, on the morning of the nineteenth and demanded a meeting with the Polish leaders. Ochab went before the plenum, informed the delegates of the situation, and requested an adjournment until that evening to permit discussions; but not before Gomulka was readmitted to the Central Committee.

It is difficult to know exactly what transpired during the Polish-Soviet confrontation that continued through the early morning hours of 20 October. Reports indicate that when Khrushchev first saw Gomulka he asked, "Who is that man?" and the proposed Polish leader replied, "I am Gomulka, and because of you I have just spent three years in prison."[50] At some point, however, the hostilities eased and the negotiating began. Perhaps the Soviets stopped threatening the Poles because Gomulka in return threatened to take the issue of Soviet hegemony versus the Polish road directly to his people.[51] But, more likely, the Soviets moderated their position because Khrushchev became convinced that Gomulka had no intention of damaging Soviet security in Eastern Europe and could be relied upon to channel the national sentiments of the Polish people in a direction that would not challenge the leading position of the Polish party. Gomulka said afterwards that the chief Soviet concern was that events might "lead to a breach of the Warsaw Pact, would lead to a break-off of Polish-Soviet relations."[52] Finally, convinced that this would not be the case, Khrushchev and his Kremlin colleagues left Warsaw twenty-four hours after their arrival, and Gomulka addressed the reconvened Eighth Plenum of what had become *his* Polish party.

First, he criticized the program of agricultural collectivization carried out under Stalin and the general failure of the party to improve living standards. Having dismissed the Soviet model as inappropriate, Gomulka proceeded to declare that the actions of the Poznan workers were fully justified and not the result of external agitation. "The causes of the Poznan tragedy and of the profound dissatisfaction of the entire working class are to be found in ourselves, in the leadership of the Party, in the Government."[53]

Gomulka then turned to the question of Polish-Soviet relations. "How did it happen," he asked, "that our Party . . . permitted the many distortions which took place in the recent past?" His answer was that the early Marxists had only established a general theory of socialism.

They never imagined their theory to be complete. On the contrary, they always maintained that theory must be always alive, must develop on the basis of practical experience and must always be enriched. Even a theory of socialism evolved in the best possible way at any given time in any given conditions cannot embrace all the details of life which is richer than theory.

What is immutable in socialism can be reduced to the abolition of the exploitation of man by man. The roads of achieving this goal can be and are different. They are determined by various circumstances of time and place. The model of socialism can also vary. It can be such as that created in the Soviet Union; it can be shaped in a manner as we see it in Yugoslavia; it can be different still.

Only by way of the experience and achievements of various countries building socialism can the best model of socialism under given conditions arise.

The Soviet Union was the first state in the world where a socialist revolution took place. Lenin and the Bolshevik Party undertook for the first time in history the gigantic task of transforming the theory of socialism into a material, a social, reality.

In the face of tremendous difficulties which accompanied the re-shaping of the system of tsarist Russia, backward from every point of view, into a socialist system, during the period when the Party was directed by Stalin, the practice was begun of liquidating in an increasingly ruthless manner the normal clash of views concerning problems brought forth by life which occurred within the Party while Lenin was alive.

The place occupied in the Party by intra-Party discussion was taken—as this discussion was gradually being eliminated—by the cult of personality. The mapping out of the Russian road to socialism passed gradually from the hands of the Central Committee into the hands of an ever smaller group of people, and finally became the monopoly of Stalin. This monopoly also encompassed the theory of scientific socialism.

The cult of personality is a specific system of exercising power, a specific road of advancing in the direction of socialism while applying methods contrary to socialist humanism, to the socialist conception of the freedom of man, to the socialist conception of legality.

After World War II the Soviet Union ceased to be the only country building socialism. . . . The Workers Parties . . . were confronted by problems which previously did not exist in practical form. To these problems belong such questions as the road to socialism in conditions proper for each country, which to a certain degree influences the shaping of the model of socialism. . . .

The mutual relations between the parties and states of the socialist camp . . . should be shaped on the principles of international working class solidarity, should be based on mutual confidence and equality of rights; on granting assistance to each other; on mutual friendly criticism, if such should become necessary; and on a rational solution, arising from the spirit of friendship and from the spirit of socialism, of all controversial matters. Within the framework of such relations each country should have full independence, and the rights of each nation to a sovereign government in an independent country should be fully and mutually respected. This is how it should be and—I would say—this is how it is beginning to be.

In the past it was unfortunately not always like this in the relations between us and our great and friendly neighbor, the Soviet Union.[54]

The key to Gomulka's success was not how far he was willing to go in establishing the Polish road; rather it consisted in the limits he placed on those who would have gone too far. This, as we shall see, was the crucial difference between the Polish and the Hungarian experiences. At the same time that he spoke of the need for the democratization of the party he also stated categorically, "The Party must and will be monolithic from top to bottom."[55] And Gomulka left no doubt about the future of Polish-Soviet relations. "The leadership of the Party gives first priority in political work to the problem of consolidating in the consciousness of the whole nation the importance of friendship between Poland and the Soviet Union. . . . That is why we must oppose the work of the rabble-rousing, provocative elements which oppose Polish-Soviet friendship. . . ."[56] Gomulka understood precisely that the interests of Poland could never be divorced from those of the USSR, and that the only guarantee of security acceptable to the Soviet leaders was the knowledge that each of the bloc states was ruled by a party apparatus that could be relied on to support Soviet foreign policy toward the West in general, and Germany in particular. For his part, Khrushchev understood that Poland under a popular leader like Gomulka was far more stable and therefore less susceptible to anti-Soviet appeals than it was under a repressive, puppet regime such as Bierut's. National communism reemerged and survived in Poland because it served, rather than challenged, Soviet interests. The fate of national communism in Hungary was to be just the opposite because it could not pass this crucial test.

Hungary: 1956

The Hungarian party leader Matyas Rakosi had managed to survive the "new course" and oust his opponent Imre Nagy when Khrushchev dumped Malenkov. But the intensification of the destalinization campaign signaled by the Twentieth CPSU Congress in February 1956 and the Soviet capitulation to Tito in June rendered Rakosi's position untenable. Rakosi had depended upon repression and purge as his means of party and social control, but Khrushchev had declared an end to that style of leadership. Imre Nagy's brand of reform economics, with its emphasis on decentralization and consumerism, was not in favor in the USSR, but Tito had supported Nagy's policies in the past and Tito had made the removal of Rakosi and the restoration of Nagy part of his price for the normalization of relations with Moscow. Finally, the spirit of reform generated among the populations of East Europe by destalinization made any former Stalinist unpopular and any prominent victim of Stalinism a potential national hero.

Thus, at the very moment that Bulganin was dispatched to Warsaw to urge caution on the Seventh CC Plenum, Mikoyan informed the Hungarian Politburo on 17 July that the interests of the party would be best served by Rakosi's "resignation" and replacement by equally loyal but less hated Erno Gero. Rakosi accepted his defeat calmly, publicly explaining that his health did not permit him to continue as party leader. Significantly, Mikoyan went directly from Budapest to Yugoslavia to consult with Tito, then returned to Hungary on 21 July when another member of the Rakosi team, the party secretary responsible for the security apparatus, was also purged.

The immediate reason for Rakosi's removal was that the Soviets had received word through their ambassador in Budapest, Yuri Andropov (later head of the KGB) that Rakosi was about to launch a new purge. However, the effect of replacing him with Gero was minimal. Tito remained dissatisfied as long as Nagy was out of power, the problems in the Hungarian economy persisted, the popular mood was turning against the party; yet the Kremlin did not trust Nagy just as it did not trust Gomulka.

Inevitably, destalinization resulted in the exposure of the crimes committed by the European Stalinists and the rehabilitation of their victims. Toward the end of September 1956 a series of "reburials" of innocent victims began, including that of former party secretary Laszlo Rajk, whom Rakosi had had murdered. These reburials provided a platform for speeches calling for exposure of those responsible and were accompanied by mass demonstrations. By that time Nagy was identified in the public mind as the most important living victim of Stalinism in Hungary, and party leaders decided that if he requested readmission to the party they would grant it without requiring an admission of past mistakes. In his letter to the Central Committee of 4 October 1956 requesting reinstatement, Nagy declared,

"I deem it necessary to restate that . . . industry, agriculture and the entire national economy should be placed on the foundations of socialism in the spirit of Marxism-Leninism in accordance with the special conditions existing in Hungary. . . ."[57] On 13 October, the party Politburo recommended Nagy's readmission.

In the week that followed, support for Nagy in the form of public demonstrations and pronouncements by reformist groups mounted. This mass support reached its crescendo when word reached Hungary that Gomulka had met Khrushchev face to face and had emerged victorious. Spontaneous and uncontrolled demonstrations broke out in support of the Polish "victory," and demands grew for Nagy to emulate Gomulka. In the midst of this domestic turmoil, which reached a head on 23 October, it was announced that Hungary and Yugoslavia had agreed that the two parties would cooperatively pursue the construction of socialism in their respective countries.[58] A conservative speech by Gero that same evening incited the mobilized population even further in the direction of radical change. The situation was clearly out of hand.

Exactly who among the Hungarian leaders decided to call on Soviet troops for assistance is not known. Both the declaration of martial law and the appeal for Soviet military aid were issued in the early hours of the morning of 24 October by the prime minister, Imre Nagy. Sometime during that morning Nagy was named head of the government, but he subsequently denied issuing any such decrees. "How," one observer of the Hungarian revolution has asked, "could Soviet tanks arrive in Budapest at 2 A.M. on October 24, in response to a request received in Moscow on the same day?"[59] And, how, we may further enquire, could Nagy have issued a request for tanks that began arriving before he knew he was prime minister? The most reasonable answer is that no official requests were made and the decision to introduce Soviet troops was made by Gero and the Kremlin through the Soviet ambassador Andropov. Whoever made the decision, the intervention was a disaster. The presence of Soviet troops to resolve a Hungarian problem converted the entire affair into a national crusade against Soviet hegemony. The attempt to resolve a political problem by military means was futile, and after days of confrontation and skirmishes between Hungarian civilians and the Soviet military, the legitimacy of the Hungarian communist party had completely vaporized.

Finally, on 28 October the party capitulated and ordered a cease fire. The people had won, or so it seemed, and Nagy announced the formation of a new government. But most momentous of all, the Hungarian Workers' Party dissolved itself, turning the affairs of the

party over to a six-member committee including Nagy and Janos
Kadar, another victim of Rakosi's purges.

Events progressed at a rapid-fire pace after that. On 29 October
it was announced that Soviet troops would withdraw from Budapest.
The next day Nagy declared the restoration of the multiparty system
in Hungary and the formation of a coalition government: "The
Cabinet abolishes the one-party system."[60] Then, on 31 October,
Nagy announced, "This day we opened negotiations for the withdrawal
of Soviet troops and for the renunciation of our obligations from
the Warsaw Treaty."[61] The very next day Nagy informed the United
Nations that the Hungarian government had notified the Soviet
government that the former "immediately repudiates the Warsaw
Treaty and at the same time declares Hungary's neutrality."[62] In an
address to his people on the same day, Nagy proclaimed:

> The Hungarian people desires the consolidation and further de-
> velopment of the achievements of its national revolution without
> joining any power blocs. The century-old dream of the Hungarian
> people is thus fulfilled. The revolutionary struggle fought by the
> Hungarian heroes of the past and present has at last carried the cause
> of freedom and independence to victory. The heroic struggle has made
> it possible to implement, in the international relations of our people,
> its fundamental national interest—neutrality.[63]

The final heresy of 1 November was the formation of a new party—
the Hungarian Socialist Workers' Party—a clean break with the
Stalinist past. The leadership of this "new" party declared that it
would

> defend the cause of democracy and socialism, whose realization it
> seeks not through servile copying of foreign examples, but on a road
> suitable to the historic and economic characteristics of our country,
> relying on the teachings of Marxism-Leninism, on scientific socialism
> free of Stalinism and any kind of dogmatism, and on the revolutionary
> and progressive traditions of Hungarian history and culture.[64]

The Hungarians embraced the two policies that Gomulka had so
scrupulously avoided: They created a party apparatus completely
independent of Soviet influence and they threatened to disintegrate
the Soviet security network in East Europe by removing Hungary
from the Warsaw Pact. With those two acts the fate of the Hungarian
revolution was sealed. At 5:20 A.M. on 4 November 1956, Imre Nagy
announced:

THIS IS IMRE NAGY, Premier, speaking. In the early hours of this morning, the Soviet troops launched an attack against our capital city with the obvious intention of overthrowing the lawful, democratic, Hungarian Government. Our troops are fighting. The Government is in its place. I inform the people of the country and world public opinion of this.[65]

Shortly thereafter, another decree was issued in the name of something called the Hungarian Revolutionary Worker-Peasant Government, headed by Janos Kadar and others, which called on Hungarians to repudiate the Nagy government "in the face of the ever growing strength of the counterrevolutionary threat menacing our People's Republic."[66] The resistance of the Hungarian people against Soviet troops and the new Kadar government were to continue for weeks after 4 November, but the fall of the Nagy government signaled the end of the Hungarian road. Nagy sought and received asylum in the Yugoslavian embassy, where he remained until 22 November. Then, under a guarantee of free passage out of Hungary, he left the embassy, but was immediately arrested by Soviet troops. Nagy never appeared in public again, and on 16 June 1958, it was announced that he and three others had been tried, found guilty, and executed for their role in the "counterrevolutionary uprising."

The use of the term "counterrevolution" is crucial to an understanding of the Soviet response to events in Hungary. It is not merely a catch phrase used by Soviet ideologists to justify Moscow's actions. Counterrevolution means an attempt by noncommunist forces to overthrow a previously established communist regime. In the case of Hungary, there were frequent references in the West to "Freedom Fighters" and the revival of "democracy" by those forces. What this meant was that Hungarians were struggling for freedom from communist control, and, consequently, Soviet control. This struggle was undoubtedly inspired by national sentiments on the part of Hungarians who wished to regain sovereignty over their nation's affairs, but not every expression of national spirit in a communist country is national communism. If the Hungarian party had managed to contain popular pressure for democratization, as had its Polish comrades a few weeks earlier, it is doubtful that the Soviets would have intervened. A resolute, unified Hungarian party probably could have convinced the Kremlin to accept Nagy within the context of a Leninist party system, just as the Poles had forced Gomulka on a hesitant Khrushchev. However, when runaway Hungarian nationalism swept aside the fundamental principles of a communist regime (i.e., party control and alliances within the bloc), the movement was transformed from

national communism to anticommunist nationalism—what the Soviets called "counterrevolution."

Even Tito, who was harshly critical of the initial Soviet intervention
and of Soviet policies that had caused the problems that resulted in
the Hungarian revolution, was forced to concede that military intervention was the only option available to the USSR. "There could
be either chaos, civil war, counterrevolution, and a new world war,
or the intervention of Soviet troops which were there. . . . And, of
course, if it meant having socialism in Hungary, then, comrades, we
can say, although we are against interference, Soviet intervention
was necessary."[67]

From the Soviet perspective, and from that of virtually every
communist leader at the time, national roads were permissible only
when they were roads to socialism. Of course, the crucial question
of who had the right to define what socialism is remained open, but
the Hungarian declaration of neutrality in the struggle between
capitalism and communism made it appear to the Soviets that
something that had been gained in Hungary was about to be lost.
This counterrevolutionary turn of events is what justified Soviet
policy within the communist world.

In subsequent statements the Soviet leadership attempted to make
it clear that its action in Hungary was not a repudiation of the right
of each socialist country to adopt policies suited to national conditions.
In fact, one article that appeared in *Pravda* shortly after the final
Soviet intervention laid much of the blame on the Hungarian
leadership for its failure to develop a Hungarian form of socialism.
"The former Party and state leadership of Hungary mechanically
copied the experience of the Soviet Union in the field of industrialization despite the fact that [they] . . . were repeatedly given comradely
advice not to do this."[68] The article continued, "The leadership of
the Hungarian Workers Party did not sufficiently respect the national
peculiarities of the country. . . . But each nation has national traditions
and customs that must be respected."[69]

The Soviet criticism of the Hungarian party for having "hurt the
national self-respect of the Hungarian people" at the very moment
that Soviet troops were repressing Hungarian "Freedom Fighters"
may appear to some as brazen hypocrisy. Yet from their perspective
the Soviets' position was consistent. They were repressing not communists in Hungary, but "counterrevolutionaries" and "bourgeois
democrats" who had attempted to wrest power from the people and
to restore the ancien regime.

Limiting National Communism:
The Moscow Declaration of 1957

For more than a decade after the Hungarian debacle the CPSU attempted to clarify this distinction between national movements within socialism and nationalism against socialism. The Kremlin wanted to evolve a policy that would combine, to the satisfaction of other socialist states, the right to develop national policies with the obligation of each party to a basic standard of communist behavior. First at a meeting of the twelve ruling parties in November 1957, and again at a convention of eighty-one parties in November 1960 (both in Moscow), the Kremlin tried to distill a set of principles to which all communists could subscribe. It was an exercise in futility from the beginning, as subsequent events would prove. The reactions of China and Albania, which were labeled dogmatists, as well as developments in Czechoslovakia and Romania would bear witness to the Soviet incapacity to impose, by means other than military force, some minimal content on the term "communism."

The Moscow Declaration of 1957, signed by the ruling parties of the time, did include a list of "general laws," which, it was proclaimed, "are manifested everywhere alongside a great variety of historically formed national features and traditions," but which are "applicable to all countries embarking on the socialist path."[70] However, the vague wording of these laws reveals the nebulous quality of these so-called universal features:

- "leadership . . . by the working class, the core of which is the Marxist-Leninist party, in bringing about a proletarian revolution in *one form or another* and establishing *one form or another* of the dictatorship of the proletariat;"
- "alliance of the working class with the bulk of the peasantry and other strata of the working people;"
- "abolition of capitalist ownership and . . . public ownership of the *basic* means of production;"
- "*gradual* socialist reorganization of agriculture;"
- "planned development of the national economy;"
- "raising the working people's standard of living;"
- "a socialist revolution in the sphere of ideology;"
- "elimination of national oppression;"
- "defense . . . of socialism against encroachments by external and internal enemies;"
- "proletarian internationalism" [*all emphases supplied*].[71]

The ambiguity of these general laws was further compounded by the declaration's call for their "creative application" by communist leaders "in accordance with the specific conditions in their countries."[72] While no mention was made of the Hungarian events, the declaration did assert that the movement considered right-wing revisionism (i.e., the attempt to restore bourgeois democracy) to be the "main danger" within the movement. Specifically, the revisionists (such as Nagy and Tito) were condemned because

> they deny the historical necessity of . . . the dictatorship of the proletariat during the period of transition from capitalism to socialism, deny the leading role of the Marxist-Leninist party, deny the principles of proletarian internationalism, demand abandonment of the Leninist principles of Party organization and, above all, of democratic centralism and demand that the Communist Party be transformed from a militant revolutionary organization into a kind of debating club.[73]

The reference to "democratic centralism" is especially important because it refers to the Leninist principle of policy making that permits debate on issues *within* the party organization *before* a decision is made, but forbids criticism or resistance to a party directive after it is issued. This is an obvious reply to the Nagist heresy that the party is neither omniscient nor omnipotent and, therefore, other parties should be permitted to participate in the policy-making process and criticize its outcome. In short, the 1957 Moscow Declaration underscored the theme, which was reiterated at the 1960 meeting, that the lowest common denominator of communism was party dictatorship.

THE CZECHOSLOVAKIAN CHALLENGE AND THE BREZHNEV DOCTRINE

Czechoslovakia had, since the communist takeover in 1948, been generally considered to be among the most reliable of the Soviet "satellites." The party leader, Clement Gottwald, it will be recalled, had died just after Stalin and was replaced by another Moscow loyalist, Antonin Novotny. Despite the reforms and ferment permeating much of the bloc, Novotny and the Czech leadership adhered to the Soviet model of economic development through heavy industrialization. Throughout Khrushchev's destalinization campaign Novotny's leadership style remained essentially Stalinist. On the surface, Novotny's policies appeared to be successful. Czechoslovakia was among the most industrialized nations in the bloc and even surpassed the USSR on numerous per capita indicators of output. However, much of this success was at the expense of the consumer and agricultural sectors, where investment was consistently low, and the regime was the target of widespread popular dissatisfaction with living standards. After some false starts at reform in the early 1960s, pressure for change, emanating largely from economists, finally began to have some impact in the latter part of 1967.

As in the Polish and Hungarian cases a decade earlier, much of the blame for the deficiencies in the Czech economy was directed at the party leadership. The major criticisms were that the regime had been unresponsive to popular demands and that it had adopted a model of economic development inappropriate to Czech national conditions. In response to these charges a division of opinion emerged within the Central Committee in late 1967 and early 1968.

At issue was the now familiar theme of the role of the communist party in Czech society. Novotny subscribed to what he considered to be the standard Leninist view. "The leading role of the party," he said in July 1967, "is and will remain the standard principle of the life of socialist society. . . . The party acts and will act as the leading, directing force in all spheres of social life without exception, beginning with the national economy and including the fields of ideology, culture and art."[74] In view of the Hungarian outcome and subsequent declarations from Moscow, it was difficult for anyone to take issue with Novotny's viewpoint. Consequently, in the earliest stages of the Czech reform debate, differences tended to focus more on leadership style than on the substance of policy. Novotny had retained both the party leadership and the presidency, and his critics commented on the "immense cumulation of power in the hands of some comrades, especially comrade Novotny."[75] Among these critics, one of the most outspoken was the Slovak leader Alexander Dubcek, who, while not disagreeing with Novotny's view of the party, reminded his colleagues that the role of the party was to "lead, not direct, society," and that "the government must govern."[76]

In the absence of any formal process of political succession, a deficiency of all communist parties, the Czech leaders were obliged to resolve the question of whether Novotny should be retained among themselves, while maintaining a public image of unity. For his part, Brezhnev, who visited Novotny in Prague on 8 December 1967, remained relatively neutral, perhaps because, having been involved in a similar struggle against Khrushchev in 1964, he was aware of the declining tenability of Novotny's position. Undoubtedly, however, the Kremlin's lack of support for Novotny was read as a signal by his Central Committee opponents that Brezhnev would not be unhappy with a change of leadership in Prague. Thus it was with at least the tacit approval of Moscow that Dubcek was elected to replace Novotny as party first secretary on 5 January 1968. Thus began the Czech Spring.

Unlike Gomulka and Nagy, Dubcek was not an obvious choice. He was not a "victim" of Stalinism or a leader with mass appeal, nor was he an innovative or radical reformer. In short, nothing in his background or early public statements as party leader gave any hint of his subsequent break with the traditional model of socialist development. It is not that Dubcek had succeeded in hiding his true colors, but that his transformation began with that of the Czech system itself. In the end the fact that Dubcek always seemed to be moving along with events, or even one step behind them, proved to be a major source of concern for Brezhnev and the leaders of the other bloc states. Quite simply, Dubcek never gave the impression that he was in control of events that were to be perceived as highly dangerous by the Kremlin.

The period from the Dubcek ascendancy to the Soviet invasion on 20 August has been voluminously documented by observers, participants, and historians. There is no need to do more than sketch the broadest outline of those days here. As with the events of 1956, our focus will be not on what the Czechs attempted to do to reform their system, but on how a legitimate effort to match socialist policies to national conditions escalated into an international communist crisis and precipitated the sudden forcible containment of a national movement.

The heart of the Czech reform was contained in the Action Program adopted by the party in April, which declared, "we are seeking our Czechoslovak manner of constructing and developing socialism. This is our internal affair, to be decided by the sovereign will of our people and their honest labor."[77] Although it was a clarion expression of national communism, the content of the Action Program was not especially radical, particularly when compared to the demands beginning to emanate from the Czech intellectual community. In fact, as Skilling has suggested, the Action Program was more of a compromise between traditional party interests and popular demand for reform than a statement of direction by the party for all to follow. The chief contribution of the Action Program, and a source of concern in the capitals of the bloc, was its emphasis on the need to "democratize" the Czech party and society.

In the social sphere "democratization" included promises of freedom of speech and assembly, an end to prior censorship, the right to travel, and a new emphasis on legal rights. In the political context, the Action Program noted that rule by the party should be based upon "voluntary support of the people. . . . The party cannot impose its authority. . . ."[78] Yet although the Action Program repudiated the notion of the party as the "universal caretaker of our society . . . to regulate every step taken in everyday life with its directives," it also warned that "the party cannot turn into an organization which would only influence society. . . . Rather," the Program asserted, the party, "with its membership and its bodies . . . has to develop the functions of a practical organization and a political force in society."[79]

The idea that probably generated the most concern in the Kremlin (as measured by the reaction of the Soviet press) was that a "National Front" composed of communists and noncommunists was the only structure that could reflect the interests of the Czech people. However, the Program did not go so far as to advocate open political competition for office. The National Front was to be a cooperative effort, but one led by the communist party. Nevertheless, this modification of the principle that the party must exercise the "dictatorship of the proletariat," which the Program characterized as a "false thesis,"[80] gave the green light to reformist elements in Czechoslovakia to demand a larger role in the policy-making process and signaled an alarm in the Kremlin.

This Soviet concern was best expressed by the leader of the Moscow party organization, V. V. Grishin, in a Lenin anniversary speech. He cautioned against "spontaneity, unlimited decentralization, and the reduction of the party to the level of a political-educational organization," and warned that "revisionist, nationalist and politically immature elements" supported by imperialist forces were attempting to reverse socialist victories.[81] Grishin left no doubt as to what the Soviet response would be to these imperialist challenges, referring at one point to "military aid" for bloc parties.[82] At the beginning of May Dubcek was called to Moscow, where the Soviet leaders expressed concern about "counterrevolution." After his regime was turned out by Soviet troops, Dubcek recalled that meeting as follows: "The Soviet comrades made no secret to us of the fact that under no circumstance was it possible to permit a development which sooner or later could lead to the liquidation of the achievements of socialism in the Czechoslovak Republic. This would be no longer only Czechoslovakia's 'internal affair,' but a matter of world socialism as a whole."[83]

Once again, Moscow had defined the issue in terms of counter-revolution and security rather than national rights. Nothing in the

Soviet statements denied the Czechs the right to experiment with socialist forms, but as Soviet President Podgorny put it in a speech to the Supreme Soviet in July, "Hostile forces in and outside the country were clearly trying to push Czechoslovakia off the socialist road and to force it away from the socialist commonwealth."[84] From this perspective, any Soviet action would be directed at keeping the party on the road to socialism, be it a Czech road or otherwise.

Events developed quickly in the late spring and summer of 1968. Just after Dubcek's departure the leaders of five socialist countries arrived in Moscow to discuss the need for unity in the bloc. The Czechs were not invited and the Romanians refused to attend on the ground that Czech developments were an internal political matter of no concern to the other parties. Then, in mid-July, these same party leaders met in Warsaw and issued a joint statement, the first, to Czechoslovakia from the rest of the Warsaw Treaty Organization, minus Romania. The essence of the message was that the Czech party leadership had let the situation get out of hand, and unless the party immediately resumed control and reasserted its leading position, capitalist counterrevolution remained an imminent danger. Underlying the Warsaw communiqué was the twofold concern that Western attempts at "bridge building" in Eastern Europe would generate a growing independence on the part of Prague from the Warsaw Treaty Organization and, equally dangerous, that reforms in Czechoslovakia would inspire antiparty feeling throughout the bloc and make life more difficult for Ulbricht, Gomulka, Kadar, and Zhivkov, all of whom adhered to the Soviet model of party leadership.

It is important to note that at no time before or after the Warsaw meeting did the Czech leadership suggest that it was considering withdrawal from the bloc. Having learned from the Hungarian disaster, Dubcek denied that the eventual goal of Czech foreign policy was neutrality. He did, however, seek to make the development of bloc foreign policy a more cooperative affair that would reflect the national interests of all parties involved, and it was patent that an essential feature of the Action Program was the promotion of closer economic ties with nonbloc countries, particularly West Germany. But, with American troops in Vietnam, the arms race in high gear, Chinese relations at a low ebb, and German influence on the increase in European affairs, the Soviet leadership was in no mood to tolerate any equivocation from one of the bulwarks of its security system.

On 29 July an unprecedented meeting of virtually the entire Soviet Politburo and its Czech counterpart convened at the frontier city of Cierna Nad Tisou. Little is known of the proceedings at Cierna except that after four days of discussion, Moscow and Prague remained divided on the issue of party control. It was decided to expand the Cierna meeting to include the other bloc parties, and less than 24 hours after the Cierna discussions ended, a new meeting convened in Bratislava, which was joined by East Germany, Poland, Hungary, and Bulgaria. Again Romania refused to participate. The Bratislava declaration, issued on 4 August 1968, contained a bit of something for everyone. It stressed "solidarity" and the mutual obligation of socialist states, but it also referred to the need to develop socialism according to national conditions. The Czechs came away from Bratislava emphasizing the latter, apparently convinced that they had survived the ordeal and that they would be permitted to continue on the Czech road. They were wrong. On the night of 20–21 August, troops representing the Warsaw Treaty Organization (not including Romania), but composed primarily of Soviet forces, entered Czechoslovakia. As with Hungary twelve years earlier, there were vague references in the Soviet press to the effect that "party and state leaders of the Czechoslovak Socialist Republic have requested the Soviet Union and other allied states to give the fraternal Czechoslovak people immediate assistance, including assistance with armed forces."[85]

Why, after months of warnings, threats, negotiations, and apparent compromises, did the Soviet leadership finally decide that military intervention was the only remaining recourse for Soviet policy in response to Czechoslovakian developments? The Soviet invasion was a last resort, not a first choice, and a symbol of weakness rather than a show of strength. The invasion was an open admission that after fifteen years of post-Stalin leadership the USSR had still not implemented a satisfactory alternative to Stalinist hegemonism in Eastern Europe. Yet all of this was considered an acceptable price to pay; hence, we must conclude that Moscow perceived the stakes to be very high. For Brezhnev and the Soviet Politburo the choice was between losing Czechoslovakia, and perhaps the rest of the bloc, and suffering the outrage of world public opinion. Under those circumstances there was no real choice. From the perspective of the occupants of the Kremlin, the issue was not what socialist path the Czechs were taking. They believed that socialism itself, which also meant alliance with the USSR, was being threatened in Czechoslovakia "by counterrevolutionary forces that have entered into collusion with external forces hostile to socialism."[86]

Three articles that appeared in *Pravda* during the week immediately preceding the invasion are extremely instructive on the motives underlying the Soviet attitude toward national communism and counterrevolution. On 14 August a piece entitled "Common Principles and National Characteristics in the Development of Socialism"[87] addressed itself to defining the common, irreducible core of socialist practice. A dozen years earlier Gomulka had declared that the essence of socialism consisted of the elimination of human exploitation and beyond that everything depended on national conditions. This vague principle had been consistently rejected by the Soviets, who insisted on Leninist party organization. But in April, the Czech Action Program referred to the idea that the party must lead the dictatorship of the proletariat as a "false thesis." The *Pravda* article checked off, point by point, what it referred to as "the basic features and principles of socialism inherent to the new society in *all* countries."[88] Four spheres of life were included:

> In the *political* sphere, it is rule by the working people headed by the working class. . . . One of the chief laws of socialism is the leadership role of the Communist Party. . . .
> In the *economic* sphere, it is . . . public ownership of the means of production in two forms—property of all the people and cooperative property. . . . The principle of centralized planning on a society wide scale is combined with . . . democratic participation by the working people . . . , i.e., the principle of democratic centralism is followed.
> In the *social* sphere, . . . society consists of two classes of working people—workers and peasants, as well as the people's intelligentsia. . . .
> In the sphere of *spiritual* life, it is . . . affirmation of Marxist-Leninist ideology in the struggle against alien views. . . .[89]

Having enumerated these essential principles, the article stated: "The fact that these features are mandatory for all countries is a logical, objectively determined development."[90] The reasoning underlying this assertion was that since socialist revolution had occurred in countries with essentially identical social systems, the construction of socialism must necessarily follow the same path. It was not a case of the USSR imposing a socialist model, but one in which conditions in prerevolutionary East Europe were the same as those extant in prerevolutionary Russia, and thus generated similar socialist systems.

What place do national characteristics have? Owing to different levels of industrialization there may be differences in "the balance of forms of public ownership" or even differences in the role of nonparty organizations owing to different political situations. And certainly there will be variances in art and culture. "However," the article declared, "it would be a deviation from science to regard these features as basic to a definition of what socialism should be in a particular country."[91] With unmistakable reference to events in Czechoslovakia, Moscow informed Prague on the pages of *Pravda:*

> It would contradict the logic of the class struggle if the working people, holding state power in their hands, allowed the "has beens" to reconstruct their reactionary parties. . . . While peasant and other democratic parties are operating in a number of socialist countries, there are no grounds whatever for reviving a party of big capital . . . even if they "traditionally" existed before. . . .[92]

The theme that the real danger to socialism consisted not in legitimate national variations, but in subversive attempts to manipulate national feelings for reactionary purposes was reiterated four days later in an article entitled "Insolent Attacks by Reactionaries" that appeared under the pseudonym I. Aleksandrov.[93] It is well known that articles by "Aleksandrov" are in reality policy statements directly from the party leaders on the Politburo. This message was succinct and clear. The problems in Czechoslovakia were ascribed completely to "fierce new efforts by right-wing, reactionary forces, encouraged from abroad by imperialist reaction, to undermine the foundations of socialism, discredit the leading role of the working class and its party and cut Czechoslovakia off from the socialist commonwealth."[94] The term socialist commonwealth was then, as it is now, synonymous with the Warsaw Treaty Organization. The Soviet leadership was raising the specter of the collapse of communist leadership in Czechoslovakia and its loss to reactionary imperialism. At the time that this article appeared military logistics would have required that the decision to invade Czechoslovakia had already been made.

On the day of the intervention, but before it occurred, an article in *Pravda* appeared under the title, "A Volcano That Is Not Extinct."[95] Filed from the Czech–West German border, the article observed, "In all the strategic plans of the German militarists the high road of the 'Drang Nach Osten'—thrust to the East—always ran through these gates."[96] This final preinvasion article stated openly what everyone knew was behind the references to foreign imperialists: "The revanchist activists are not dawdling in the area bordering on Czechoslovakia."[97] Upon leaving the area, the authors of this article stopped at a crater of a long-extinct volcano near the border and concluded, "Nearby, only a few kilometers away, there is an active volcano. Its name is Sudetendeutsche Landsmannschaft, the revanchists of West Germany. This must not be forgotten."[98]

The combination of internal liberal reform, uncertainty about Dubcek's ability to maintain control over his party, the party's unwillingess to maintain control over Czechoslovakia, and the presence of hostile forces in Germany seeking to take advantage of an unstable situation was more than Brezhnev was willing to tolerate.

The invasion of Czechoslovakia was not, therefore, a repudiation of national communism but a reaffirmation of the Soviet determination to keep the socialist commonwealth socialist.

Nearly three months after the intervention, Brezhnev used an address to a Congress of the Polish United Workers' Party to enunciate what has come to be referred to as "the Brezhnev Doctrine." Actually, the first clear statement of this policy appeared in *Pravda* on 26 September 1968 in the article "Sovereignty and the Internationalist Obligations of Socialist Countries," by S. Kovalev.[99] There was little, if anything, new contained in either the Kovalev article or the Brezhnev speech, but they set forth in no uncertain terms the limits of national communism in the postinvasion era.

The Brezhnev Doctrine is often referred to as a theory of "limited sovereignty," since the right of socialist states to act independently of all external influence was circumscribed. But perhaps it is more instructive to view the doctrine as one of "collective responsibility" rather than limited sovereignty. Collective responsibility is a doctrine of parliamentary politics that holds all members of the government individually responsible for collective acts and the government as a whole responsible for the acts of its individual members. Although Brezhnev never used the term collective responsibility with reference to international communism, it is obvious that this is what he had in mind when he said in Warsaw, "When a threat arises to the cause of socialism in [one] country—a threat to the security of the Socialist commonwealth as a whole—this is no longer merely a problem for that country's people, but a common problem, the concern of all socialist countries."[100] Kovalev put it this way: "Every Communist party is responsible not only to its own people but also to all the socialist countries and to the entire Communist movement."[101]

The conclusion that flows from this notion of collective responsibility is that while "each Communist Party is free in applying the principles of Marxism-Leninism and socialism in its own country, . . . it cannot deviate from these principles (if, of course, it remains a Communist Party)."[102] The act that places a party outside the acceptable limits of national variation is the repudiation of communism itself. Anything that a party does to apply Marxist-Leninist principles in a national context is beyond the legitimate concern of other parties, but the application of communist principles and their abandonment are entirely different matters. The Brezhnev Doctrine invokes the international obligation of all parties to preserve the gains of socialism, i.e., collective responsibility for the survival of the movement and its integral parts, on the theory that "if the enemy plants dynamite under our house, under the commonwealth of socialist states, our patriotic, national and international duty is to prevent this by using any means that are necessary."[103] When the forces of counterrevolution within a country conspire with external forces of imperialism, as in Czechoslovakia, it ceases to be an internal matter. Deviation within socialism does not, according to the Brezhnev thesis, include deviation from socialism. In the latter case the use of "military assistance to a fraternal country" is justified. In Brezhnev's words: "The C.P.S.U. has always advocated that each socialist country determine the concrete forms of its development along the path of socialism by taking into account the specific nature of their national conditions. But it is well known, comrades, that there are common natural laws of socialist construction, deviation from which could lead to deviation from socialism as such."[104]

Is all this rhetoric about sovereignty and noninterference in internal affairs to be taken seriously, or is it merely a subterfuge to disguise Soviet hegemony and great power chauvinism? The thesis put forth here is that the Brezhnev Doctrine and Soviet action in Hungary and Czechoslovakia were unquestionably intended to preserve Soviet national security interests, but did not exclude national communism. Were the Soviets incorrect when they branded the Hungarian Freedom Fighters and the Czech independence movement "counterrevolutionary"? Was Western support for these forces motivated by the fact that they were national communists or by the hope that they were national anticommunists? Is not the logical alternative to Soviet influence in Central Europe German influence? In the answers to these questions we have the answer to whether national communism or national counterrevolution was the target of Soviet action.

Whatever the personal sympathies of noncommunists may be toward the right of the Czechs, Hungarians, or Poles to determine their own national fate, that fate is presently inextricably tied to that of world socialism. The course of one cannot be determined without affecting the course of the other. To ignore this political reality is to romanticize nationalism within the socialist bloc and elevate it to the level of a moral struggle between good and evil. To label this form of nationalism as national communism and then conclude that by repressing it the Soviet Union and its leaders denied the legitimacy of national roads is a serious mistake. What the Hungarians and Czechs wanted was independence from, not independence within, the socialist commonwealth, and in both cases the Soviets correctly appraised the potential consequences of such an occurrence, not just for the USSR but for the movement as a whole. Even those in the West who support the goals of national communists generally do so because they interpret variation within the movement as a prelude to the eventual disintegration of that movement. That Brezhnev and his predecessors have understood this and have demonstrated a willingness to take action to prevent such disaggregation does not constitute a recantation of the rights of communists to pursue national roads, i.e., national communism.

In the 1950s the late Italian communist party leader, Palmiro Togliatti, coined the term "polycentrism" to describe the new situation in the international communist movement. Polycentrism means that rather than there being any single source of communist authority, numerous national parties can claim to be legitimate spokesmen for the movement. Tito in Yugoslavia, Mao in China, Gomulka in Poland, Hoxha in Albania, and Brezhnev in the Soviet Union each claimed to be pursuing the true Marxist-Leninist path. Often such claims have contradicted each other. One might well ask, Why hasn't the USSR invaded the other countries that promote polycentrism? The answer is that polycentrism means many centers of the *same* movement, which precludes the restoration of capitalist democracy. In threatening to divorce themselves from the socialist bloc, Hungary and Czechoslovakia were not testing the limits of polycentrism, since one cannot be a central point in a system to which one does not belong.

In order to comprehend the limits of national communism today it is necessary to look at a system that has not removed itself from the movement but has exercised an extraordinary degree of national control over its domestic and foreign policies nevertheless. This is Romania.

ROMANIA: THE EPITOME OF NATIONAL COMMUNISM

The Romanian system has had only two leaders under socialism: Gheorghi Gheorghiu-Dej, who served until his death in March 1965, and Nicolae Ceausescu. Both have been extremely popular national figures, yet both amassed an enormous amount of personal power and exercised it in an authoritarian manner. At present probably no leader in the communist world holds as much formal power within his own system as does Ceausescu, who is head of the party secretariat, a member of the party Permanent Presidium (equivalent of the Politburo), president of Romania, head of the Socialist Unity Front (which includes all major social organizations), commander in chief of the armed forces, and chairman of the Supreme Council for Socioeconomic Development (which coordinates planning and production).[105] One of the closest contenders for the title of "most powerful" is Brezhnev himself. This undoubtedly protects Ceausescu from criticism of his leadership style, which is distinctly Stalinist.

Romania, however, is not only Stalinist in its leadership pattern. With the possible exception of Albania, about which detailed information is difficult to obtain, Romania remains the most illiberal East European system with respect to domestic political practice. Few of the reforms associated with the post-Stalin era, even in the USSR, have been implemented in Romania. Romania's tightly controlled system illustrates the point made earlier that national communism must not be confused with political liberalism. The Romanian experience demonstrates that national communism is simply the demand of a socialist state for the right to make its own socialist policies. In fact, the truly successful national communists have been not the "liberals" like Nagy and Dubcek, but the "conservatives" like Ceausescu, Hoxha, Kadar, Gomulka, and, of course, Tito. Their conservatism derives not from obedience to Soviet directives but from their domestic political style.

In the case of Romania, the initial point of national departure came over the issue of the industrialization model. Unlike Poland, Hungary, and later Czechoslovakia, Romania welcomed the Soviet model of heavy industrialization as the most appropriate weapon against economic underdevelopment. Romania had an agrarian economy, but it possessed numerous natural resources including iron ore, oil, and gas, which the Romanian leadership believed could provide the foundation for a modern industrial economy. In short, Gheorghiu-Dej's goal for Romania was virtually identical to that of Stalin for the USSR: the creation of an autarkic industrial economic system based upon communist principles.

The major obstacle to the Romanian plan was the fact that if each bloc country pursued the same development model each would be a duplicate of all the others, and since the members of the bloc traded primarily among themselves, no country would have anything to trade that the others could not produce. Poland, Czechoslovakia, East Germany, and the USSR already had, by the late 1950s, developed industrial systems capable of supplying the needs of the bloc; hence, duplication of those capacities in Romania was wasteful from the perspective of an integrated socialist commonwealth.

In 1949 the Council for Mutual Economic Assistance (CMEA, or Comecon) was organized to meet the perceived challenge of the Marshall Plan, but through the 1950s it never served as a coordinating agency for intrabloc economics. However, in the early 1960s Khrushchev devised a plan whereby the economic redundancy of autarky would be replaced by what he called the "socialist division of labor," and Comecon was proposed as the vehicle for the integration of the bloc economic systems. Khrushchev's theory was relatively simple: Have the industrial nations produce industrial goods, the agrarian nations agricultural goods, and have each purchase from the others what it does not produce. Naturally, this meant that the economic status of each state would be frozen at the level it had achieved when the program was adopted.

Under a system of "socialist division of labor" Romania would sell its industrial raw materials to the USSR or Czechoslovakia and buy them back in the form of manufactured goods or refined petroleum products. Furthermore, Romania, with a relatively successful agricultural sector, would provide food for the rest of the bloc. Romania, in other words, would become the "permanent vegetable garden" of Comecon. The Romanian view, as developed by Gheorghiu-Dej, was that rather than sell resources and produce to East Germany, for example, and buy back steel, Romania should have its own steel mills to process Romanian ore, and its own petroleum refineries as well. In sum, while economic integration was more efficient when viewed from the perspective of the commonwealth's needs, it was definitely contrary to Romanian national interests.

Gheorghiu-Dej refused to respond to Soviet pressure in the political arena also. As Khrushchev's anti-Stalin campaign picked up steam in 1961, it was inevitable that the Romanian leader would be required to destalinize his own party. But Gheorghiu-Dej was a Stalinist who had purged his opponents with Stalin's approval. In what can only be described as masterful obfuscation, Gheorghiu-Dej launched an attack against the "Moscovites" who had taken refuge in the USSR during the war and whom he had subsequently eliminated, such as Pauker and Luca. By identifying this faction as Stalinist, Gheorghiu-Dej completely reversed the definition established by Khrushchev. He equated Stalinism with "Moscovite imperialism," which meant Russian interference in Romanian affairs. In the process of destalinization, Gheorghiu-Dej was accusing Khrushchev of being a Stalinist for his attempt to impose the Comecon plan.[106]

The plan for the socialist division of labor was officially adopted by Comecon in June 1962 in the form of a declaration called "The Basic Principles of the International Division of Labor." The key provision of this program, to which the Romanians strenuously objected, was that Comecon should serve as a supranational planning agency for the bloc and all planning decisions should be approved by majority vote. This meant that Romania, along with the other members, would have to surrender its sovereign control over its own economy.[107]

For all its potential impact on the economic character of Romania and the bloc in general, the Soviet-Romanian debate over integration was, at bottom, political, not economic. Those within the international movement who supported Dej's position did so because they believed in his right as the leader of Romania to determine his nation's policies, not because they agreed with his economic program.

The reaction of the Chinese leadership is a case in point, and China became an important element of the Soviet-Romanian confrontation. For reasons that will be discussed in the next chapter, the Sino-Soviet conflict was a public issue when Romania decided to resist Comecon integration. It is not surprising, therefore, that Mao Zedong would support another party leader who was resisting Soviet control. Yet the Chinese never addressed themselves to the content of Dejism. Rather, the Chinese Central Committee declared, "It would be great power chauvinism . . . in the name of 'international division of labor' or 'specialization,' to impose one's will on others, infringe on the independence and sovereignty of fraternal countries. . . ."[108] In return the Romanian party adopted the official position that developments in China were an internal affair to be resolved by the Chinese; therefore, Romania would remain neutral in the Sino-Soviet conflict. In fact, however, Gheorghiu-Dej began to lean toward the Chinese side in the dispute. First Romania subscribed to Peking's view that the 1960 Moscow Declaration was an express guarantee of the right of national sovereignty within the communist movement. Then, in early 1963, Romania published the Chinese "twenty-five point" criticism of the USSR, which was the severest attack on the Soviet position to date.

By playing the "China card" Gheorghiu-Dej hoped to force the Kremlin into concessions on the Comecon issue in exchange for Romanian support on the China issue. The open conflict with China and Moscow's recent humiliation in the Cuban missile crisis undoubtedly weakened the Soviet position and contributed substantially to Romania's ability to maneuver for advantage within the bloc. Nevertheless, Gheorghiu-Dej seems to have overplayed his hand when he suggested that as a neutral party, Romania could mediate the Sino-Soviet dispute. This attempt resulted in a fruitless expedition by Romanian representatives to Peking and Moscow in early 1964. Khrushchev was patently displeased with the prospect of having to cope with a second Tito and he began to refer to Soviet territorial claims outstanding against Romania in a not-so-subtle effort to put a lid on Gheorghiu-Dej's offensive behavior.[109]

Khrushchev's heavy handedness had the opposite result. Rather than bend to Soviet pressure, Dej took the opportunity to issue the

strongest statement thus far on the subject of national sovereignty
in the bloc. Published on 22 April 1964, this "Statement on the
Stand of the Romanian Workers' Party Concerning the Problems of
the World Communist and Working Class Movement" is generally
referred to as the Romanian "Declaration of Independence." In
reference to the Comecon integration plan, the Romanians declared:

> Our party has very clearly expressed its point of view, declaring
> that since the essence of the suggested measures lies in shifting some
> functions of economic management from the competence of the re-
> spective states to that of super-state bodies, these measures are not in
> keeping with the principles underlying relations between the socialist
> countries. The idea of a single planning body for all CMEA countries
> has the most serious political and economic implications. The planned
> management of the national economy is one of the fundamental,
> essential and inalienable attributes of the sovereignty of the socialist
> state—the state plan being the chief means through which the socialist
> state achieves its political and socio-economic objectives, establishes
> the directions and rates of development of the national economy, its
> fundamental proportions, the accumulations, the measures for raising
> the people's standards and cultural level. The sovereignty of the socialist
> state requires that it effectively and fully avails itself of the means for
> the practical implementation of these attributes, holding in its hands
> all the levers of managing economic and social life. Transmitting such
> levers to the competence of super-state or extra-state bodies would
> turn sovereignty into a meaningless notion.[110]

Then, in more inclusive terms, the statement went on to argue that
although there might be universally applicable general laws of socialist
development, each socialist state could operationalize them differently.

> In establishing the best forms and methods of building socialism,
> the Communist and Workers' parties take into account both the
> objective laws and the concrete historical conditions prevailing in their
> own countries. They carry on an intense creative activity, grasping the
> requirements of social development, synthesising their own experience
> and studying that of fraternal countries. . . . There are not and there
> cannot be any unique patterns and recipes. Nobody can decide what
> is and what is not correct for other countries and parties. It is up to
> every Marxist-Leninist party. It is a sovereign right of each socialist
> state to elaborate, choose or change the forms and methods of socialist
> construction.[111]

But it remained for Gheorghiu-Dej's successor, Nicolae Ceausescu,
to convert the pragmatic expression of Romanian national interest

into an ideological principle. In July 1965, a few months after Dej's demise, Ceausescu told the Ninth Congress of the Romanian party: "Following the disappearance of the exploiting classes the nation has grown stronger. . . . It is only under socialism that the real community of economic interests, the common socialist culture of all citizens who live in the same territory can fully express themselves. . . ."[112] Ceausescu's thesis went beyond the basic Marxist-Leninist notion that nations would survive for an indefinite period after the revolution. What the new Romanian leader postulated was that only under socialism could the nation develop to its fullest potential. George Schöpflin has suggested that Ceausescu converted the doctrine of "national in form, socialist in content" into "socialist in form and national in content." According to Schöpflin, "Lenin is alive and well, and living upside down in Bucharest."[113] Whether Ceausescu's national policy had indeed turned Marxism-Leninism on its head, or whether he was merely the first to admit what had been true throughout the entire history of the socialist movement, Ceausescu's theory represented a fresh challenge to the Soviet position. Moreover, in subsequent pronouncements, Ceausescu has come close to declaring that the vehicle of social progress is not the proletarian class but the proletarian nation, a subtle but important distinction. This theory completely undercuts Brezhnev's doctrine of the right of one socialist nation to intervene in the affairs of another in the name of proletarian internationalism. As the 1974 Program of the Romanian Communist Party states, "The tendency to oppose, in one form or another, internationalism to the thriving of the nation and of the independent national state would be a serious error and would greatly prejudice the interests of building socialism in every country. . . ."[114]

Romania's move toward independence was in response to Khrushchev's scheme for the "division of socialist labor." Yet when the Comecon scheme for supranational planning was abandoned at the end of 1963 because of Romania's refusal to participate, Romanian national aspirations were only beginning to become manifest. Undoubtedly, the Sino-Soviet conflict contributed to Gheorghiu-Dej's successful resistance to Soviet pressure, but another ingredient in that success was that the Romanian party's national (if not nationalistic) stand was extremely popular with the average Romanian. Despite their continued Stalinist political styles, Gheorghiu-Dej and Ceausescu were able to convert the national issue into strong domestic support for the regime. Though popular support is not essential to a communist regime, such support undeniably facilitates the party's leadership. In other words, national communism had domestic political payoffs for the Romanian party that made the risks of alienating the Soviet party acceptable.

In addition to the China factor and popular support for national communism, a third element contributed to the Romanian position— the willingness of some Western nations to underwrite the Romanian initiative. For example, as part of their program of economic autarky, the Romanians proposed the construction of a steel mill at Galati and requested Soviet assistance for the project. Because of Khrushchev's integration plan, the USSR held back on any commitment to the Galati project, although in June 1960, Gheorghiu-Dej did make reference to aid from the Soviet Union for the Galati steel mill, perhaps to force the Soviet hand.[115] Soviet hesitance was understandable in view of the fact that Romania would have had to import iron ore from the USSR to supply Galati, reducing Soviet reserves and also cutting into Czech imports, which the Soviets would have to make up. Whatever the motive was for the Soviet refusal to help build Galati, the steel mill became symbolic of Romanian autarky. Only the offer of an Anglo-French consortium to construct Galati, which Dej accepted, made it feasible for the Romanians to succeed in their economic development plan. Without this participation by Western interests, of which the Romanians have continued to avail themselves, Gheorghiu-Dej might have been forced to capitulate to Soviet pressure for integration. As Tito had done a decade earlier, Dej demonstrated that it was possible for a communist regime in the Soviet sphere of influence to survive and prosper if two key ingredients were present—popular support for regime policies and Western willingness to underwrite independence from Soviet economic control.

The Romanian decision to accept Western assistance was only the beginning of a pattern of consistent deviation from the Soviet line in foreign policy. As Aurel Braun has observed, Dej's decision to build economic bridges to the West "was a form of political defense" in Romania's general attempt to free itself from Soviet control; hence, a network of trade agreements with nonbloc states provided Romania with the foundation for its political independence.[116] Early trade agreements with Italy (1961) and France (1963) were followed in the Ceausescu era by oil deals with Iran in 1968 and 1969, and an iron ore arrangement with India in 1969. In 1966, Renault agreed to build an auto factory, and this contract was followed by large-scale trade agreements with Israel in 1967, West Germany in 1969, and France in 1970.

After President Nixon's precedent-shattering visit to Romania in 1969, U.S.–Romanian economic ties also improved. In 1971 a joint

U.S.–Romanian corporation was established for the first time, and in 1972 Romania and Yugoslavia became the first two communist countries to receive loans from the U.S. Overseas Private Investment Corporation. Romania was also the first communist country to join the International Monetary Fund and the International Bank for Reconstruction and Development in 1972. A year earlier, Romania had become a member of GATT (General Agreement on Trade and Tariffs). Finally, in 1975 Romania was granted Most Favored Nation (MFN) status by the United States. As a consequence of these policy initiatives Romania has been less dependent on intrabloc trade than any other Comecon member.

Politically, Romanian policy has been equally independent. In January 1967 Romania established diplomatic relations with West Germany, despite Soviet and East German insistence that only one Germany, the German Democratic Republic (GDR), could be recognized at a time (the Hallstein doctrine). In that same year Ceausescu refused to break diplomatic relations with Israel along with the other bloc states in response to the Six-Day War. Perhaps the most courageous decision of all was Romania's refusal to participate in the Warsaw Treaty Organization's Czechoslovakian intervention. Ceausescu asserted that the purpose of WTO was to defend the member states against Western invasion, not to police the actions of its members. From Ceausescu's perspective, the Czech reforms were an internal matter, and he rejected the Soviet argument that the WTO's action was justified by the threat of counterrevolution. Romania first consistently declined to participate in any of the multilateral meetings that dealt with the Czech situation, and then not only refused to join the invasion, but denied use of Romanian air space and territory to invading troops, seriously complicating Bulgarian participation.

The risks involved in this decision were enormous. The evidence suggests that Ceausescu believed that the Soviets might really invade Romania. On 21 August Ceausescu announced the formation of an armed Patriotic Guard composed of all the people to defend Romania.[117] Ceausescu's threat to mobilize his population probably did not deter the Kremlin from an invasion, but it did reveal the depths of his national sentiment and his commitment to Romanian independence.

Subsequent policy initiatives, while less dramatic, continued to underscore the Romanian insistence on an independent foreign policy suited to the needs of Romania rather than to those of the USSR. The Nixon visit in 1969 was reciprocated by Ceausescu's trip to the United States in October 1970. To the extent that the Soviet invasion of Czechoslovakia was a message to the West that any "bridges" built to East Europe would have to be approved by Moscow, these visits were a challenge to Soviet policy. Yet in the era of emerging détente, Moscow could not afford to criticize Ceausescu's contacts with the United States very strongly.

What was perhaps more disturbing to the Soviet leadership than the American connection was Ceausescu's continuing flirtation with Peking at a time when Soviet-Chinese relations were at an all-time low. Ceausescu visited China in June 1971 and upon his return launched what became known as the "mini cultural revolution." This was an attempt, along the lines of the Chinese model, to regenerate ideological fervor and commitment to revolutionary goals. The Soviets were extremely unhappy with Ceausescu on this score and went so far as to perform military maneuvers on the Romanian border. This Soviet threat eventually resulted in the Romanian adoption of an "all horizons" defense law in December 1972, to ensure that the Romanians would not get caught in the same position as Czechoslovakia in 1968. No one actually believed that Romania could resist a Soviet attack, but Ceausescu calculated (correctly) that the USSR had no stomach for a prolonged guerrilla war within the bloc.

Romania has continued to keep its participation in the activities of the WTO at a minimum. On numerous occasions Romanians have not participated in military exercises as required, and in 1978 Romania refused to increase its military budget to conform with WTO directives. Romania is the only WTO member to refuse to endorse the Soviet intervention in Afghanistan. Romania has never hinted at the prospect of withdrawal from WTO, but her halfhearted membership renders Romania's role in the future actions of the alliance marginal at best.

The outstanding issue, however, remains Romania's stance against the economic integration of the Soviet bloc. Romania's resistance to the 1962 Khrushchev plan was successful, but in 1971 Brezhnev revived the idea in the form of a "Comprehensive Program" for the integration of Comecon. Unlike its predecessor the new program called for "voluntary" associations and agreements rather than unanimous decisions and avoided the question of supranational coordination. This robbed Romania of its veto over integration, as the other states could enter into voluntary agreements without Romania's approval; hence, in order to protect its interests in the bloc, Romania was forced to participate in some of the integration proposals. But the real blow to Romanian economic autonomy came in 1973 on the heels of the world-wide oil crisis. The sudden escalation of oil prices throughout the world had several negative effects. First, the USSR, an oil exporter, continued to sell oil within Comecon at prices substantially below Organization of Petroleum Exporting Countries (OPEC) levels. Although Soviet prices increased in the years following 1973 they have never reached world levels. Therefore Romania, along with the other members of Comecon, is tied to Soviet oil exports. Second, the economic slump that followed the oil crisis made Romanian goods less competitive in Western markets, and the cost of Western goods to Romania jumped dramatically, in turn putting a heavy strain on hard currency reserves. These problems were not unique to Romania, but as the chief opponent to integration, Bucharest found it increasingly difficult to withstand the economic pressures exerted by the USSR.

Ironically, at the same time that Romanian autarky was threatened by Brezhnev's integration program, that policy was becoming much more expensive for the USSR to pursue. The Soviet Union was subsidizing the East European systems by artificially keeping the price of energy and industrial commodities low in order to tie those economies to her own. However, by 1975 the advantages of Comecon membership had shifted in favor of the East European states, and Moscow was losing enthusiasm for integration. Hence Romania has never had to choose whether to resist a concerted Soviet drive for supranational authority and integration *at the expense of* its national economic interests.

Throughout this entire Soviet-Romanian contest two political facts have remained constant—the party has been the unchallenged leader of Romanian society, and Ceausescu has been the unchallenged leader of the Romanian party. Not only has the party continued to assert its hegemony, but toleration for dissent has actually decreased during the 1970s. In June 1977, for example, responsibility for all press censorship was centralized in the party rather than in the former system of nonparty press committees, and dissident writers have been consistently silenced in recent years. "We do not have," Ceausescu announced to the Central Committee in June 1977, "I am repeating, for I don't know the how-manyeth time—more than one single philosophy in Romania: dialectical, historical materialism. . . . We cannot make any sort of concession about our philosophy of the world or life."[118]

Is the Romanian case inconsistent with those of Hungary and Czechoslovakia? The Romanians have refused to destalinize their leadership; they pursue what must be described as an independent foreign policy; their position in WTO is ambivalent; they have refused to side with the USSR in the dispute with China; the appeals of the leadership are not simply national, but nationalistic and are often directed against the Soviet Union itself. To some, it appears that Romania is "getting away" with a great deal. Yet the Romanian case is not anomalous, because unlike Hungary and Czechoslovakia, the Romanians have never given any of their fellow members of the socialist commonwealth reason to fear that Romanian national communism might be transformed into "counterrevolution."

Romania's marginal strategic importance to the USSR (i.e., its distance from West Germany) could conceivably account for the fact that it has not been invaded. But more to the point, previous Soviet interventions occurred only after all other options were exhausted; they were last-resort policy choices. The fact that the USSR disagrees with the policies of another socialist state has never been held to justify invasion. It is not surprising that the interests of the USSR and Romania differ, nor should it be surprising that Moscow attempts to influence the policies of the bloc states. The USSR is a great power with critical regional interests to protect. But these policy differences do not negate the legitimacy of national communism, they confirm it. The reason the USSR has not invaded Romania is that Romanian national communism is not an intolerable aberration in international communism, but an acceptable, normal pattern of behavior.

THE POLISH CRISIS RENEWED: FROM GDANSK TO GDANSK

The Polish road charted by Gomulka proved to be a rocky one. The stumbling block for the Polish party had always been effective organization and management of the economy. Although Gomulka broke with the Soviet model, he never successfully replaced it with an efficient Polish one. In addition, what began as an apparent liberalization of Polish politics in the post-Stalin era became more of the same control and repression under Gomulka. Finally, in late 1970, after demonstrations broke out in Gdansk and elsewhere in protest over government-announced food price increases, Gomulka was forced to step down. The Polish United Workers' Party (PUWP) had lost touch with the national spirit that had carried it through the 1956 crisis, and Gomulka's successor, Eduard Gierek, vowed to restore the people's trust in the party's ability to lead Poland. Unfortunately for Gierek, and for Poland, international economic factors, such as the decline in Western markets after the 1973 energy crisis, and continued abuses within Poland, such as widespread corruption and party privilege, rendered Poland's economic situtation increasingly serious.

Throughout this period, but particularly in 1970 and again in 1976 (when the government again attempted to increase prices), the workers' movement gradually developed. Each time a local or national confrontation occurred, the party promised reform and the people returned to work. But as the situation worsened in the late 1970s the party's ability to control workers' demands declined, and finally, on 1 July 1980, when the government once again attempted to increase food prices to cover a growing deficit, the situation exploded. That the Polish leadership tried to raise food prices in the midst of extreme shortages and general economic stagnation, and after having twice provoked mass demonstrations in response to such a policy in the past, is indicative of how isolated from the public mood the PUWP had become.

This time, however, the workers of Gdansk, Radom, Warsaw, and other industrial centers were determined not to permit the party leadership to retreat without a firm commitment to general economic reform. What began as spontaneous worker protests coalesced around embryonic workers' organizations and individual leaders, such as Lech Walesa, into a unified workers' movement—Solidarity. Once this institutional base was established to challenge party hegemony, the issue quickly shifted from the narrow problem of food shortages and prices to a broader and far more profound controversy over the rights of workers in Poland and the role of the communist party in the system.

The strikers contended that the PUWP did not adequately represent workers' interests, and the central demands that emerged were for the right to organize independent, self-governing trade unions and to strike over economic issues. The crucial question was whether the PUWP would or could accept the legitimacy of autonomous worker organizations in which it had virtually no influence. This demand patently transgressed the well-established limits of party jurisdiction. Recognition of Solidarity as an independent union would be a tacit confession that the communist party had failed to represent the proletariat and would be in direct conflict with the principles of proletarian dictatorship. It is not surprising, therefore, that initial Polish (and Soviet) responses to the unionist demands equated Solidarity with potential "counterrevolution."

After weeks of intense negotiation and continued strikes, the "Gdansk Agreement" was approved by the government and Solidarity on 30 August 1980. The key provisions of this unprecedented agreement read:

In setting up the independent, self-governing trade unions, the Interfactory Strike Committee [the workers] states that they will observe the Polish Constitution. The new unions will defend the social and material interests of working people, and they have no intention of playing the role of a political party.

They accept the principle of nationalized means of production, which is the basis of Poland's socialist system.

They recognize that the Polish Communist Party plays a leading role in the state and they do not challenge existing international alliances.[119]

The explicit rejection by Solidarity of any challenge to the WTO alliance or to the PUWP's leading role in Polish politics was in strict conformity with the principles of the Brezhnev Doctrine. Walesa was acutely aware of the need for extreme caution in these sensitive areas so that Moscow would not conclude that this was the beginning of another Czechoslovakia. In response to a question from a Western reporter about Poland's future relationship with the Soviet Union, Walesa told the following story:

There are these two rabbits at our border, one Polish and the other Russian. The Russian rabbit is running as fast as he can. The Polish rabbit asks him why and the Russian rabbit replies, "because they're castrating all the bears." "But you're a rabbit," the Polish friend says. "Yes," the Russian rabbit answers, "but I'm not sure if that's a good enough explanation."[120]

It was imperative that Solidarity maintain the image of a workers' organization concerned exclusively with economic reform in order for the PUWP leadership to maintain its vanguard image. Whatever ultimate intentions the Solidarity leadership may have had, they recognized that an open assertion of political equality with the party was an invitation to disaster. Behind the scenes, however, the political situation was rapidly changing.

One week after the Gdansk Agreement the Central Committee of the PUWP replaced Gierek as first secretary with Stanislaw Kania. A long-standing member of the party Politburo with a professional background in internal security, Kania did not represent any radical change in policy, but simply replaced a discredited and ineffective leader. To Kania fell the task of forging a party-Solidarity relationship that would balance demands for enhanced worker participation in management and decision making with the need to maintain the PUWP's leading role in Polish society.

However, the fragile partnership broke down almost immediately when Solidarity attempted to become a legal organization by registering its charter and bylaws with the Warsaw provincial court as required by the Gdansk Agreement. Because Solidarity's bylaws did not specifically recognize the party's leading role, the court unilaterally amended them to include such a reference and approved the amended version. The Solidarity leadership countered that the Gdansk Agreement provided for both the party's "leading role in the state," and "independent, self-governing trade unions," which, when taken together meant that the party would play no *direct* role in the union leadership. In other words, the party could lead the state, but the unions were to be independent of both state and party control. When the government exhibited no willingness to resolve the controversy, Solidarity leaders threatened strikes in retaliation. Finally, on 10 November 1980, the Polish Supreme Court stepped in and ruled in support of Solidarity's right to independence, thus averting an open confrontation for the moment.

Solidarity won this battle for independence, but a dangerous pattern began to emerge. Each time an issue led to a confrontation with the government, whether it pertained to hours, wages, working conditions, or participation, Solidarity resorted to the threat of strikes in order to force concessions. Although Kania apparently understood the necessity to restore confidence in the party, he was concerned that repeated capitulation to Solidarity demands might be interpreted in Moscow as a sign that the party was losing control of the situation. Kania had to avoid any indication that the PUWP was becoming part of the reform movement, even when it responded to legitimate grievances. This confrontational rather than cooperative approach made normalization virtually impossible, and Poland passed from one crisis to another throughout 1980 and early 1981.

The turning point for Kania, Solidarity, and Moscow was the Bydgoszcz affair in March 1981. When police in the city of Bydgoszcz used strong-arm tactics to break up a sit-in of workers and farmers who were demanding local government reforms, Solidarity threatened a nationwide general strike unless the government punished the offending officers. One day before the scheduled strike the government acceded to Solidarity's demands, but the Bydgoszcz settlement prompted a strong negative reaction from Moscow. For the first time the Soviet media criticized Kania's leadership, reporting that Solidarity had "wrestled away new concessions," and concluding that the Bydgoszcz events "have proven that the creeping counterrevolution has risen to its feet and attained its full height. It has not thus far met with perceptible resistance, and this is why it has become increasingly impudent. . . ."[121]

From Moscow, the Bydgoszcz settlement appeared to be a dangerous capitulation to counterrevolutionary forces, and Soviet criticism of the PUWP's inability or, worse, unwillingness to crack down on Solidarity intensified dramatically. That criticism subsided somewhat in July when, at the Ninth Extraordinary Congress of the PUWP, Kania was reelected first secretary in an unprecedented secret ballot in which more than one candidate competed for the post. But at that congress Soviet Politburo member V. V. Grishin criticized Kania's predecessors for their "deviation from the Leninist principles of party activity," and warned that "anywhere a deviation from the general laws of Marxism-Leninism occurs, hostile forces will not miss a chance to exact revenge and move toward the restoration of the old order." In an unmistakable reference to the Brezhnev Doctrine, Grishin added, "The cause of the defense of socialism in Poland is inseparable from Poland's participation in the socialist countries' collective organizations and its ties of alliance."[122]

In addition to stressing the themes of party control, socialist internationalism, and the danger of counterrevolution, Moscow railed against what it referred to as Solidarity's "campaign of anti-Sovietism." For example, on 17 September the Polish media made public a message from the Central Committee of the CPSU demanding that the Polish government "immediately take determined and radical steps in order to cut short the malicious anti-Soviet propaganda and actions hostile toward the Soviet Union" that the CPSU attributed to "coordinated efforts by enemies of socialism."[123] The statement referred specifically to a message issued by the national congress of Solidarity on 9 September to the working people of Eastern Europe, suggesting that they organize their own independent unions. Referring to this call as a "revolting provocation," the CPSU Central Committee demanded that the Polish government limit the activities of the Solidarity congress, which TASS labeled "an anti-socialist and anti-Soviet orgy."[124]

Moscow's emphasis on anti-Sovietism in the midst of all the ideological transgressions was not merely a nationalist outburst. By targeting anti-Soviet nationalism in its criticisms of the Polish leadership, the Kremlin was establishing a justification for its own involvement if that should become necessary. The Soviet Union would be far less subject to accusations of interfering in the internal affairs of Poland if Solidarity's activities were identified as blatantly anti-Soviet. Its ideological challenges to the PUWP made Solidarity an enemy of the USSR by extension, but its anti-Sovietism made Solidarity a direct enemy of the Soviet Union.

The CPSU Central Committee warning was followed on 13 October by a blast straight from the Soviet Politburo in the form of a *Pravda* article by the nonexistent Politburo alter ego Alexei Petrov. Solidarity was labeled a "counterrevolutionary" movement that would not be tolerated anywhere else in the socialist commonwealth. Petrov charged that Solidarity was a political organization that was attempting to replace the government, calling for Polish withdrawal from CMEA and WTO, and indulging in "blatant anti-Sovietism."[125]

In view of the universal lack of confidence in Kania's ability either to improve Poland's deteriorating economic condition or to control Solidarity, it came as little surprise when the Central Committee of the PUWP replaced him as party leader on 18 October 1981. What was surprising was the choice of General Wojciech Jaruzelski as Kania's successor—not because Jaruzelski was unqualified, but because for the first time a military leader was made first secretary of an East European communist party. Furthermore, Jaruzelski had been named prime minister on 9 February 1981 and had retained his post as minister of defense. Not since the days of the Stalinists had the control over the party, government, and military of a communist system been concentrated in the hands of a single leader.

Jaruzelski's elevation to party leadership undoubtedly came with Moscow's approval, if not at its insistence, although during his brief tenure as prime minister he had been part of the leadership team that the Soviets had criticized for not having maintained control over Solidarity. However, as a military man, Jaruzelski was not associated in the public mind with the long-term economic and political failures of the party, and he appeared to command the respect of Solidarity leaders and Polish officials alike. In the highly charged nationalist atmosphere of the time, with the PUWP in total disrepute among both Poles and Soviets, only national institutions like the military (and the church) were capable of drawing popular support. From the Soviet point of view, Jaruzelski must have seemed the only remaining hope for normalization, short of direct intervention by Soviet troops. Despite the Bonapartist implications of his appointment, therefore, it was generally conceded that Jaruzelski was the only Polish leader who could stand up to Walesa and the Catholic Church. There is no evidence that the martial law that was eventually declared in December was being contemplated in either Warsaw or Moscow at the time of Jaruzelski's appointment as party leader. Nevertheless, when martial law was imposed, Jaruzelski's multiple leadership roles made it possible to assert that the party was in control, because the party first secretary was at the head of the military government. In form, if not in substance, the vanguard role of the party was preserved.

Despite the leadership change, the political and economic situation continued to deteriorate. Jaruzelski had previously promised that Polish troops would never fire on Polish workers, and the moderate Walesa found it increasingly difficult to control Solidarity's radicals, who, convinced that the Soviet Union would not invade Poland, saw little reason to exercise self-restraint in their demands for reform. The major obstacle in the continuing negotiations was the issue of "workers' self-management." With the goal of increasing worker participation in production, Solidarity demanded that workers' councils within enterprises be given a management role and the power to appoint managers. These demands were a direct threat to two fundamental principles of Leninist (Soviet) organization—*Nomenklatura* and *Edinonachalie* (one-man management). The former provides that all managerial appointments be made by the party apparatus. The latter guarantees that each enterprise has one boss, who is, in turn, responsible to the party that appoints him. In short, the demand for workers' self-management was another challenge to the leading role of the communist party, and it could not be conceded without causing Moscow to invoke the Brezhnev Doctrine.

In the realization that further capitulation to Solidarity demands was impossible and that his regime was the last chance the Poles would have to resolve their own problems, Jaruzelski moved slowly, but surely, toward the militarization of the government. From late October to early December 1981, military units were gradually introduced in the countryside and urban centers, and a crackdown on dissidents began. Although there is no reason to assume that Jaruzelski or the Kremlin had already definitely decided on martial law, the swiftness and efficiency with which martial law was finally implemented leaves no doubt that plans for such an eventuality had been carefully prepared beforehand.

The immediate provocation, or excuse, came on 12 December when Solidarity leaders meeting in Gdansk demanded a national referendum that would declare that "society cannot any longer tolerate the existing situation in the country," and would put four questions to a popular vote:

- Are you for a vote of confidence in General Jaruzelski?
- Are you for establishing a temporary government and for free elections?
- Are you for providing military guarantees to the Soviet Union in Poland?
- Can the Polish United Workers' Party be the instrument of such guarantees in the name of the whole society?[126]

Between Gdansk August 1980 and Gdansk December 1981, Solidarity had reversed itself on virtually every point. The Gdansk referendum proposal was an open repudiation of the Gdansk Agreement that the Jaruzelski government could ignore only at the risk of Poland's national survival. Its response was a declaration of martial law on 13 December, which resulted in the arrest or detention of virtually the entire Solidarity leadership and the end of all independent union activity. But it also included the arrest of Eduard Gierek and other former party officials on suspicion of corruption. Everything was done in the name of the Military Council for National Salvation, not the PUWP.

Strictly speaking, military council is a misnomer because the troops that imposed martial law were primarily security forces, not regular army. These security forces had demonstrated their loyalty to the government on 2 December when they broke up a strike of cadets at the Warsaw Firemen's Academy. That preliminary action also proved that military force could be used against striking workers without inciting widespread popular resistance. Of course, once he declared martial law Jaruzelski could not possibly have turned back even if his troops had been disloyal, or if the population had risen up in protest. In either of those events he would have had to call in Soviet support. Consequently, there can be no doubt about Soviet cooperation in the operation, but this cannot be interpreted to mean that the Soviets ordered martial law to be imposed. All the currently available evidence suggests that both Polish and Soviet leaders concluded that further negotiation with Solidarity was a losing proposition, both economically and politically.

The fundamental difference betwen the Polish case and the Hungarian and Czech ones that preceded it was that in Poland the leadership never became a part of the reform movement. Neither Kania nor Jaruzelski was a Nagy or a Dubcek. The Polish leaders may have mishandled the Solidarity challenge, but in not joining the "counterrevolutionaries" they never gave the Soviets a reason to intervene with military force. The Polish experiment from Gdansk to Gdansk was truly a revolution from below, whereas the Hungarian and Czech ones came from above. Walesa, as leader of Solidarity, was certainly a threat to Soviet hegemony in Poland, but far less so than if he had been the leader of the party, as was Dubcek. In 1981 it was Walesa and Solidarity that raised the question of Polish withdrawal from the WTO; in 1956 it was Nagy and the Hungarian party. For all its failures, the PUWP kept Poland in the socialist commonwealth, thus avoiding Soviet intervention. In so doing,

however, the party lost whatever national support it had and therefore
had to be replaced by a Military Council for National Salvation.

The very name of the military government evokes nationalist
rather than Marxist emotions. National salvation, not communist
construction, is the goal of this government. Furthermore, it is a
"military" council, not a "party" council or even a "party-military"
council, that is responsible for saving the Polish nation. All of this
raises the crucial question, What is the present and future status of
the Polish communist party?

Although Jaruzelski is ostensibly head of both the party and the
military council, the declaration of martial law represents the end
not only of Solidarity as previously constituted, but of the PUWP
as well. There have been vague references to the continued role of
the party Politburo on the military council, but that role has not
been specified. From a strictly Leninist viewpoint, there can be but
one role for the party—the leading role—but this was clearly not
the case under martial law.

While nothing about the future of Poland is certain at this point,
it is likely that national salvation will include the restructuring and
renaming of the Polish party. In the early months of 1982, numerous
party officials have been removed by the military council and many
others have apparently resigned. The party hierarchy is in disarray.
What is certain is that military government is only temporary. The
leadership will be turned back to the party at some point, but that
party is bound to be a very different organization from the old
PUWP.

Solidarity, too, will have to be rebuilt. With Walesa's status in
question, it is impossible to say what role he will play. Nevertheless,
Jaruzelski's military council has consistently maintained that martial
law does not mean a return to pre–Gdansk Agreement conditions.
How independent Solidarity, or its successor, will be, and what limits
will be imposed on the right to strike, are issues that can be resolved
only after the economic crisis is brought under control. No one in
or out of Poland believes that martial law can solve all of Poland's
problems, but if martial law does not succeed, nothing short of Soviet
intervention will.

The most recent Polish crisis demonstrates that even in a nationalist
environment, with an organized workers' movement backed by a
strong church, the limits of national communism within the Soviet
bloc are still inscribed by Moscow. This and the next generation of
Soviet leaders will continue to face the Polish problem, but no matter
how much the solutions to that problem vary from the Soviet model,
they will be implemented within the confines of the socialist com-

monwealth. The failure of the Gierek and Kania regimes lay in their inability to adjust party policies to national realities, and those national realities exploded in the form of Solidarity. The failure of Walesa and Solidarity lay in their inability to adjust their demands to international realities, and those international realities exploded in martial law. What remains is for Poland's leaders to come up with a formula that will satisfy both the Marxist and the national imperatives that constitute the current Polish reality.

What the Romanian, Hungarian, Polish, Yugoslavian, and Soviet developmental experiences prove is not that it is possible for a national communist regime to survive, but that *only* a national communist regime can survive. All these national communists "knew that the national feelings of the people and also their anti-Soviet sentiments would outweigh the antipathy which they themselves inspired. They relied on the idea of national pride and reaped a useful harvest."[127]

However, the national path is extremely narrow and has proved a difficult one to walk. On one side is the danger of falling victim to uncontrollable national forces unleashed by the party. Such was the fate of Dubcek. On the other side is the danger of taking national support for granted once having established the national character of the regime. In 1970 Gomulka made this mistake when he alienated the population by proposing food price increases that appeared unjustified. Gomulka, the national communist *sans rival* of the 1940s and 1950s, had been one of the motive forces behind the Czech invasion, and this fact, combined with his callous disregard for the economic problems of the Polish people in 1970, lost him the popular support upon which his regime depended. He was forced by his own party to step down in December 1970 because he was no longer viewed as a national communist leader. The irony of Gomulka's downfall was that the father of national communism *redux* became its most prominent victim. His successor, Eduard Gierek, put Poland back on the national path and pursued Gomulkaism without Gomulka, but eventually made the same mistake of losing touch with Polish national sentiment. There are, indeed, tremendous political benefits to be reaped by those who adhere to the national road, and dramatic costs to those who abandon it.

National communism, which reemerged under the personal tutelage of powerful political leaders, has become an institutionalized phenomenon. Ceausescu's continuation of Dejism and even Kadar's policies in Hungary, Husak's in Czechoslovakia, and Honecker's in East Germany demonstrate that national communism is not simply a fact of political life but a permanent necessity of political survival in the socialist commonwealth.

NATIONAL COMMUNISM AND EUROCOMMUNISM

Thus far, the protagonists in this chapter have been communists who used their power as leaders of communist states to assert their claims of autonomy. Hence, those national appeals have stressed rather traditional (non-Marxist) principles of national sovereignty: specifically, the right of states to be free from interference in their domestic political affairs. This claim, now universally recognized within the bloc, has been denied only when the exercise of national sovereignty resulted in the possibility of counterrevolution, i.e., the disestablishment of a ruling communist party. In other words, the "rules of the national road," which derived from the post-Stalin autonomization process, applied to parties in power. However, as has been shown in Chapter 2, national communism had Marxist roots that predated the establishment of communist states, and it was not only within the bloc that national communism was revived in the post-Stalin era. Hence, although they premised their arguments on different doctrines, the leaders of the nonruling parties also sought to establish their independence from Soviet hegemony.

The position of the nonruling parties was ambiguous. While they could not appeal to doctrines of national sovereignty to legitimate national independence claims, neither could the USSR (or any other ruling party) assert the right to interfere in their affairs on grounds of counterrevolutionary threats since a party not in power cannot be overthrown. The ambiguity was heightened by the fact that with no power to preserve, the nonruling parties could be permitted more control over their ideological destinies, but being out of power and lacking the legitimacy derived from domestic political control, these parties were more susceptible to influences and control by foreign parties in power, particularly that of the Soviet Union.

This created much the same dilemma for the leaders of the nonruling parties as that faced by those in power. As long as they identified their political fortunes with those of a foreign nation (especially a major power like the USSR), they could not generate sufficient domestic support to bring them to power. Surrounded by suspicion as to their true loyalties because they slavishly subscribed to Soviet (or Chinese) doctrines, many of which were totally alien to their own political cultures, the nonruling parties, particularly in the industrialized West, were strangers in their own lands. These parties derived their ideological legitimacy from their international associations, but lost their national legitimacy as a result. Therefore, the major task of the nonruling parties, especially after the dissolution of Cominform in 1956, was to establish domestic bases of support. The focal point of this effort was Western Europe, where Marxism was born. It had become obvious to all but the most diehard radicals that communism would not be established in the European democracies by means of proletarian revolution. As early as the 1930s, the European communists had been forced to reconcile themselves to parliamentary participation. Although this was justified as an expedient necessary to aid the USSR in its struggle against fascism, it was actually the beginning of a new pattern of communist behavior. In the post-Stalin era Khrushchev openly recognized the possibility, first voiced by Marx and Engels, of a nonrevolutionary road to socialism under certain favorable conditions. For their part, the leaders of the major Western European communist parties, particularly in the Latin nations of France, Italy, Spain, and Portugal, gradually came to believe that only by divesting themselves of their image as "foreign agents" could they hope to win even a share of power. This phenomenon of communism coming to power in a democratic, parliamentary national context via the electoral process has been labelled Eurocommunism.

Like the more generic concept of national communism, Eurocommunism has no universal substantive content. In fact, Eurocommunism is a misnomer—first, because non-European parties such as the Japanese have undergone many of the same changes experienced by the parties of southern Europe; and second, because there are marked differences in the theories and practices of the "Eurocommunists" as communists seeking to develop in conformity with national conditions. There is French communism, Italian communism, and Spanish communism, and the only factor common to all is the need to develop a communist model consistent with the patterns of parliamentary democracy in their respective nations. In that sense, what binds the Eurocommunists together is their common rejection, to a greater or lesser extent, of the Leninist Soviet model, rather than their common adoption of any program of development. Some, like the Spanish party leader Santiago Carillo, have completely repudiated the Soviet model, and have even suggested that the USSR is not a socialist system at all. Others, like the French leader George Marchais, are willing to grant to the Soviets the legitimacy of their system, and simply contend that it is inappropriate for democratic societies.

In order to appreciate fully the Eurocommunist thrust it is necessary to consider briefly the Leninist view of state power. Lenin's position was that it was the historical right of the working class to seize state power from the capitalists in order to build socialism. Borrowing from Marx, Lenin asserted that this "dictatorship of the proletariat" was a legitimate regime because it was in conformity with the dialectical process of historical development. In a social system such as Russia, which had only begun the process of industrialization and thus had only a small proletariat, the responsibility for exercising this dictatorship fell upon the "vanguard of the proletariat," the communist party. The party could impose its will upon the population because it ruled in the name of the class destined to reign in the final stage of history—the communist epoch. While the term dictatorship had not been totally corrupted by the excesses of Hitler, Mussolini, and Stalin, in Lenin's time it meant more than authoritarian rule. A dictatorship is a system that imposes the values of the political leadership on a population that does not share those values. In view of Marx's claim to have discovered the scientific law that revealed communism to be the culmination of human social development, the legitimacy of proletarian rule did not have to be established by popular support. To the true believer, the number of people who agree with him is inconsequential to the rectitude of his thought. This Leninist notion of the right of the party to dictate its value system to a hostile political culture is the cornerstone of Soviet political power.

The Eurocommunists have (for the most part) rejected the principle of proletarian dictatorship. They have argued that the development of industrial capitalism has resulted in the continuous growth of the "working class" until today it includes virtually everyone in society except the few, wealthy monopoly capitalists. The party of the working people, therefore, represents the interests of the majority rather than those of an exploited minority and can come to power by democratic means. Rather than attempting to exclude segments of society, the Eurocommunists seek to make the party's appeal as wide as possible and do not find it necessary to eliminate political forces that they cannot control directly. In other words, the political legitimacy of the Eurocommunist party derives from popular support rather than historical destiny.

Antonio Gramsci, the Italian communist theorist, developed the concept of "the hegemony of the proletariat" to replace that of the "dictatorship of the proletariat." This hegemony notion has been adopted most completely by Carillo, who developed it in his controversial, anti-Soviet treatise *Eurocommunism and the State.*[128] Hegemony departs from Leninism in that it rejects force as a basis of political authority. In Lenin's view the ultimate task of the party is

Eurocommunism

to mobilize a minority to seize power and impose socialism on an unwilling majority. In Gramsci's view the task of the party is to mobilize the will of the majority against the exploiting minority and come to power on the shoulders of a democratic mandate. In response to the charge that the abandonment of the idea of the dictatorship of the proletariat is tantamount to the abandonment of communism, Carillo has argued: "The essence of all the various political forms of transition to socialism is . . . *the hegemony of the working people,* while *the diversity and abundance of political forms* likewise entails the possibility of *the dictatorship of the proletariat not being necessary.*"[129] At the heart of Carillo's argument is the national communist belief that "Marxism is based on the concrete analysis of concrete reality,"[130] and the concrete reality of modern Europe (and Japan) is a democratic political culture. Marchais echoed this sentiment at a meeting of European communist parties in East Berlin in June 1976.

> Because the term "dictatorship of the proletariat" does not match the reality of political power in the Socialist France for which we are fighting, we have decided . . . to dispense with it.
> In choosing our path to Socialism, we are carefully taking into account our national reality, the special conditions of our country, its traditions. Every country has its own. Ours have led us to envisage a different path than the one taken by the peoples who have already transformed their countries into Socialist ones. Socialism in France will be Socialism in French colors.[131]

Undoubtedly Brezhnev, who listened to Marchais speak, had believed that all socialism was colored red, and that was probably the color he was seeing as the Eurocommunists, one by one, asserted their independence from Leninism. The Spanish party carried the process of autonomization to its ultimate conclusion in April 1978 when, at its Ninth Congress, the membership voted to drop all references to Lenin from the party's program on the ground that Leninism was uniquely suited to Russian development.[132]

Carillo's heretical assertion that Lenin's theory of the role of the party in socialist construction is incorrect has naturally not been seconded by the Kremlin. Yet the Soviet leaders have been quite circumspect in their criticism of even the extreme expressions of Eurocommunism. Richard Lowenthal has characterized the Soviet response to Eurocommunism as "cautious to the point of ambiguity" and suggested that Moscow would prefer not to alienate the European communists because they are "actually and potentially supportive of Soviet foreign policy interests."[133] For example, the Soviet campaign in 1981 to prevent the deployment of American medium-range missiles in Western Europe received strong support from all European communist parties. However, Soviet restraint may simply derive from the lack of an alternative. In the absence of any international organization from which the Eurocommunists might be expelled, the most that the Soviet party could do would be to "excommunicate" the most vociferous anti-Leninist Eurocommunists. But Soviet hostility could serve only to promote the interests of those who are attempting to project an independent image. An open Soviet attack against Carillo, for example, would enhance his national popularity and make it more difficult to replace him with a more pro-Soviet leader in the future. While Moscow does not support all of the particulars of the Eurocommunist argument, the counterproductivity of a frontal assault has resulted in a general acceptance of the nonrevolutionary path to socialism as a realistic approach in democratic societies.

From another perspective, there are those who believe that the USSR is not as tolerant as it seems, because Eurocommunism is not as democratic as it claims to be. Jean-Francois Revel, for example, has observed in *The Totalitarian Temptation* that the French communists "verbally defend freedom, but they do it in totalitarian fashion."[134] Revel's view is that communism by its very nature is dictatorial and totalitarian; hence, if the communists of Europe are truly adopting reformism as a means to achieve socialism they will, by definition, become social democrats rather than communists. The Eurocommunists, of course, deny that there is an inherent incompatibility between democracy and communism and assert that any apparent contradiction is with the Leninist model, not "true" communism. Yet there are ambiguities in the Eurocommunist position that would seem to lend support to Revel's position.

The issue of pluralism is a case in point. Carillo has stated, along with the other Eurocommunists, that "the fight for Socialism in our countries will not take the form of dictatorship but will base itself upon respect for political and ideological pluralism, without the rule of one party, and in complete accordance, at all times, with the results of general elections."[135] He followed this affirmation of pluralism with an expression of hope that this will be a peaceful process, warning, "We cannot exclude the possibility of a use of force to defend democratic liberties, in case reactionary minorities, defeated in popular elections, should threaten those liberties through coup d'etat."[136] Although he did not employ the term, Carillo was obviously referring to "counterrevolution." The Eurocommunist position appears to be that if a communist government is elected, it has the right to preserve its gains by force if the capitalists seek to return to power. The promise to abide by the outcome of general elections seems to be limited to the stage of building socialism; hence, once socialism has been achieved the Eurocommunist commitment to pluralism could be abrogated.

Similarly, Marchais has described French socialism as a system "which includes the possibility of a democratic alternation [of governments]—recognition of the right of political parties to exist."[137] But does a "democratic alternation" include the restoration of capitalism, or will that be described as counterrevolution? And does the "right of political parties to exist" mean the right of *any* party to exist or just the ones whose ideas are in conformity with those of the "working people"? The misuse of the term "democracy" in the Soviet bloc has made many noncommunists extremely skeptical of its use among the Eurocommunists. Despite their protestations to the contrary, the Eurocommunist spokesmen have done little to clarify their position on the key issue of whether democratic pluralism is a means to power or a way of life for Eurocommunism.

In view of this ambiguity, the Soviet leadership can criticize the most extreme forms of anti-Leninism as it did in the case of Carillo's *Eurocommunism and the State,* about which the Soviet journal *New Times* said: "The concept of Eurocommunism is erroneous. There is only one communism. Its foundations were laid by Marx, Engels, and Lenin and its principles are adhered to by the present-day communist movement."[138] Yet at the same time Brezhnev can sign a document, such as that adopted at the 1976 Berlin Conference, stating, "The participants . . . emphasize that their parties, on the basis of a political line worked out and adopted by every party in complete independence in accordance with the socioeconomic and political conditions and the specific national features prevailing in the country concerned, are firmly resolved to . . . achieve the objectives of peace, democracy and social progress. . . ."[139]

The Soviet position on Eurocommunism is that as long as the Eurocommunist parties are not openly anti-Soviet and Eurocommunism does not contaminate relations within the socialist commonwealth, Moscow will not insist that the dictatorship of the proletariat, the Leninist form of party control, be implemented by communist parties in democratic societies. However, as has been previously observed, there is a distinction between a "national road *to* socialism" and "national communism." What the Soviets and the Eurocommunists are willing to accept in the drive toward power, they may find intolerable once in power. This does not mean that the Eurocommunists will adopt the Soviet model at the first opportunity. What it does mean is that Eurocommunism is just one form of contemporary national communism and, as such, is not inherently liberal or conservative. As Carillo has said many times, the essence of Marxism is the "concrete analysis of concrete conditions," not any particular doctrine. The Eurocommunists share the desire of all national communists—to be independent of any foreign power in order to make policy appropriate to the realization of communism in their national contexts. In the case of the Eurocommunists, this means independence from the CPSU.

In the words of Italian communist party leader Enrico Berlinguer:

> The solidarity among our parties is based on recognition that each party elaborates autonomously and decides in full independence its own political line, both international and national. It is based . . . on respect for the right to freely choose different roads in the struggle for the transformation of society and the building of socialism. . . .
>
> The truth is that, just as there is not and cannot be any leading party or leading state, on the theoretical level as well, the development of Marxism requires the concurrence of many different contributions. . . .[140]

It is significant that the term "proletarian internationalism," which has always been the code word for a Soviet-led international movement, never appeared in the document adopted at the 1976 Berlin conference of European parties. Instead, the phrase "voluntary cooperation and solidarity" was substituted. At least insofar as the nonruling parties are concerned, Moscow has not enunciated any equivalent of the Brezhnev Doctrine, which places internationalist obligations above those of national sovereignty. Whether this distinction will remain viable if, or when, socialism is established by a Eurocommunist party remains to be seen. There has always been a difference in the Soviet view between socialist internationalism, which regulates relationships among socialist states, and proletarian internationalism, which guides interparty relations. The Brezhnev Doctrine was intended to apply only to socialist international relations, and no Eurocommunist party has arrived at that stage yet.

Ironically, the independence strategy of the Eurocommunist parties has not reaped the expected harvest, and, in fact, appears to have been counterproductive in some significant instances. The general expectation that the Eurocommunist decision to work within the system and cooperate with other political forces of the Left would ultimately result in communist participation in, and perhaps leadership of, a European government by 1980 has not been realized.

In France, the Common Program of the Union of the Left did indeed result in significant gains for the communists in the 1973 parliamentary elections. However, many old-line communists believed that their party had compromised too many of its ideological principles for the sake of electoral success. In an attempt to mollify the left-wing critics within the party, Marchais unilaterally reinterpreted the goals of the Common Program late in 1977 and the socialists withdrew from the Union just before the 1978 parliamentary elections. The communists capitulated at the last minute and managed to work out electoral agreements with the socialists that enabled the communists to retain their parliamentary representation, but the returns were a stunning defeat for the party that many believed might win the election and be a part of the new government. The declining fortunes of the French communist party continued in the elections of 1981. Although the communist party supported the presidential candidacy of the socialist Francois Mitterand after its own candidate failed to qualify for the second ballot runoff, Mitterand's victory, and that of the socialist party in the succeeding parliamentary elections, represented serious setbacks for French communism. In their poorest parliamentary election showing since World War II, the communists received only about 16 percent of the popular vote and their representation in the national assembly declined from eighty-six to forty-four. Although Mitterand rewarded the communist party for its support in the presidential race by appointing four communists to minor posts in his forty-four member cabinet, this could hardly compensate for the fact that the transformation of the French communist party had resulted in an overwhelming social democratic victory largely at the expense of the communists.

A similar situation prevailed in Italy. The communists had entered into a so-called historic compromise with the ruling Christian Democratic Party in parliament. In a reversal of its traditional opposition role, the Italian communist party attempted to prove to the Italian electorate that it was a responsible political party willing to participate in mainstream Italian politics. As a result of this transformation, many observers expected a clear-cut victory in the parliamentary elections in 1979, at least one that would make the communist party a partner in a ruling coalition. Instead, it lost seats in the parliament and its proportion of the popular vote declined by about 4 percent. In 1980 the decline of the party continued in regional, provincial, and municipal elections, where the proportion of the communist vote declined roughly 2 percent compared to 1975 returns.

The cause of these failures, and of similar declines in Spain, is the same: the disaffection of the rank and file members of the party, working people, who believe that their party compromised proletarian principles for the sake of political expediency. The Eurocommunist parties have not managed to attract enough new supporters from the left and center by their new moderate stances to compensate for the number of traditional supporters who were alienated by what appeared to be revisionist opportunism. In January 1981, for example, the Catalonian branch of the Spanish communist party voted to break with the center and to reject the Eurocommunist line in favor of a pro-Soviet position. Undoubtedly, many European communists still consider the USSR to be the center of international communism, but even those who support autonomization are not necessarily convinced that Leninism itself is incompatible with Eurocommunism. Since all the nations in which Eurocommunism has developed already had strong socialist parties that adopted the nonrevolutionary strategy of parliamentary reform decades ago, many communists, such as the French leftist Louis Althusser, have expressed serious doubts that communists can establish a distinctive position on the left if they abandon the fundamental principles of revolutionary Leninism.

In view of their continuing electoral disappointments, it may well be that Eurocommunists will be forced to reevaluate their strategies for the 1980s if they wish to retain leadership of their own parties, much less attain leadership of their national governments. This does not mean that they must necessarily become less nationalist or more pro-Soviet. Berlinguer, Marchais, and Carillo have continued to speak out against Soviet intervention in Afghanistan and Poland. In fact, none of these leaders attended the Twenty-Sixth CPSU Congress in February 1981, and the Italian delegate was not permitted to address the congress because his speech was critical of the Soviet role in Afghanistan. But at some point the Eurocommunists may have to decide whether there is indeed a minimal content to the notion of communism over and above "concrete analysis of concrete conditions," and whether that content does not include the idea of the leading role of the communist party and the elimination of political competition through the dictatorship of the proletariat.

In short, while everyone may agree that European communism must develop in conformity to national conditions, it remains problematic what those national conditions require in the way of concrete political action. To borrow from Marchais, France will have socialism with French colors, but it is unclear what those colors will be. What is clear is that change can be just as threatening to the survival of a communist party as refusal to change. The absence of a clearly defined strategy is just as threatening as the absence of national consciousness, and when one works against the other national communism cannot survive.

NATIONAL COMMUNISM AND PROLETARIAN REVOLUTION

This chapter on the rebirth of national communism has focused exclusively on developments in Europe. Marx, of course, had predicted that the proletarian revolution would break out in Europe because it was there that bourgeois capitalism was most developed. Whatever effect the emergence of the first communist system in Russia had on Marx's theory of proletarian revolution, and whatever effect Stalin's theory of "socialism in one country" had on proletarian internationalism, Europe has remained the focal point of the Marxist movement. This is not to deny the importance of the development of communism in Asia, Africa, and Latin America, which will be considered at length in the following chapter. But European communism represents the mainstream of socialist development in its Marxist proletarian orientation, whereas communism elsewhere has taken on a distinctly different, although no less important, character.

The theme running throughout this and the previous chapters is that national communism has, from the outset, been the dominant mode of the Marxist movement. Despite the efforts of those who refused to recognize the universal right of communists under Marxist doctrine to formulate national programs, national communism has not merely survived as one form of communism, it is communism. Even Stalin's aberrant attempt to stifle national movements within the new Soviet bloc was nothing other than an extreme form of national communism. Stalin, for all his proletarian internationalist pretensions, was merely denying the right of other communist leaders to exercise independent control over their domestic affairs, a right that he had established in the most extreme degree within the USSR.

There has always been national communism, but today it is universally recognized as a right of all parties, ruling and nonruling. The Soviet invasions of Hungary and Czechoslovakia were not abrogations of this right, nor did they establish the limits of national communism. What these events demonstrated is that the Soviet Union has not been willing to tolerate any challenge to the security network it has constructed in Eastern Europe. From the Soviet point of view the loss of one of the members of the socialist commonwealth constitutes such a challenge. In other words, the road to socialism is a one-way street. Once a party embarks on the socialist path it is free to veer right or left but not to make a U-turn. Any suggestion

that an established party may wish to leave the international proletarian movement is labeled "counterrevolution" and ceases to qualify
as an issue of "national roads."

Is there, from the Marxist perspective, a difference between "national communism" and "national roads to socialism"? Thus far,
"national roads to socialism" has been universally recognized; national
communism has not. National communism goes beyond variations
deriving from national peculiarities in the process of socialist construction and includes the possibility of the permanent existence of
nations under communism. The ambiguity of Marx's thoughts on
this subject does. not contribute to a satisfactory resolution of this
question. Few contemporary communists, even the most national,
are willing to concede that national variations will persist indefinitely.
Only Ceausescu and Carillo have suggested that the national state
is a permanent institution. Since the final achievement of communism
is generally conceded to be in the far distant future, there is no great
need to resolve this highly theoretical problem. Only time will tell
whether "national communist" will become an acceptable appellation
in the socialist world.

Despite all this variation and confusion over doctrine, there is
one common element in the national communisms discussed thus
far. All are concerned with the problems of how to bring about and
complete a proletarian revolution in an established, generally industrialized, nation. In effect, we have been considering national
communism as proletarian revolution, and all variations have been
adaptations of this theme to local circumstances. National communism has thus far been analyzed from the perspective of European
communists seeking to gain control over their national parties in
the face of overwhelming Soviet influence. That is why national
communism, irrespective of its content, is so closely associated with
anti-Sovietism.

Yet there is another form of national communism that has only
barely been touched upon. This is the brand of communism that
has emerged in societies without any domestic capitalist history and,
therefore, without a proletariat. If the national communism that has
been analyzed heretofore consists, at bottom, of variations on the
theme of proletarian revolution, then the type to which we now turn
must be markedly different, owing to the absence of any industrial
proletariat in those systems. This variation will be labeled "national
communism as national liberation."

SUGGESTIONS FOR FURTHER READING

Albright, David, ed. *Communism and Political Systems in Western Europe.*
Boulder, Colo.: Westview Press, 1979.

Carillo, Santiago. *Eurocommunism and the State.* Westport, Conn.: Lawrence Hill and Co., 1978.

Fejto, Francois. *A History of the People's Democracies.* Translated by Daniel Weissbrot. New York: Praeger Publishers, 1971.

Gyorgy, Andrew, and Kuhlman, James, eds. *Innovation in Communist Systems.* Boulder, Colo.: Westview Press, 1978.

Ionescu, Ghita. *The Breakup of the Soviet Empire in Eastern Europe.* London: Penguin Books, 1965.

Lange, Peter, and Vannicelli, Maurizio, eds. *The Communist Parties of Italy, France and Spain: Postwar Change and Continuity.* London: George Allen and Unwin, 1981.

Rakowska-Harmstone, Teresa, and Gyorgy, Andrew, eds. *Communism in Eastern Europe.* Bloomington, Ind.: Indiana University Press, 1979.

Rusinow, Dennison. *The Yugoslav Experiment: 1948-1974.* Berkeley: University of California Press, 1977.

Skilling, H. Gordon. *Czechoslovakia's Interrupted Revolution.* Princeton: Princeton University Press, 1976.

Sugar, Peter, and Lederer, Ivo, eds. *Nationalism in Eastern Europe.* Seattle: University of Washington Press, 1969.

Zinner, Paul, ed. *National Communism and Popular Revolt in Eastern Europe: A Selection of Documents on Events in Poland and Hungary, February-November 1956.* New York: Columbia University Press, 1956.

5
National Communism as National Liberation

The relationship between communist revolution and the transformation of nonindustrial systems into modern societies has always posed problems for Marxists. Ostensibly, Marxism was a solution to the problems engendered by industrialization that promised social justice to the industrial proletariat. Marxism was not, however, a theory of industrialization. Many interpretations of Marx are possible, but the one undeniable constant is Marx's conviction that only mature capitalism could give birth to revolutionary communism.

Undoubtedly, as we have seen in Chapter 2, even Marx recognized that the people of the nonindustrialized world could contribute to the ultimate downfall of capitalism if their actions disrupted the economies of the industrial nations that were becoming increasingly dependent on the resources and manpower in their colonies. Nevertheless, Marx never envisioned a situation in which the peasantry could take the lead in the revolution. In fact, the evidence indicates that Marx believed colonialism contributed more to the proletarianization of the East than to the downfall of Western capitalism. In any event, Marx never altered his basic position that communist revolution was the product of, rather than the requisite for, industrialization, and that the importance of events in the colonial world was to be measured solely in terms of their contribution to the efforts of the industrial proletariat of Europe.

Lenin, as we saw in Chapter 3, did not depart from this Marxist position on the role of underdeveloped societies, although his theory of imperialism was unquestionably a major alteration of the Marxist revolutionary program. It will be recalled (see pp. 53–59) that Lenin's notion of imperialism as the "highest stage of capitalism" explained why the revolution that Marx believed was imminent had never occurred in the most industrialized states of Europe, but could occur in Russia. However, it must also be remembered that Lenin's explanation placed Russia in the capitalist-imperialist chain, albeit as its "weakest link." The revolution, Lenin argued, could break out in Russia because that country had been unsuccessful in the worldwide scramble for colonies, not because it was the victim of colonial exploitation. The Russian revolution would "spark" the proletarian movement throughout Europe because workers would be inspired by the success of their Russian comrades and because the system of imperialism had begun to unravel. For all her backwardness, Russia was a European system in Lenin's view, and communism remained, in his eyes, a phenomenon of industrial capitalist society.

Lenin's confrontations with Sultan-Galiev and M. N. Roy, described in Chapter 3, make it abundantly clear that Lenin's Western orientation, which he shared with Marx, was a conscious political strategy. Lenin rejected the Roy thesis that the future of communist revolution depended on the success of the Eastern communists in their anticolonial struggle. This difference did not stem from any disagreement over the status of Russia. Lenin and Roy agreed that Russia was a European, imperial state, not a colonial possession or an Eastern underdeveloped society. Roy's Eastern strategy, which held that the revolutionary process begun in Russia could be completed only in the colonial world, was his point of departure from Lenin. Lenin continued to adhere to the Western strategy, insisting that communism could be realized only in the industrialized West.

One contemporary Western scholar, John Kautsky, has argued that the goal of the Russian Revolution was, among other things, "the rapid introduction of industry without economic and political dependence on Western capital. We can, in short, classify it as a nationalist revolution in an underdeveloped country. . . ."[1] In other words, Kautsky contends that Lenin transformed Marxism into a national liberation movement by adapting Marxist theory to an underdeveloped society. No doubt Lenin's revolution was national. Indeed, it has been argued here that the national character of the Russian Revolution did not represent a departure from the Marxist model, but was consistent with it. Further, from the perspective of historical hindsight, and in purely economic terms, Russia was indeed an underdeveloped country.

Nevertheless, these facts alone do not make the Russian Revolution the first national liberation struggle. True, Lenin internationalized the revolutionary struggle by reidentifying the enemy as imperialism, rather than capitalism, and in so doing provided the break with Marxist analysis that was later to be carried to a decidedly non-

Marxist conclusion by the advocates of national liberation. But even this fact does not mean that Lenin was personally responsible for the transformation. Although he created a role for the colonial revolutionary intellectual in the world communist revolution, Lenin never conceived of that role as anything more than contributory to the victory of the industrial proletariat. Roy envisioned anticolonial communism as an end in itself, but Lenin explicitly rejected that strategy. As Kautsky himself argued, the essence of nationalism is "the desire to be rid of alien rulers and have [one's] own government,"[2] and this was never a significant goal of Lenin's Russian Social Democratic Party. In short, it was Roy and Sultan-Galiev, not Lenin, who laid the groundwork for the development of national communism as national liberation. Lenin's belief that the revolution could begin in a nonindustrialized system and that communism could facilitate the process of industrialization was decidedly un-Marxist, but since the underlying motivation of national liberation is not economic development per se but anticolonialism (i.e., opposition to foreign control of domestic wealth and resources) Lenin's movement, while undeniably national in character, cannot be classified as national liberationist.

Furthermore, implicit in the national liberation concept, but absent in Leninism, is the notion that the revolutionary struggle is one of *all* the people of a nation exploited by imperialism. Lenin never abandoned his theory (and Marx's) that the industrial proletariat must be the vehicle of revolution. Lenin created the Bolshevik Party to serve as the revolutionary vanguard of the proletariat and to rule until such time as the proletariat developed enough in size and consciousness to justify proletarian self-rule. Although the Russian proletariat was only a small fraction of the Russian labor force, Lenin insisted that the revolution was being carried out in its name. While it is true that Lenin was willing to grant the peasantry a far greater measure of participation than Marx considered possible, his enlistment of the rural masses in the revolution amounted to a recognition of political reality, not a transformation of ideological principles. In short, Lenin mobilized the Russian peasants in the cause of proletarian revolution, but he did not transform the movement into a rural-based, peasant-oriented people's revolution. The later reorientation of communist revolutionary strategy toward the peasant masses assumes an antiurban, populist bias that was never an element of either Marx's or Lenin's thought, but is implicit in all national liberation movements that pursue the Eastern strategy. In sum, while Lenin undoubtedly contributed to the process by adapting Marxism to Russia and focusing on the effects of imperialism, the marriage of Marxism and national liberation represented a departure from, rather than an outgrowth of, Leninism.

In his analysis of the relationship between socialism and tradition, S. N. Eisenstadt has compared the transfer of Marxist socialism to traditional, non-Western societies with the evolutionary process of selective adaptation, which he called "selective diffusion."[3] The Eisenstadt thesis is that the extent to which Marxism will be adapted in traditional societies is dependent upon the degree of congruence between traditional values and communist ideology. Those elements of Marxism that are in harmony with a cultural heritage will be selected and diffused, while those elements at odds with the host tradition will be rejected. Only rarely, according to Eisenstadt, and never successfully, have revolutionary movements "attempted to accept the whole 'package deal' of socialism, or to make it the predominant element in the symbols of their collective identity."[4]

As for the factors that account for the degree of a traditional culture's receptivity to socialist symbols, Eisenstadt provided a twofold explanation. First, receptivity depends "on the degree to which the traditions of the receptive society . . . contain within themselves strong universalistic elements . . . as well as strong utopian elements." Second, "Receptivity to the central symbols of socialism is dependent on the degree to which these universalistic orientations and elements existed within their own Great Tradition. . . ."[5]

However, unlike the random, mindless process of biological evolution, ideological evolution requires the conscious, purposeful selection of compatible dogma by strong revolutionary leaders. One cannot explain why a particular system becomes socialist solely in terms of the culture's receptivity to socialism, without reference to the revolutionary will of the leadership. Socialism does not just happen. In each instance where a national movement has incorporated socialist doctrine the phenomenon has been associated with a strong-minded revolutionary leader such as Mao Zedong, Ho Chi Minh, Fidel Castro, Gamal Nasser, or Julius Nyerere. Without the force of these personalities, socialism would have wilted, no matter how fertile the ground.

Therefore, this analysis of the relationship between communism and national liberation will lay heavy emphasis on the contributions of the revolutionary personalities around whom the movements were shaped. Just as Russian socialism became inextricably identified with Leninism, the national liberation struggle in its communist orientation is synonymous not with national movements but with personal ones, particularly Maoism and Castroism. Only after their contributions to national communism have been identified will it be possible to understand the intimate connection between national liberation and charismatic movements of the type so prevalent throughout the so-called Third World.

Undoubtedly, the primary persona in the process was Mao Zedong, for it was he who first effectively forged the merger between Marxism and national liberation, and this was unquestionably his major contribution to communism.

MAO AND THE CHINESE REVOLUTION

Two questions dominate all discussions on the role of national tendencies in Mao's Chinese revolution. First, to what extent was Mao Zedong an authentic nationalist, as opposed to Marx and Lenin, who permitted national considerations to influence but not dominate their goals? Second, what were the relative contributions of national and socialist symbols to Mao's campaign to mobilize the Chinese people before and after the 1949 Revolution? The first question is an inquiry into the importance of national symbols to Mao personally, and the second into their significance in the collective mind of the Chinese peasantry. On the one hand, Mao might have employed national sentiment in order to appeal to the masses without having been affected by it himself. On the other hand, Mao might have been a nationalist who merely employed socialist symbols to legitimate his movement in terms of a universalist tradition.

Nationalism and the Mobilization of the Peasants

On the first question, concerning Mao's personal orientation, a consensus appears to have developed, which will be discussed below. There is, however, some controversy over the second question, on the importance of nationalism as a mobilizer of popular support. The focal point of the controversy is the now classic thesis propounded by the American scholar Chalmers Johnson in *Peasant Nationalism and Communist Power.*[6] Johnson's theory was that neither the Chinese Communist Party (CCP), established in 1921, nor Mao's faction that splintered from the CCP in 1927 generated popular enthusiasm among the peasant masses until the Japanese invaded China in 1937.[7] Specifically, the harsh treatment inflicted on the Chinese people by their Japanese conquerors provided the communists, but especially Mao, with a mobilizing issue to exploit.

According to Johnson, the major obstacle to the CCP's efforts before 1937 was the parochial mentality of the Chinese peasant, which socialist appeals for land reform failed to transform. However, the presence of Japanese forces on Chinese soil imposed a Chinese identity on the people: the "we-they" mentality that is the essence of nationalism. Once that spirit of "Chineseness" began to spread among the peasants, the communists under Mao's leadership "eschewed their old slogans of class warfare and violent redistribution of property in their post-1937 propaganda and concentrated solely on national salvation."[8]

> In other words, from 1921 to 1937 Communism failed in China because the Chinese people, in general, were indifferent to what the Communist Party had to offer. After 1937, it succeeded because the population became receptive to one particular kind of political appeal; and the Communist Party—in one of its many disguises—made precisely that appeal; it offered to meet the needs of the people for leadership in organizing resistance to the invader and in alleviating war-induced anarchy in rural areas.[9]

Two points in this argument are particularly noteworthy. One is Johnson's view that the CCP had failed to attract widespread support before 1937, and the other is his contention that the CCP's national appeal was a "disguise" that concealed its true goal—socialist transformation. The second point relates to Mao's own national inclinations and will be discussed shortly; the first requires further examination. Some of Johnson's critics have accused him of underestimating the early successes of the CCP, particularly during the period referred to as the Jiangxi Soviet from 1931 to 1934 when Mao established a formidable stronghold under communist leadership, and during the Shaanxi period in 1936. Johnson has responded to this criticism by explaining that his reference to Mao's "failure" pertained to the inability of the party to generate widespread popular support, not to the CCP's organizational skills or Mao's leadership ability. The Long March of 1936, for example, when Mao led his followers on a 6,000-mile journey to safety from Chiang Kai-shek's pursuing Guomindang (KMT) is generally considered a major achievement because it galvanized Mao's leadership as well as the commitment of the party cadres who survived. In these senses it was a success. But Johnson's view is that the very fact that the Long March occurred indicates that the CCP was in retreat because it did not have the support of the people against the nationalist Guomindang.[10]

Essentially, Johnson's critics have charged, in one form or another, that he has reduced the communist success among the Chinese peasantry to a single causal factor, and that he has consequently overemphasized the pre-1937 isolation of the CCP.[11] Because Johnson chose 1937 as the birth year of Chinese nationalism, he has been accused of ignoring the Chinese perennial preoccupation with foreign "barbarians" and the Chinese historic memory of exploitation by foreigners since the Opium Wars.[12] Furthermore, Johnson has been criticized for underestimating the strength of anticommunist forces in China that accounted for Mao's defeats before 1937. Finally, Johnson has been chastised for refusing to recognize just how strong the CCP really was in those preinvasion years. "Long before Japan invaded China," asserted one critic, "the Chinese Communist Party enjoyed the support of the masses, owing largely to its policy of advancing their social and economic interests."[13]

However, Johnson never contended that nationalism was absent before 1937, only that it was not "mass nationalism." Contemporary nationalism, according to Johnson, is not merely a state of mind or an elite phenomenon, it is a movement whereby the masses establish their identity as a people. Thus, mass nationalism comprises two essential elements: social mobilization, whereby a political community takes shape; and ideology, "which serves to idealize the activities undertaken by the people in common."[14] The ideology serves as a "national myth" and is "drawn from doctrines that are independently respected in society."[15] Before 1937 only the elites shared the national sentiments and the ideology; they were not sufficient to spark the mobilization process. Elite nationalism, in Johnson's view, became mass nationalism only when the Japanese invaded.

Johnson further maintained that in terms of developing mass nationalism the cases of Yugoslavia and China were quite similar, because both established the legitimacy of the communist party in the context of resistance to foreign invaders, and both parties enlisted a mass following on the basis of an ideology that functioned as a national myth. "China and Yugoslavia, from the time of the invasions to the present, offer typical examples of mass nationalist movements in which Communism serves as an official rationale for nationalist policies."[16]

There was, however, a significant difference between Titoist and Maoist nationalisms that Johnson appears to have ignored. Tito was a Comintern agent who remained loyal to Soviet leadership until Stalin forced him to choose between domestic popular support and Soviet friendship. Tito did not nationalize communist ideology in the context of mass mobilization; rather, he and the Yugoslav elites developed the so-called Titoist model long after they had mass support. Mao, on the other hand, never seems to have doubted the need to adapt Marxism to Chinese conditions. From the mid-1920s Mao rejected the Comintern strategy of cooperation with the Guomindang in the belief that the Soviet urban-based revolutionary strategy was inappropriate in rural China. In other words, the fact that the Chinese people did not accept Mao's appeal until 1937 does not mean that the Chinese elites nationalized their strategy in order to bring it into conformity with postinvasion realities as Johnson contended.[17] In both the Yugoslav and the Chinese cases the emergence of national communism did not coincide with invasion, and Johnson's conclusion that national communism "is a natural outgrowth of the politicization of the masses in China and Yugoslavia during the war" is incorrect.[18] In Yugoslavia national communism followed by at least five years the partisan victory over the Nazis, while in China, it will be argued here, national communism, in the form of national liberation, preceded the Japanese invasion by a decade or more.

Nationalism and Mao Zedong Thought

This brings us to the first question raised earlier: To what extent was Mao an authentic nationalist? Although the thesis of this study is that national considerations have always been an implicit element of Marxist socialism, it has also been argued here that neither Marx nor Lenin was a nationalist. Rather, national communism, in its European mode, has been ultimately oriented toward class struggle and international proletarian goals, although it employs the nation as a vehicle of social transformation. The logical conclusion of this line of reasoning is that if Mao was an authentic nationalist, he could not have been an authentic Marxist-Leninist. However, this is where the European model breaks down and Mao's ideological contribution becomes crucial. Unquestionably, Mao Zedong's most significant contribution to socialist ideology was the successful integration of nationalism and socialism through the merger of class struggle and national liberation.

Marx and Lenin refused to recognize the value of the national struggle apart from its international context. Mao, on the other hand, refused to recognize the value of the international struggle apart from its national context. Therefore, if we eventually conclude that Mao was, indeed, an authentic nationalist, this will not mean, as it would have in Lenin's case, that he was not *simultaneously* a communist. What abrogates this apparent contradiction is Mao's realization that in the colonial world, of which China was a part, class struggle for the liberation of the working class and national struggle against foreign exploitation and control, i.e., antiimperialism, were one and the same. Mao was not the author of the doctrine of either the class struggle or imperialism, but he was the first to synthesize them into a powerful variation of national communism, and therein lies Mao's importance.

Chinese Nationalism Before Mao. In order to comprehend fully the nature of Mao's achievement it is necessary to investigate the origins and development of his thought. Unquestionably, the twentieth-century Chinese revolutionary intellectual tradition was dominated by nationalist themes. Although never a colony in the formal sense, China had been exploited by the Western powers in the nineteenth century to the point of collapse. The intellectual community, while still certain of China's cultural superiority over the West, began, around the turn of the century, to inquire as to the root causes of its inability to withstand Western incursions. Although a number of responses emerged, the consensus among China's intellectuals was that Western industrial, technical, and military superiority, as opposed to superior culture, accounted for the Western advantage. All of this can be summed up in the single word, *modernization,* which became the overriding goal of China's revolutionary elites. But it had to be modernization within the context of traditional Chinese values and culture. Thus, the twentieth-century Chinese intellectuals have been termed "revolutionary nationalists" rather than "cultural nationalists" because rather than simply wishing to expel the foreigners and return to traditional patterns, they recognized that the only way to dislodge the imperialists was to transform China's own economic and social system into one equal to that of the West. Consequently, when the imperial dynasty finally collapsed in 1911, virtually every segment of the intellectual community rallied around the leadership of Sun Yat-sen and his modernizing nationalist Guomindang. Sun's new republic was to be guided by what he referred to as the Three People's Principles—Nationalism, Democracy, and People's Livelihood.[19] The first emphasized the unity of China in opposition to foreign control, the second focused on the popular nature of the new regime, and the third stressed the need to develop an economic system capable of satisfying human needs.

Sun was not a communist. In fact, before the 1917 Russian Revolution there were no Chinese communists. Yet Sun's unsuccessful struggle to implement his principles, combined with Lenin's electrifying success in Russia, drew the attention of the Chinese revolutionary intellectual elite toward the theories of Marxism-Leninism. It must be emphasized that when Chinese communism began to take shape after the Russian Revolution it was an outgrowth of the revolutionary nationalist tradition. In fact, the first Marxist-Leninist center emerged at Beijing National University among those intellectuals who had instigated the May Fourth Movement. This movement was an emotional and spontaneous response on the part of faculty and students in Beijing to the Versailles Conference's decision to turn former German concessions in Shantung over to the Japanese, rather than return them to China. The issue that led to street demonstrations on 4 May 1919 was clearly nationalist. The Versailles decision was an affront to Chinese national pride and another indication that the West would continue to dismember China as long as she remained weak. But after the 1917 revolution in Russia, Chinese intellectuals began to consider a new explanation for Western behavior—Lenin's theory of imperialism.

Early Maoist Nationalism. Although it appeared two years before the May Fourth Movement, Mao Zedong's first published article in the journal *The New Youth,* which was published by the man who would become the first head of the Chinese Communist Party, was permeated with this new spirit. The theme of this twenty-four-year-old student was national strength. "Our nation is wanting in strength. The military spirit has not been encouraged. . . . The principal aim of physical education [the subject of the article] is military heroism."[20] Mao and his comrades recognized the elemental truth that in military strength and in personal commitment lay the independent future of China.

Mao was among about a dozen Chinese revolutionaries who met in July 1921 to organize the Chinese Communist Party. However, aside from their revolutionary commitments to proletarian principles borrowed from the Soviets, they had no clear conception of Marxist ideology. The major issue for this new faction was its relationship to the Guomindang. Since the purpose behind the formation of the CCP was to establish a distinction between Marxist, class-oriented antiimperialism and Sun Yat-sen's diffuse antiforeign, national unity movement, it came as a rude surprise to the CCP leadership in July 1922 when the Comintern representative in China, Maring, advised them to cooperate with the Guomindang. The CCP's problem was that by 1922 Sun Yat-sen had been frustrated in his attempt to enlist the cooperation of either China's warlords or foreign interests in his modernization program and had accepted an offer of assistance from the only willing source, the Comintern. From his perspective, Lenin saw Sun's nationalist movement as the best hope for rending capitalist control out of Asia, thereby unraveling the imperialist network upon which the capitalist system depended. This policy was an outgrowth of Lenin's Western strategy, according to which any national cause merited support if it served to hasten the revolution in the West, to which the Russian revolution was only a prelude.

Despite the fact that they felt betrayed, the CCP leaders accepted Maring's advice and agreed to join the Guomindang while maintaining the identity of their own party. Ultimately, the strategy called for infiltrating the KMT and transforming it into a communist tool, but in 1922 none of the communists deluded themselves that this was an imminent prospect. Thus, on both sides of the new "United Front" the interests of nationalism and communism in China were fully integrated. For their part, the Guomindang nationalists were willing to accept communist support (and, indeed, Sun became more radical himself) from within China and from the USSR, in order to eliminate foreign control. On their side, the communists, both Soviet and Chinese, accepted the necessity to ally with nonproletarian, bourgeois interests in order to defeat imperialism and bring about the real *social* revolution to come. The common theme was nationalism.

At first Mao and others in the CCP concurred in this United Front strategy because of its antiimperialist orientation, but events inside China and the USSR in 1926 and 1927 rendered this strategy increasingly unacceptable. In March 1926, shortly after Sun Yat-sen's death, the leadership of the Guomindang was seized by Chiang Kai-shek. At approximately the same time the struggle between Stalin and Trotsky for the post-Lenin leadership of the Soviet Union took shape, and one important issue in that conflict was the Comintern strategy in China. Despite Chiang's increased willingness to cooperate with patently bourgeois elements in China, Stalin contended that the Comintern should continue to support him. Trotsky, on the other hand, was more inclined to encourage independent revolutionary action by the CCP. Thus, although it became increasingly apparent in 1927 that Chiang was himself a representative of the bourgeoisie, Comintern under Stalin's influence virtually abandoned the CCP. Even if he had been encouraged by developments in China to switch support to the CCP, Stalin was forced by his own political situation vis-à-vis Trotsky to maintain the United Front strategy.

Mao was among the first of the CCP leaders to recognize that their nationalism was being used by the general secretary of the CPSU and that the Comintern strategy was incorrect insofar as the interests of Chinese communism were concerned. Despite the continuation of the United Front, Mao returned to his native Hunan province in 1926 to study the activities of the peasants and appraise the possibility of organizing a peasant-based movement under communist leadership. In March 1927 he produced his "Report on the Investigation of the Agrarian Movement in Hunan," which was the first solid proposal emphasizing the revolutionary potential of the rural masses.[21] One month later Chiang Kai-shek's Guomindang forces turned against their United Front communist allies in Shanghai and slaughtered 10,000 CCP supporters. The Shanghai Massacre destroyed the United Front, decimated the urban base of the CCP, and threw into sharp focus the necessity to concentrate on rural organization. The fact that Stalin remained willing to support the

Guomindang after Shanghai confirmed in the minds of most communists that the Comintern path was a dead end for the CCP. The communists had permitted their antiforeign sentiments to trap them into support for a Western revolutionary strategy—the Soviet model. The combination of Stalin's cynical manipulation of Comintern and the increasingly obvious shortcomings of the model in the Chinese setting created sharp disagreement within the CCP. The Shanghai Massacre vindicated Mao's skepticism about Comintern strategy and shifted the attention of the CCP leaders to Mao's peasant-based strategy.

Nothing in Marxism-Leninism, with which Mao was only vaguely familiar anyway, justified his shift to the mobilization of the countryside. Rather, it must be counted as one of Mao's major contributions to communism, albeit based on M. N. Roy's earlier Eastern strategy, that he recognized that Marx's deification of the urban proletariat and Lenin's fixation on elitist party organization could not survive in the Chinese environment. Mao's instinctive mistrust of Chinese urban interests and his faith in rural people and values propelled him inexorably from being a secondary figure in the CCP—an ideological outcast—to the leadership of the new CCP. The "Autumn Harvest" uprising and the Nanchang uprising of August–September 1927, the former led by Mao, represented the first efforts to put this new policy into practice. However, Mao's instincts were not matched by his organizational and military skills. These early attempts to mobilize the peasants for military action in the name of land reform were dismal failures, and Mao lost his party leadership as a consequence. The lesson of the Autumn Harvest failure was threefold. First, commitment was not enough; leaders needed experience in military organization. Second, the masses were not ready for mobilization by any group. And third, revolution in China would entail a prolonged struggle that only a close association between the party and the people could win.

Mao was operating in an ideological and experiential vacuum. Having abandoned the Soviet model, he had to develop a Chinese one. Referring to those early years, Mao later observed, "nobody knew how to conduct the revolution or how to carry on the struggle; only later did we acquire some experience. Our path gradually emerged in the course of practice."[22] Mao gained his organizational and military experience during the period of the Jiangxi Soviet, which he established after the failure in Hunan, in the Long March, and, after 1937, in his campaigns against the Japanese from his base in Yanan. The ideological development to match that experience came in the years following the Long March, when he was isolated in the mountains of Shaanxi province. It was there, beginning in 1938, that Mao began to write and lecture seriously on ideological subjects and to develop what was to be known as "Mao Zedong Thought."

The Japanese Invasion and Mao's New Democracy. Mao was originally drawn to communist ideology in his search for a means to liberate China from foreign control. He remained committed to communist dogma in the early years for lack of a viable revolutionary alternative. In the view of Stuart Schram, a leading scholar on Mao's thought, the pre-1927 commitment to the United Front "demonstrated that he attached (at least for the moment) a higher priority to the national revolution than to the social revolution."[23]

After 1927, and especially after 1937, Marxism-Leninism continued to appear a viable model for the modernization of Chinese society, and, perhaps more importantly, antiimperialism served as a sound justification for the new national sentiment that was permeating the Chinese masses. Schram summarized Mao's position thus: "While Mao was a genuine communist revolutionary, and while the categories in which he reasons are Marxist categories, the deepest springs of his personality are, to a large extent, to be found in the Chinese tradition, and China's glory is at least as important to him as is world revolution."[24]

Mao was, after all, Chinese, and the Japanese invasion of 1937 unleashed his own patriotic attachment to the Chinese national tradition just as it encouraged nationalism among the general population. Mao had intuitively rejected the Comintern strategy a decade earlier, but the Japanese aggression stimulated him to formulate his own revolutionary strategy in the context of the Chinese cultural experience. Mao's lurking awareness that Marxism-Leninism would have to be adapted to Chinese conditions surfaced in 1938–1940 as Mao undertook the "sinification of Marxism."

The dominant theme of this period was that Marxism-Leninism had to be reshaped to conform to unique national conditions. But it was not sufficient for Mao simply to assert that China was different and leave it at that. The sinification of Marxism that marked Mao's emergence as a national communist was couched in antiimperialist terms. In Mao's view, what was specifically different about the Chinese case was that China's troubles could be traced directly to colonial exploitation, the latest instance being the Japanese occupation. In short, the "sinification of Marxism" was, in essence, the Maoist transformation of communist revolution into a struggle for national liberation. All of the remainder of Mao Zedong Thought grows out of this fundamental alteration in the goal of communist revolution. Later, in his attempt to universalize the Chinese experience and to promote the so-called Chinese model of revolution, Mao would downplay this sinification period. But in a 1938 speech, he summarized his view thus:

> If a Chinese Communist, who is part of the great Chinese people, bound to his people by his very flesh and blood, talks of Marxism apart from Chinese peculiarities this Marxism is merely an empty abstraction. Consequently, the Sinification of Marxism, that is to say, making certain that in all of its manifestations it is imbued with Chinese peculiarities . . . becomes a problem that must be understood and solved by the whole Party without delay.[25]

Echoing those who had embarked on the national communist path before him, and encapsulating what all those who were to follow would express in one form or another, Mao stated: "Our theory is made up of the universal truths of Marxism-Leninism combined with the concrete reality of China. We must be able to think independently."[26]

Mao's rather simplistic theoretical attempt to come to terms with China's "concrete reality" was his 1940 tract *On New Democracy,*[27] which has been characterized as the "classic document" of Mao's sinification effort.[28] What Mao attempted in *On New Democracy* was to resolve the debate between those who argued that China would have to go through the stage of bourgeois development before entering socialism and those, whom he characterized as "left phrasemongers," who insisted that revolution in China would lead directly to socialism, the so-called single revolution theory. Mao conceived of a new stage, between semifeudalism and socialism, which he termed "New Democracy," during which Chinese politics, economics, and culture would be transformed and made ready for the introduction of socialism. Although vague, the New Democracy was a modified version of Sun Yat-sen's Three Principles of Nationalism, Democracy, and People's Welfare, combining the restoration of Chinese national greatness with socialist transformation. Mao argued that his new version of the Three People's Principles, which required "alliance with Russia, cooperation with the Communists and assistance to the peasants and workers,"[29] was in full conformity with the "Communist Party's minimum programme."[30] Mao explained the merger of Sun's nationalist principles and communist revolution in terms of the new conditions extant in China:

> The Chinese revolution is virtually the peasants' revolution, the resistance to Japan now going on is virtually the peasants' resistance to

Japan. New Democratic politics are virtually the granting of power to the peasants. The new or genuine Three People's Principles are virtually the principles of the peasants' revolution. . . . The anti-Japanese War is virtually a peasants' war. . . . So the peasant problem has become the main problem of the Chinese revolution, and the strength of the peasants constitutes the principal force of the Chinese revolution.[31]

In other words, fighting against Japan was, in Mao's view, synonymous with struggling for communism, and the peasants could do both simultaneously.

Mao explained that three types of systems had emerged: "(1) republics under bourgeois dictatorship; (2) republics under the dictatorship of the proletariat; and (3) republics under the joint dictatorship of several revolutionary classes."[32] The third type, to which China belonged, was a transitional form for colonies and semicolonies and was characterized by "the joint dictatorship of several anti-imperialist classes."[33] "In China," Mao went on to explain, "this new democratic form of state assumes the very form of the anti-Japanese united front. It is anti-Japanese and anti-imperialist; it is also in the nature of a coalition of several revolutionary classes, of a united front."[34]

Mao's New Democracy differed from Leninism in that Mao rejected proletarian dictatorship in favor of a "joint dictatorship of all revolutionary classes," which, in effect, included all anti-Japanese forces. It was similar to Leninism in that Mao accepted democratic centralism as the fundamental principle of political organization. In contrast to Lenin's exclusionary approach to revolutionary organization (over which the break with the Mensheviks occurred) Mao adopted a conciliatory, inclusionary approach that permitted as wide a cross section of the Chinese population as possible to identify with the New Democracy. Yet Mao managed to maintain the Leninist emphasis on centralized party control and unquestionable authority by equating national independence with communist revolution. "Such are the internal political relations," Mao insisted, "which a revolutionary China, an anti-Japanese China, ought to and must not fail to establish, for these constitute the only correct direction for our present work of 'national reconstruction.' "[35]

Maoist New Democracy was totally eclectic, not only in embracing ideas from non-Chinese culture and ancient Chinese culture but in adapting Marxism-Leninism as well. Mao was willing to select and adapt any aspect of foreign or domestic culture that would contribute to social transformation, and he did not hesitate to alter communist ideology for the same reason. "China," Mao advised, "should absorb

on a large scale the progressive cultures of foreign countries. . . .
We must absorb whatever we today find useful, not only from the
present Socialist . . . cultures of other nations, but also from . . .
the various capitalist countries in the age of enlightenment."[36] Similarly, he suggested that "we must respect our own history and not
break it up." He reminded his countrymen that a "splendid ancient
culture was created during the long period of China's feudal society,"
and that to "absorb its democratic essence, is a necessary condition
for the development of our new national culture and for the increase
of our national self-confidence. . . ."[37] Mao was equally clear on the
role of Marxism in China's New Democracy:

> Likewise, in applying Marxism to China, Chinese Communists must
> fully and properly unite the universal truth of Marxism with the specific
> practice of the Chinese revolution; that is to say, the truth of Marxism
> must be integrated with the characteristics of the nation and given a
> definite national form before it can be useful; it must not be applied
> subjectively as a formula. Formulistic Marxists are only fooling with
> Marxism and the Chinese revolution, and there is no place for them
> in the ranks of the Chinese revolution. China's culture should have
> its own form, namely a national form. National in form, new democratic
> in content—such is our new culture today.[38]

No clearer expression of national communism is possible.

Maoist National Communism: The Mass Line. Mao's determination to fashion a uniquely Chinese revolutionary movement was
not, however, matched by any significant ideological adaptations.
Mao and his comrades in Yanan were revolutionary practitioners,
not theoreticians. No Djilas or Trotsky emerged in China to bolster
the CCP's commitment to a Chinese version of Marxism. Hence,
the uniqueness of the Chinese movement developed as revolutionary
method rather than theory, and Mao's contribution to the development
of communist philosophy was meager.[39] The essence of Mao's contribution to Marxist revolutionary practice was his reorientation of
the revolution to the rural peasantry, his emphasis on class unity
based on an antiimperialist united front tactic, and his realization
that the revolution in China would take on the character of a
protracted guerrilla war. While these ideas emerged in response to
the pressures of revolutionary struggle, they were eventually transformed into a foundation for the development of postrevolutionary
China. Mao never distinguished between revolutionary action and
national development. He believed that the same strategy and commitment that brought the communists to power in China could

eventually transform China into a modern socialist system. In this regard the source of his revolutionary success was the seed of his postrevolutionary failure, but Mao never abandoned his commitment to the revolutionary principles of what became known as the "mass line."

The mass line has been described as "the most pervasive concept in CCP doctrine,"[40] and as "the heart . . . of Mao Tse-Tung's lifelong revolutionary strategy."[41] Through it Mao expressed his fundamental belief in the importance of the people (not necessarily individuals) of China to the success of any revolutionary effort. The mass line was an affirmation of voluntarism as opposed to impersonal historic inevitability, and of a system of political leadership that required constant interaction between the party and the people. Mao's classic statement of the mass line formula includes the following key passage.

All correct leadership is necessarily "from the masses, to the masses." This means: take the ideas of the masses (scattered and unsystematic ideas) and concentrate them (through study turn them into concentrated and systematic ideas), then go to the masses and propagate and explain these ideas until the masses embrace them as their own, hold fast to them and translate them into action, and test the correctness of these ideas in action. Then once again concentrate ideas from the masses and once again go to the masses, so that the ideas are persevered in and carried through. And so on, over and over again in an endless spiral, with the ideas becoming more correct, more vital and richer each time.[42]

Although on occasion Lenin also referred to the necessity for the party to maintain contact with the workers, Mao's mass line is unique in its underlying conceptualizations as well as in its application. The mass line is not in conflict with Lenin's "vanguard" theory because the formulation of policy and the issuance of directives remain the prerogatives of the party. What is different about Mao's mass line is the notion that the *source* of policy must be the masses rather than the bureaucratic intelligentsia or the party elite, and that all policies must be made understandable to the masses, who will approve or disapprove on the basis of some instinctive understanding of the correct path of revolutionary development. Mao condemned both policy making without concrete guidance of the masses and mass mobilization without effective policy making. The former resulted in bureaucratism and the latter in subjectivism. The mass line was not simply a propaganda mechanism that enabled the party to rule absolutely while giving the people a false sense of participation. It represented Mao's profound belief that leadership separated from the needs and will of the masses simply could not transform Chinese society, and that the people, without party guidance, would remain adrift. The people needed the party as much as the party needed the people. If people and party were in conjunction, Mao believed, nothing could deter the revolutionary development of China; if they were divided, nothing—not personal leadership, bureaucracy, the military, or the force of the vanguard party—could realize the revolutionary goal.

It was the mass line that distinguished Maoist from Leninist party organization. The belief in the party's need for mass support and a profound distrust of bureaucracy remained persistent themes in Maoist leadership throughout Mao's lifetime. The Great Leap Forward, Mao's 1958 campaign to enlist the masses of China in the nation's economic development, was a patent manifestion of the Maoist conviction that the concerted exercise of popular will, guided by the party, could surmount any obstacle.[43]

The failure of the Great Leap, with its ensuing economic chaos, resulted in a repudiation of the Maoist approach and a reemphasis on management skills, bureaucratic organization, and centralized control by party and government elites—an accommodation that Mao was personally unwilling to make. While he openly admitted that the idea of producing steel in backyard blast furnaces throughout the country was mistaken and that he had been in error when he pushed the commune system for Chinese agriculture, he continued to pursue the mass line in his relations with the people.[44] Mao distinguished, in other words, between specific radical tactics that had failed and his basic strategy of direct communication with the people rather than relying on party and government bureaucracy.

However, Mao had less opportunity to demonstrate his commitment in the years after the Great Leap failure, owing to the emergence of more moderate forces within the party, including Zhou Enlai, Liu Shaoqi, and Deng Xiaoping. Undaunted by the failure of radicalism, Mao continued in the years 1960–65 to appeal to those within the party who shared his mistrust for bureaucratic authority. Whether they joined Mao out of a genuine commitment to the mass line or whether they used his campaign to enhance their personal power, the radicals around Mao launched a new assault on bureaucratic centralism in 1966, a movement that was dubbed the Great Proletarian Cultural Revolution. Once again Mao went directly to the people, in this case students and young workers, for support, but this time his goal was to destroy the party that he had created and subsequently lost.

Much debate continues to center on the motives of Mao and his followers in the Cultural Revolution, particularly with respect to whether power or policy was the uppermost concern for the radicals. What remains beyond question is that Mao's last revolutionary gasp employed the same mass line strategy as his first efforts three decades earlier. The so-called red vs. expert controversy that characterized the Cultural Revolution was essentially a contest between revolutionary mass will and planned, rational management of the Chinese system. Mao viewed the power of mass voluntarism among those whom he referred to as "the poor and the blank" as potentially unlimited. If the party and the masses in unison could conquer the forces of imperialism and reaction, then surely they could overcome the obstacles to Chinese economic development. This was Mao's view throughout his tenure as China's leader, but as we have seen, while it proved an effective strategy for mobilizing the Chinese people against foreign invasion and exploitation, it was ill suited to the complex tasks of economic management and public administration. Mao never seemed to grasp the crucial distinction between strategies aimed at the revolutionary overthrow of the existing order and strategies directed toward the revolutionary transformation of the economy—between, in other words, national independence and national development. The problem for all successful revolutionaries is the transition from a life committed to the destruction of a society to one of construction. Marx never faced the problem, and Lenin died before he had to make the painful metamorphosis. Mao lived long enough to seize power and use it, and therein lay his dilemma. To pursue a path of rational development would have been to abandon his revolutionary principles, but to have abandoned these principles for the sake of material benefits would have been to lose his *raison d'être*.

The essence of Maoism as a form of national communism is its unrelenting commitment to revolution through a process of increasing mass mobilization by a leadership constantly in contact with its peasant base. In this respect, Maoism was the direct product of Chinese conditions and culture; however, this fact does not render Maoism applicable exclusively to China. The conditions to which Mao adapted Marxism-Leninism are common to most nations that perceive themselves to have been victims of colonial exploitation. Mao preached antiimperialism and national salvation just as Marx had preached anticapitalism and proletarian salvation a century earlier. And just as Marx's original message was adapted to particular conditions in Europe, so Mao's message, with adaptations, has applicability among nations that perceive their essential problem to be neocolonialism or economic imperialism. As Stuart Schram has observed: "Mao may have indeed Sinified the *form* of Marxism, but his contributions to the substance of Leninist theory represent an adaptation of Marxism to Asian conditions rather than a Sinification of Marxism."[45] This is a subtle, yet crucial distinction. The "Chineseness" of Maoism necessitated its own adaptation in its application to other national conditions, but its transnational quality lies in the fact that Maoism is, in the final analysis, an ideology of national liberation from colonial exploitation for rural masses anywhere.

It is not surprising, therefore, that in a comprehensive appraisal of Mao's policy commitments between 1921, when he first joined the CCP, and 1966, when he died, Michel Oksenberg found that Mao Zedong's "performance was best when he was making revolution, when he was dealing with the countryside, and when he was enunciating policies that had popular support."[46]

According to Oksenberg, Mao undertook thirty-three major policy commitments during his fifty-five-year political career, of which 55 percent could be termed successful. However, 59 percent of his pre-1949 decisions were successful as compared to only 45 percent of those after 1949. And 73 percent of his policies concerning revolutionary strategy succeeded, while only 33 percent of his economic policies did. Finally, 79 percent of his rural policies but only 23 percent of his urban policies were successful.[47] These figures leave little doubt that the salience of Maoism lies in its promise of national revolution to an exploited rural populace rather than in its proffer of social and economic development to an urban proletariat.

The Central Committee of the CCP has done its own appraisal of Mao's performance, the findings of which are surprisingly similar to Oksenberg's. On 29 June 1981, the Central Committee approved a 119-page assessment of Mao's contributions in which he was highly praised for his early years and severely criticized for his later performance. The overall judgment of the party's report was that Mao's contributions to the Chinese revolution "far outweighed his errors," but that the Cultural Revolution was an unnecessary and costly deviation. In fact, the report goes to great lengths to distinguish between legitimate Maoist ideology and the excesses of the Cultural Revolution. "The erroneous left theses, upon which Comrade Mao Zedong based himself in initiating the Cultural Revolution, were obviously inconsistent with the system of Mao Zedong Thought, which is the integration of the universal principles of Marxism-Leninism with the concrete practice of the Chinese revolution. These theses must be thoroughly distinguished from Mao Zedong Thought."[48] In other words, the current view is that the essence of Maoism is national communism and this is the path that the post-Mao leaders intend to follow.

Chinese National Communism in the Post-Mao Era

The irony of the post-Mao era in China is that the apparent repudiation of Maoist revolutionary practice in favor of what is viewed as a more national model of economic modernization has put China back on the course of national development that Mao himself charted. By its rejection of Maoist radical populism, the post-Mao leadership, specifically Deng Xiaoping, has repudiated the universalist pretensions of postrevolutionary Maoism that contributed to its decline as an effective model for Chinese development. Contrary to the present Chinese explanation, it was not a change in Mao's approach but his refusal to change that rendered his thought inappropriate for postrevolutionary China. Maoism became counterproductive because China moved from the stage of national liberation to that of national development, not because Mao became the captive of the radical "Gang of Four."

Whether the post-Mao leadership continues to pursue the goals of the "four modernizations" program or abandons it for some less ambitious scheme of national development, as appeared to be the case by late 1981, one fact will remain constant—Chinese communism will continue to adapt itself to Chinese conditions, even if this requires abandoning the fundamental principles of Maoism. As the Chinese journal *Red Flag* declared on 1 November 1980:

> During the "Great Cultural Revolution" [the Gang of Four] . . . proclaimed themselves "the center of the world revolution" and "the standard," and judged the nature of other parties—Marxist-Leninist or revisionist—according to whether they supported the "Great Cultural Revolution." . . . Communist parties must support and learn from each other, and at the same time uphold the principle of complete equality and self-determination. Questions of revolution in various countries can only be decided by the parties and peoples concerned. Any act of issuing orders to other parties and countries and interfering in the internal affairs of other parties and countries is a deviation from Marxism.[49]

One Western analyst has characterized the Chinese communist course as perfectly consistent with the traditional quest for *Fu-Chiang* (wealth and power).[50] The success of the Chinese communists is explained by the fact that they were more efficient at pursuing this goal than their predecessors or competitors. This view explains the

Chinese break with the Soviet Union in the 1960s and the Chinese rapprochement with the United States in the 1970s as evidence of the willingness of the Chinese to do what is necessary to preserve their national independence and promote their national development, ideology notwithstanding.

In fact, China's longstanding and often violent dispute with the USSR is understandable only in terms of the CCP's continuing pursuit of national greatness. The Sino-Soviet dispute is too complex to review here, and has numerous sources that do not lend themselves to brief analysis.[51] Suffice it to say here that any attempt to distinguish between ideological and national issues in this dispute is artificial. Since both the Soviets and the Chinese have followed the national communist tradition of interpreting Marxist principles and adapting them to national conditions, ideological and national motivations are indistinguishable, and are, in fact, one and the same. The problem is more complex than one of Maoism versus Leninism. If it were merely a question of the Maoist model being unacceptable to the Soviet leadership, the dispute would be more amenable to reconciliation now that Maoism has become less acceptable to the Chinese as well. But it is not, nor is it likely to be. The post-Maoist leadership, despite its reputation for moderation in matters of economic development and policies toward the West, is as disinclined as Mao himself was to come to a reconciliation with the USSR. In fact, the moderate leader Deng Xiaoping has a deep-seated anti-Soviet animus that is not explainable in terms of revolutionary theory or socialist economic interpretation.

Numerous issues divide the Soviet and Chinese parties. Mao's rural-based revolutionary strategy, his penchant for mass mobilization, and his antibureaucratism were undoubtedly dramatic departures from the Lenin-Stalin model. Similarly, Mao's postrevolutionary strategies, such as the Great Leap Forward, were blatant repudiations of Soviet developmental strategy. The Cultural Revolution was not simply a rejection of bureaucratism and vanguardism in China, but an open attack against these phenomena in the USSR where they were perfected. Finally, Mao's view that the future of the international communist movement is inextricably linked with and dependent on the success of national liberation struggles, as opposed to the Soviet position that the established system of communist party-states was the foundation of the movement from which it would grow, was an important source of disagreement over general revolutionary strategy.

However, these issues do not compose the core of the Sino-Soviet dispute. For example, on the issue of support for national liberation movements, the Chinese consistently chided the Soviets for their support of the Vietnamese national liberation struggle. Mao argued that the Soviet pursuit of détente with the United States while American troops were the major obstacle to communist victory in Indochina was a repudiation of Moscow's obligation to international communism. For their part, the Soviets contended that open East-West confrontation made national liberation more difficult and only when the two blocs agreed to compete peacefully would communism stand a real chance of success. Yet the virtual collapse of détente precipitated by the Soviet intervention in Afghanistan (the Soviet position is that détente was destroyed by forces within the American system long before Afghanistan) has not resulted in a Sino-Soviet rapprochement. Quite on the contrary, the political distance between Moscow and Washington has been inversely proportionate to that between Beijing and Washington, while the distance between Moscow and Beijing has remained constant.

Revolutionary strategies, détente, economic policies, and leadership personalities are not the causes of the Sino-Soviet conflict; they are merely its manifestations. China, as a function of its continuing process of national development, and the Soviet Union, as a function of its own emergence as a nation, are motivated by geography, history, and ideology to exert themselves in roughly identical spheres of influence. It is pointless to attempt to distinguish what either system does out of national interest or ideology, because neither makes such a distinction in its own policy-making process. It is not irrelevant that both China and the Soviet Union are communist systems, but neither does that ideological fact function as the determinant force in their relationship. Maoism was one form of Chinese national communism; the post-Mao era has generated its own national variations that fundamentally alter the Maoist approach. Chinese national communism has changed because conditions in China have changed, but Maoism will continue to remain a viable model where current conditions and perceptions match those of prerevolutionary China.[52]

Chalmers Johnson has observed that "virulent nationalist movements have always found it opportune to incorporate transnational values" such as communism to motivate their supporters.[53] And Robert Scalapino has expressed the view that "the nationalist quotient in the political programs of all Asian States . . . is likely to remain high, reflecting the fact that the nationalist and the Communist revolutions are reaching their peak in these societies at approximately the same time."[54] But no one has put it more clearly or succinctly than Mao himself when he declared, "In the final analysis, a national struggle is a question of class struggle."[55]

In this one statement Mao's version of national communism as national liberation actually stands Marxism on its head but retains the essential ingredient of class warfare. In the Communist Manifesto, it will be recalled, Marx and Engels declared that "the struggle of the proletariat with the bourgeoisie is at first a national struggle," and pointed out that "its own country is the immediate arena of its struggle." The emphasis was clearly on class struggle in a national context, which has been identified as the essence of national communism in its anticapitalist, Marxist-Leninist form. Contrariwise, what Mao said was that the national, antiimperialist struggle is also a class struggle, but the starting point of Maoism is national rather than class liberation. This is not simply a different emphasis, it is a different type of national communism. Because Maoism retains the fundamental principle of class struggle (unlike some socialist-oriented national liberation movements that will be discussed below), it retains its links with Marxism and qualifies as national communism despite the reversal of the national and class priorities.

ANTICOLONIAL NATIONAL COMMUNISM IN ASIA

China was not the only system in which national liberation served as a focal point for communist movements. Indeed, because unlike China most of the Asian states had been colonial possessions, there was greater cause for antiimperialism in Indochina or Korea, for example, than there had been in China. As in the case of China, long-standing anticolonial grievances were aggravated and precipitated by Japan's domination of Asia in the 1930s and 1940s. Whatever else it accomplished, the Japanese sweep across Asia dislodged Western imperialism and provided a focal point for national mobilization. No less importantly, the eventual defeat of Japan created a power vacuum in Asia that the former colonial powers never managed to refill and that national liberation movements used to establish political footholds in their respective systems. In short, the same forces that engendered the emergence, rise, and eventual success of the Chinese communists worked to the advantage of Asian communist movements that were willing to make the necessary adaptations to their peculiar national circumstances. However, these movements, such as that in Indochina, were not mimicking the Maoist model. In most instances the Asian movements took shape at the same time as, or even before, the emergence of Maoism. They developed along similar lines because they developed under similar circumstances and in response to similar needs. If they had merely copied Maoism, they would not have been national communist, as they were.

What each of these movements has in common is the shifted

priority of national and class struggle. It is not surprising, therefore, that the strongest manifestations of national communism as national liberation would be in the two Asian nations that were physically divided—Vietnam and Korea. In each of these two cases national unification became synonymous with communist-dominated national liberation. The national development of these systems had been thwarted by an externally imposed division of the nation that had to be overcome before the system could develop. Just as Mao had merged national and social development under communist leadership in China, so these movements integrated national unification and communist revolution.

Similarly, the necessity to forge this unity of purpose among a rural, politically unaware population required a strong personality to lead the party. It is not coincidental that where communist parties have emerged as the focal points of national unity movements, those parties have been dominated by charismatic national leaders. Although the experiences of Vietnam and Korea have differed in a number of crucial respects, both Ho Chi Minh and Kim Il Sung were essential to the mobilization of their populations on the path toward national liberation and social transformation. Nevertheless, the experience of Vietnam since the death of Ho in 1969 demonstrates, just as does that of China since Mao's death in 1976, that national communism is not dependent on the presence of a single figure, no matter how charismatic. The forces that created these movements persisted beyond those who shaped them, and the communist parties have institutionalized that personal power.

Vietnam

There was never any question or debate concerning Ho Chi Minh's national commitment. He began, pursued, and ended his political career as a nationalist. Yet there has also never been any question about Ho's commitment to communism. In fact, unlike many of his national communist counterparts in Asia, such as Roy and Mao, Ho never deviated from the Comintern course laid down by Moscow. This is not to say that Ho was Stalin's puppet or that Ho willingly sacrificed the interests of the Vietnamese national movement for the sake of the international movement. Rather, Ho so completely integrated nationalism and communism that pursuing one to the detriment of the other was never an issue. In this respect it may be argued that Ho captured the essence of the Marxist synthesis of national sentiment and communist revolution. However, it is also true that Ho was among those who, in pursuit of the Eastern strategy, contributed to the reversal of the national and class priorities.

When Ho left French Indochina in 1911 at the age of twenty-one, he was already embittered by the colonial experience of his people. Although he settled first in London and participated in some political action there, Ho was eventually drawn to Paris in 1917, because it became apparent that he could most effectively influence the future of his nation in the capital of its colonial master. Indicating his political mood at the time, Ho (only the last of a series of pseudonyms) adopted the alias Nguyen Ai Quoc—Nguyen (the most common patronymic in his country) the Patriot. Despite an early association with the Young Socialist movement, most of Ho's attention was focused on national problems. His first public acts consisted of attempts to contact President Wilson at Versailles in order to persuade him to apply his Fourteen Points to the people of Indochina.

Ho was active in the French socialist party in the early 1920s, and participated in the formation of the Intercolonial Union. This was a period of decision for Ho, as it was for all socialists. Should he remain a part of the badly damaged Second International or should he associate with Lenin's newly organized Comintern? According to Ho, the turning point came when he read Lenin's *Thesis on the National and Colonial Questions.* "What emotion, enthusiasm, clear-sightedness, and confidence it instilled in me!" Ho remembered in 1960. "I was overjoyed. Though sitting alone in my room, I shouted aloud . . . 'Dear Martyrs, compatriots! This is what we need, this is the path to our liberation.' "[56] Summarizing this period in his development, Ho recalled,

> At first, patriotism, not yet Communism, led me to have confidence in Lenin, in the Third International. Step by step, along the struggle, by studying Marxism-Leninism parallel with participation in practical activities, I gradually came upon the fact that only Socialism and Communism can liberate the oppressed nations and the working people throughout the world from slavery.[57]

Ho the patriot became Ho the communist because he believed that Leninism could liberate his people from French colonialism, but in becoming a communist, he became no less a patriot. Although Ho did not return to Indochina until 1941 to lead the Japanese resistance movement, spending the years between his conversion to Leninism and his return serving as a Comintern representative in China and East Asia, he never lost his primary commitment to Vietnamese national liberation. When he returned to Vietnam his initial political act was to convene a plenum of the Central Committee of the Indochinese Communist Party in order to change the name of the organization to the League for Vietnamese Independence—Vietminh, for short. The Vietminh called upon a "broad National Front uniting not only the workers, the peasants, the petit bourgeois and the bourgeois, but also a number of patriotic landowners" to join together under the banner of *Cuu Quoc* (National Salvation).[58] The stated purpose of the new Vietminh was to unite "all patriots, without distinction of wealth, age, sex, religion or political outlook so that they may work together for the liberation of our people and the salvation of our nation."[59] Although the immediate target of this nationalist outpouring was the Japanese, the long-range goal remained liberation from all foreign control. Even when the Japanese were defeated and Ho installed a provisional government in Hanoi before the French could reestablish themselves, he placed control of the government in the hands of a National Liberation Committee, rather than a communist party. In fact, the formal organization of a Vietnamese Communist Party did not occur until December 1976, after the reunification of the nation. In 1945, Ho's appeal was purely national. One of Ho's biographers, Jean Lecoutre, described Ho's wartime impulses thus:

> Ho revealed his true character as an active believer in the patriotic revolution. For twenty years his nationalist tendencies had been oppressively curbed by the Third International. . . . The man who had been compelled to haul down the banner of the Vietnamese Communist Party . . . , the man who had been pained by the suppression of all references to the Vietnamese nation now deliberately conferred the name *Cuu Quoc* (National Salvation) on the movement. Henceforth the emphasis would be on Vietnam's history, its flag, its culture—and, necessarily on the peasantry rather than the proletariat.[60]

This virulent national strain did not, however, prevent Ho from sacrificing short-term gains for Vietnam to long-term international interests as defined by Moscow. At Geneva in 1954, Ho accepted a compromise settlement with France that divided Vietnam, despite the fact that the Vietminh had defeated the French. He did so because the French premier Mendes-France had staked his leadership on a quick settlement at Geneva, and Moscow wanted to keep Mendes-France in power because he was opposed to admitting Germany to the European Defense Community. In short, Soviet interests in Europe required that Ho accept less than he could have had, and Ho agreed. This concession to Soviet interests was consistent with Ho's earlier conformity to the Comintern line and his later acceptance, in the era of emerging Soviet-American détente, of the USSR's restrained support for the war in the South against the United States.

This pragmatic strain did not make Ho any less a nationalist; rather, it made him an extremely effective national communist. Unlike Tito and Mao, who locked horns with Stalin and his successors over national issues, Ho maintained both national integrity and Soviet support, and his successors appear to have learned this lesson well. Vietnam joined the Soviet-sponsored Comecon in 1978, but has not adopted the Soviet economic model. Further evidence of the continued Vietnamization of the movement is the fact that while the reunification of Vietnam occurred much more quickly than most observers expected, postunification policy in the South has been cautious, reflecting once again Vietnam's hesitance to apply pat ideological formulae to new and unique problems.

Now that unification has been accomplished, social transformation has undoubtedly moved to the top of the Vietnamese policy agenda. The change of the party's name to include the word "communist" is symbolic of the reorientation of the party's goals from national liberation to national development. Ironically, however, there are indications that although this development will conform to Vietnamese conditions and needs, the Hanoi leadership has already begun the process of extending the Vietnamese revolution to the rest of Indochina. Just as Mao moved from the sinification of Marxism to the notion of a Chinese revolutionary model, the Marxism Vietnamized by Ho Chi Minh is becoming, once again, an Indochinese communism. The Vietnamese occupation of Kampuchea (Cambodia) and the overthrow of the Pol Pot regime, which precipitated a Chinese attack against Vietnam, suggest that Hanoi is willing to pay a substantial price in order to establish control over Indochina. The fact that Kampuchea under Pol Pot was also a communist party-state makes it impossible to justify the extension of Vietnamese control on antiimperialist grounds. For reasons of history, national security, and ideology Vietnam wants to unify (or reunify) the entire Indochinese peninsula under its control—proving that the line between national development and national chauvinism is as difficult to establish under communism as in the realm of imperialism. Since the extension of Vietnam's influence will continue to be viewed dimly by China, Hanoi's pragmatic attitude toward Soviet leadership will remain a necessity if not a preference.

Despite Vietnam's denial of Kampuchea's right to develop its own national path, Ho's spirit of national communism persists. As the leader of the party, Le Duan, said in 1976: "Nation and socialism are one. For us Vietnamese, love of country now means love of socialism."[61] Whatever the content of Vietnamese national communism in the future, the guiding principle of its development will remain creativity and adaptability. As one party pronouncement put it, "Each revolution has its creativeness. This is the rule. Without creativeness, a revolution cannot succeed. With dogmatism, a revolution will fail."[62]

Korea

Strictly speaking, there was no communism in Korea until it was introduced under Soviet occupation in 1945. Under the circumstances the Democratic Republic of Korea (DRK) could be expected to be a true Soviet satellite. Yet, even in Korea, totally dependent on Soviet support for its existence, it was not long before the emphasis on national needs emerged as a dominant theme of Korean communism and the DRK began to pursue its own national road. Ironically, the very artificiality of communism in Korea necessitated the national readjustment that has promoted its continued survival.

However, the fact that there was no communism in Korea until 1945 does not mean that there was no Korean communism. The existence of a strong Korean communist movement can be traced back to the time of the Russian Revolution and the subsequent establishment of Comintern. Korean communism was inspired by the same antiimperialist motivations that existed throughout Asia. What was unique about the Korean instance was that the antiforeign sentiment was directed not against a European power or "Western imperialism" but against the Japanese occupation. Anti-Japanese animus, which, as we have seen, was largely responsible for the eventual success of the Maoist forces in China and Ho's efforts in Indochina in the 1930s, inspired Korean communists decades earlier. Although the repressive tactics of the Japanese occupation forces prevented the emergence of a viable communist movement within Korea, Comintern-sponsored Korean communist groups operated openly within the Soviet Union in the areas inhabited by ethnic Korean citizens of the USSR, and in China, particularly in Shanghai. Thus, when the USSR created a communist regime in Korea in 1945 its leadership was not drawn from indigenous guerrilla fighters, but from functionaries of Comintern sections who had spent their entire "revolutionary" careers outside Korea, involved in what can best be described as localized, bandit-like raids on Japanese positions in occupied Manchuria. The Soviet choice to lead the new DRK, Kim Il Sung, was a virtual unknown in Korea and originally the object of some resentment among those anti-Japanese nationalists who objected to the imposition of a "Soviet puppet."[63] Under these circumstances, the transformation of Kim Il Sung into a national communist is remarkable testimony to the absolute necessity for communist movements to become national if they are to survive.

Unlike Mao, Ho, or Tito, Kim was not a leading figure in the development of his national communist party, nor was he a hero of his people's national liberation struggle. In addition, neither Kim nor any other Korean communist developed any original doctrinal variations of Marxism-Leninism during the years of struggle against Japanese occupation. Because it lacked a domestic base and many of its leaders were citizens and residents of the USSR, Korean communism was organizationally and ideologically a creature of Comintern. When Comintern adopted the strategy of supporting national struggle against imperialist domination in the East, as the first stage in its eventual communist transformation and more importantly, as an essential ingredient of the imminent collapse of Western capitalism, Korea proved a perfect example of Lenin's tactic of manipulating the national spirit of colonial people to the advantage of socialist revolution. Bolshevism's attractiveness to the Korean nationalists lay in the willingness of the Russians (later Soviets) to underwrite the Koreans' effort to expel the Japanese from their homeland (an interest the Russians shared, as evidenced by their own efforts to dislodge the Japanese from the mainland of Asia). Hence, the coincidence of Korean and Soviet national interests vis-à-vis Japan facilitated the acceptance of Marxism-Leninism, especially among Soviet Koreans, and guaranteed Comintern a major role in the development of Korean communist policies.

In their definitive analysis of Korean communism, Scalapino and Lee have argued that the policy of a communist-dominated united front of antiimperial groups, with heavy emphasis on the role of the peasantry, originated in the Comintern's strategy for Korea in 1927–28, years before Mao formulated his doctrine.[64] The implication of this assertion is, of course, that it is within Leninism, not Maoism, that one finds the true roots of national communism as national liberation. Aside from the question of historical accuracy (it will be recalled that by 1928 Mao had already analyzed the importance of peasant activities in Hunan, participated in the Autumn Harvest uprising, and moved to establish the Jiangxi Soviet), the fact is that the Comintern strategy elevated, but did not make central, the role of the rural masses, and, more importantly, did not work in Korea. Mao was the first to operationalize the strategy successfully in a rural society, which is undoubtedly why Mao is remembered and the 1928 Comintern theses on Korea are not.

In any event, Korean communism must be understood as a national struggle against Japanese occupation that employed Marxist-Leninist dogma in exchange for Comintern support. There is simply no evidence of communist appeal within Korea or of any significant attachment to communist principles on the part of the Korean revolutionary intelligentsia. Even at the time of the Soviet occupation "the number of individuals affected by communism had not exceeded a few thousand through the years, and even the idea of communism was alien to most of the essentially conservative population."[65]

Ironically, when a communist regime was finally established in Korea it was in the northern, Soviet zone of occupation, which had traditionally been the area least hospitable to radical activity. Seoul, the capital of the South, was the center of radical intellectual activity, but internal divisions in the leftist movement and American influence made the emergence of an indigenous communist movement impossible in Seoul. Korea was, by any standard, an alien environment for the establishment of communism, but North Korea was most inappropriate from a sociocultural perspective and South Korea was eliminated for political reasons. The only remaining vehicle for communist revolution in Korea was the Soviet military.

The price that the communist Korean Workers' Party (KWP) had to pay was strict obedience to the Soviet Union in all matters, domestic or foreign. But, in reality, this was no price at all because in these early, unstable years the KWP had no place else to turn and no goal to pursue in conflict with Soviet interests. Kim Il Sung was loyal to the USSR because it suited his own and his party's interests to be so. Compulsion played a role in the erection of a communist regime in Korea, but not in the relationship between Stalin and Kim. Nevertheless, later developments suggest that Kim's total dependence on the USSR was a source of deep resentment and wounded his personal and national pride. Ultimately, dependence on any foreign power became objectionable to Kim, ideology to the contrary notwithstanding. It was this sense of national pride rather than any disagreement over policy or doctrine that eventually impelled Kim to pursue the Korean road.

Moreover, Kim began to face increased criticism and opposition from within his own party organization over questions of development strategy. The early history of Korean communism was marked by strong disagreements and power struggles between factions based in the USSR and those in China. Comintern eventually subdued this factionalism, but it reemerged when the communist regime was established and the Soviet and Chinese groups were merged into the KWP. Whether this factionalism was issue-based or simply the result of power ploys by rival groups with different backgrounds, Kim viewed it as a threat to his own position and to the security of the party. It was in response to this factionalism, rather than to any pressure from the USSR, that Kim Il Sung launched his national communist campaign at the end of 1955. Essentially, his tactic was to accuse the Soviet and Chinese factions within the party of being disloyal to the interests of the Korean revolution because they borrowed ideas and practices from the two communist powers. "We are not," Kim informed his comrades, "engaged in the revolution of another country, but in our Korean Revolution."[66]

Chuch'e (self-sufficiency) became the guiding principle of Kim's campaign. The new requirement would be to make the interests of Korea the central concern of the KWP and not mechanically copy the experience of any other party. In a key address to the party in December 1955 Kim echoed a theme that has a familiar ring to it.

> To love Korea is to love the Soviet Union and the socialist camp and, likewise, to love the Soviet Union and the socialist camp means loving Korea. . . . He who does not love his own country cannot be loyal to internationalism, and he who is unfaithful to internationalism cannot be faithful to his own country and people. A true patriot is an internationalist and vice versa.[67]

While it is true that the Soviets had by this time recognized the compatibility of patriotism and internationalism, and therefore Kim's declaration was not heretical, it was, nonetheless, remarkable. Kim was not a "closet nationalist" who emerged to show his true colors because Khrushchev had legitimated Tito's actions. Rather, Kim came out of necessity to the realization that nationalism was an effective vehicle for his personal career as well as for the mobilization of the Korean people. Korea as a carbon copy of the Soviet Union was not viable, and the assertion of Korean independence from the Soviet model was just as essential to the continued development of Korean communism as Korean conformity to that model had been to its establishment. In short, the Korean experience establishes once again that national adaptation is an integral and necessary component of communism, regardless of the sources of the revolution. Kimism, in the form of *Chuch'e,* came just as forcefully and, it might be said, inevitably, to Korea with its nonindigenous revolution as did Titoism to Yugoslavia, Maoism to China, and, as we shall see, Castroism to Cuba. National communism is not the byproduct of repressed national revolution; it is a response to the universal necessity to make the revolution, whatever its source, respond to national conditions.

What began as socialist patriotism rapidly developed into full-fledged national communism as Kim perceived the effects of his national campaign on the population. Further, Kim's allegiance to the USSR faded as Khrushchev pursued his new policy of peaceful coexistence with the United States, while the Koreans still perceived the Americans as the principal obstacle to the unification of their country. North Korea's anti-Americanism was shared by China, which also viewed the United States as a direct threat, and this sentiment provided a mutuality of interest that resulted in Korea's aligning with China in the emerging Sino-Soviet split. In other words, North Korea's stance in the Sino-Soviet dispute (it has the privilege of a common border with both) derived from a calculation of Korean national interest rather than from historical debts or ideological principles. Above all else, Korean dependence on the USSR and China through 1953 was interpreted by Kim as a sign of weakness to be eliminated.

Why did national themes so quickly emerge in Korea? First, the Korean revolutionary movement was national in its anti-Japanese origin. It was never possible to distinguish Korean communism from Korean nationalism. Second, the postwar presence of superpowers in both North and South made all Koreans extremely sensitive to their dependence on foreign forces. Third, communism was imposed by Soviet troops on an unenthusiastic population and the regime had to establish its legitimacy with its own people by appealing to national symbols. Fourth, Korea was a divided nation, and if the North were to have any hope of unifying the country under its control, it had to base its appeal on nationalism. Fifth, the continued American presence in the South is constant grist for the antiimperialist propaganda mill, particularly in view of the repressive character of the Seoul government. Finally, there is the presence of the charismatic Kim Il Sung, who has been glorified in his own time more profusely than any other communist leader. Kim is a national leader without equal, and regardless of his background as a minor Comintern agent he has managed, through the manipulation of national symbols, mass rallies, parades, and ceremonial events, not simply to survive but to develop into a recognized national hero. At the same time, Kim is promoted as a master of Marxism-Leninism, and the equal of any leader in the international communist system.

In sum, all of the ingredients necessary to nurture a national communist system were present in Korea. The historical and social factors generated a leader who quickly recognized the importance of national sentiment as a means of mobilizing a population for which Marxist-Leninist doctrine was irrelevant. Kim's explanations of the realtionship between national tradition and socialist revolution were in the classic tradition of all the national communists who preceded him, from Marx onward.

One who does not love one's own country and nation cannot cherish a warm passion for the revolution of one's country and cannot devote oneself to its victory. That is why we Communists love our Fatherland and nation more ardently than anyone else, determinedly fight for national independence and prosperity, treasure national culture and all the fine heritages and traditions of the nation and endeavor to carry forward and develop them.[68]

FROM NATIONAL LIBERATION TO NATIONAL COMMUNISM: CASTROISM

In December 1961, almost three years after he assumed power in Cuba, Fidel Castro publicly declared for the first time, "I am a Marxist-Leninist." Never before had a noncommunist revolutionary nationalist movement converted to communism after it had seized power. Never before had a noncommunist leader taken over a previously established, functioning communist party and made it a part of his own movement. Fidel Castro's conversion to communism was truly unique.

Three explanations of Castro's extraordinary 1961 declaration are possible. First, Castro had always secretly been a Marxist-Leninist and had merely chosen that time to reveal the fact. Second, Castro had not really converted to communism but said he had for pragmatic political reasons. Third, Castro had become a believing Marxist-Leninist between the Cuban revolution in 1959 and his statement at the end of 1961.

In support of the first possibility is Castro's admission that he was exposed to Marxism during his university days in the 1940s and his implication in the 1961 "I am a Marxist-Leninist" speech that he had always been intuitively Marxist although he did not realize it. This statement, in the midst of a rambling, five-hour speech, was incorrectly translated and interpreted by the American press as an admission by Castro that he had always been a communist, but had concealed the fact.[69] The rationale for this explanation is that Castro kept his communist beliefs secret in order to attract a broad cross section of the Cuban people to his own 26th of July Movement. Only when he was firmly entrenched in power did he dare reveal the truth to the Cuban people. The lie could be justified as a strategic necessity in a Latin environment that was hostile to ideology in general, and atheistic Marxism in particular. In other words, Castro was a communist who used a national appeal to mobilize support for revolution. The problem with this view is that there is no evidence to support it. A close reading of Castro's 1961 speech reveals that he was, in fact, apologizing for not having recognized the merits of Marxism-Leninism before the revolution in spite of the fact that he had been exposed to it.[70] Nothing in Castro's prerevolutionary statements suggests any sympathy for communism. In fact, the Cuban communist Popular Socialist Party (PSP) viewed Castro as a bourgeois revolutionary, and relations between the PSP and the 26th of July Movement were generally strained before the revolution.

The second possibility, that Castro never did become a communist, also supposes that Castro lied. Andrés Suarez, who was with Castro in the early years of his regime, has contended that Castro was not a committed Marxist in 1961. Rather, Suarez has argued, after the disastrous Bay of Pigs invasion in April 1961, Castro realized that he needed the support of the Soviet Union to protect his revolution from American attack. However, the Soviets were extremely reluctant to involve themselves openly in the "backyard" of the United States. Only by becoming a member of the communist movement could Castro extract a commitment of support from the USSR of the size and duration necessary to save the Cuban revolution from economic ruin and American interference.[71] Central to Suarez's argument is that Castro did not become a communist in 1961; he simply moved the Cuban revolution into the communist movement in order to protect and extend his own political power.[72]

In further support of this argument it can be added that the generally poor results of Castro's early radical economic policies might have weakened his position and thereby encouraged the PSP, which Castro did not control at that time, to attempt to seize power independently, or at least establish a strong independent position in Cuban politics. Rather than compete with the Cuban communists, Castro may have decided to legitimate his control over them by declaring his personal allegiance to Marxism-Leninism. This explanation implies that Castro was and remained an opportunistic nationalist revolutionary who used communism to his personal political advantage without internalizing its principal tenets. Support for this position lies in the fact that it is generally conceded by those who know him that Castro has never been ideologically motivated. He has always excelled as a revolutionary practitioner, but not as an ideologue. There is also the fact that his "conversion" coincided closely with a critical period in the development of the Cuban revolution (the Bay of Pigs), which casts some suspicion on his motives for making his declaration at that time. Furthermore, the "I am a Marxist-Leninist" speech was not greeted with enthusiasm in either Beijing or Moscow. In fact, it was not until early 1963 that Moscow was willing to publicly concede Havana's entry into the communist bloc. In short, if Castro had indeed become a Marxist-Leninist in December 1961 this would have represented not just a change in beliefs, but a fundamental alteration of his political personality, an alteration that few within Cuba or the world communist movement recognized as sincere and lasting.

The problem with denying that Castro had become a Marxist by late 1961 is that there is a great deal of evidence pointing to significant changes in his movement during the preceding two years. In order to understand this, it is necessary to consider the third explanation: that Castro began his revolutionary career as a noncommunist (not an anticommunist), but was gradually drawn to Marxism-Leninism because it offered a coherent ideological justification for his revolutionary spirit. In Theodore Draper's oft-quoted words: "Castroism is a leader in search of a movement, a movement in search of power, and power in search of an ideology. From its origins to today, it has had the same leader and the same 'road to power,' but it has changed its ideology."[73]

Castro's prerevolutionary political rhetoric and action were consistently non-Marxist. He never employed communist explanations of Cuba's position, although Cuban-American relations could easily have been cited as an example of Lenin's theory of imperialism. "Fidel Castro's anti-Yankeeism," Herbert Matthews has written, "his diatribes against 'Yankee imperialism'—are not the result of his Marxism-Leninism. They come from Cuban nationalism with its complex historic, economic and political background."[74] In the famous "History Will Absolve Me" speech that Castro made in his own defense at his trial for having raided the Moncado Barracks in 1953 (a speech he may have rewritten after the trial itself), Castro set forth every justification for his action, but made no reference to Marxism. In fact, Castro identified Jose Marti, the Cuban national hero, not Marx, as "the intellectual author of the 26th of July action."[75]

Suarez has argued that the only ideological principles evident in Castro's prerevolutionary thought were "the ideas of democracy, nationalism, and social justice" expressed in his 1956 Mexican Program.[76] The earliest date at which an alliance between Castro and the communist PSP can be placed is the summer of 1958, only months before Castro's victory, and that alliance was primarily the result of concessions made by the communists to Castro. The principal issue that divided the PSP and Castro was the strategy of armed revolutionary struggle being pursued by the 26th of July Movement. The position of the PSP, like that of virtually all the established communist parties of Latin America, was that violent revolution was premature and inappropriate in Latin America; thus, Castro was pursuing what was labeled a "putschist" policy contrary to objective economic conditions. Only when it began to appear that Castro was having an impact on the Cuban population and just might succeed in contributing to Batista's overthrow did some elements of the PSP concede that an alliance might be beneficial. But it was the communists' willingness to capitulate to the Castro strategy that served as the basis for the alliance.

In 1959 Castro persistently denied that either he or his movement was communist. "Every people has the right to its own ideology," he said. "The Cuban revolution is as Cuban as our music." Later he asked, "When we say that our revolution is not communist, when we show that our ideals do not belong to Communist doctrine, that the revolution is original, . . . why then is there this determination to accuse our revolution of being something which it is not?"[77] Yet, despite such denials, Castro's radical development strategy, which included widespread nationalization of industry and collectivization of agriculture, appeared to many to be disturbingly similar to Marxist-Leninist practice. What Castro set about doing in 1959 was to enlist the broadest possible participation of the Cuban people in a massive nation-building effort that was premised on a new nonmaterialist work ethic, independence from all foreign control (particularly by the United States), and national glory.[78] The missing element in his attempt to forge this new national ethos was a unifying ideology that could provide a foundation for national development.[79] "Communism," in Draper's words, "gave Castroism an ideology of total power."[80] What is unique about Castroism in Latin America is not the personalistic rule of Castro or his development goals, but the need that Castro apparently felt to justify his movement in ideological terms.[81]

In an interview with Herbert Matthews in October 1963, Castro said, "I gradually moved into a Marxist-Leninist position. I cannot tell you just when; the process was so gradual and so natural."[82] Yet Castro did concede that the transformation could have occurred in the summer of 1960.[83]

More important than *when* Castro became a communist is *why*. Again, Matthews quotes Castro: "It was a gradual process in which the pressure of events forced me to accept Marxism as the answer to what I was seeking. . . . With my ideas and my temperament, even in my school and university days, I could not have been a capitalist, a democrat, a liberal. I always had it in me to be a radical, a revolutionary, a reformer, and through that instinctive preparation, it was easy for me to move into Marxism-Leninism."[84] Matthews, like Suarez, labeled Castro's decision to declare his Marxist commitment "pragmatic," but, unlike Suarez, believed that the transformation was real. The consensus of those closest to Castro, such as Osvaldo Dorticos (Cuba's president), Armando Hart, and Fidel's brother Raul Castro, appears to be that Castro was not ideological before 1961, that his commitment was intellectual, not emotional, and that the change was very gradual, but that Castro is, indeed, a communist despite the peculiar nature of his conversion.[85]

We must conclude, therefore, that although the details surrounding Castro's conversion to Marxism-Leninism have been kept vague and are the subject of continuing debate, the third explanation of Castro's 1961 declaration would appear to be closest to the truth. Fidel Castro was a revolutionary Cuban nationalist without ideological inclinations who converted to Marxism-Leninism during the early years of his regime. The specific factors that entered into what he referred to as the "pressure of events [that] forced me to accept Marxism" included his deep feeling about social justice for the common man, his antiimperialism, his desire to mobilize the Cuban people in their own development effort, his commitment to modernize the Cuban economy as rapidly as possible, his need to justify his own 26th of July Movement ideologically, and the growing need to bring Cuba under the defensive umbrella of the Soviet bloc.

Whether Castro's conversion to communism was the inevitable byproduct of the historical development of the Cuban revolution, as some Marxists have argued, or whether Castro merely exercised one of a number of available options is problematic. What was inevitable, given his nationalist mentality, his nonideological character, and the rather pragmatic considerations that led to his conversion, was that once converted, Castro would be an outspoken national communist. He adopted Marxism-Leninism because of what he believed it could do for the Cuban revolution, rather than for what the Cuban revolution could contribute to the international communist movement. He was determined to maintain the Cuban character of his regime despite his more recently assumed obligations. "Marxism," Castro said in 1965, "is a revolutionary and dialectical doctrine, not a philosophical doctrine. It is a guide for revolutionary action, not a dogma. To try to press Marxism into a type of catechism is anti-Marxist."[86] Castro, like Marx, viewed ideology as something to be used by a revolutionary as a guide to action, not something that imprisoned the revolutionary in universal strategies or, worse, inaction.

Because Castro came to Marxism-Leninism after his own national revolution had been won, he never had to struggle with questions of revolutionary strategy such as the role of the peasant or the bourgeoisie. Revolutionary timing and the status of objective economic conditions supporting revolutionary action were never ideological problems for him. Unlike Lenin, Tito, Mao, Ho, or Kim, all of whom unquestionably dominated their revolutions, Castro never had to contend with the institutionalized power and doctrine of a communist party organization. The Cuban revolution was not a party's revolution, or a liberation front's revolution; it was exclusively Castro's revolution.

The essence of this Castroist revolution turned communist is that it has been unwaveringly Cuban. Herbert Matthews has observed that "there is a Cuban Revolution that has taken a communist form while always remaining Cuban."[87] Castro has said of his movement: "This is true Marxism-Leninism as we see it, but it is not Communism as it is practiced in Russia, Eastern Europe or China. We are working out our own Cuban system, to meet our problems and satisfy our people."[88] Although Matthews has concluded that the movement is not Marxist-Leninist at all, but what he calls *Fidelismo,* Theodore Draper disagrees. "It is just as logical to say that Fidel Castro cannot be a communist because he is a Castroite as to say that Mao Tsetung cannot be a communist because he is a Maoist or that Tito cannot be a communist because he is a Titoist. . . ."[89] "In short," Draper concludes, "Castroism today represents a tendency within the world Communist movement. There is no such thing as Castroism per se. . . ."[90] Whether one agrees with Matthews that Castroism is communism only because Castro says it is,[91] or with Draper that Castroism can be understood only as a communist variant, the fact remains that he is a national communist. "Let each build his Socialism or Communism as he sees fit," said Castro in 1966, "but please let him also respect our right to build our Socialism or Communism as we wish."[92]

Numerous unique features have characterized the Cuban road: Castro's dominance over the party; the fact that he came to communism as an outsider; Cuba's position as the only successful Latin American, Spanish-speaking communist system; the fact that Castro's revolution was neither bourgeois nor peasant-based, but what Draper described as a movement of the déclassé.[93] But the one outstanding feature of Castroism has always been the emphasis that the movement has placed on armed revolutionary struggle as the only road to power.

The question of whether it was possible for change to occur in Latin America or anywhere else in the colonial world without armed revolution was one that eventually divided Castro from many in his own movement, from most of the other Latin American communist parties, and, most importantly, from the Soviet Union. On this issue Castro fell into the ideological trap that had ensnared Lenin, Mao, and Tito: namely, the attempt to generalize from a unique revolutionary experience. The issue was not whether violent revolution in the form of guerrilla warfare was appropriate for Cuba; no one could deny that it had succeeded. Even the PSP eventually conceded that Castro's strategy was correct. The question concerned the implications of the Cuban experience for the rest of Latin America. Castro, and his most revolutionary colleague, the Argentinian Che Guevara, believed that bands of guerrillas could mobilize the rural masses of Latin America and make revolution regardless of economic conditions. Throughout Latin America the long-established communist parties had developed a reputation for patriotism and parliamentarianism that was supported by the Soviet leadership, which did not believe that communist revolution in Latin America was an immediate prospect. Castro changed all that in Cuba, but could Castro's success be repeated elsewhere? Castro's answer, at least until 1968, was yes.

The major elements of this revolutionary strategy can be found in Che Guevara's *Guerrilla Warfare,*[94] Castro's "Second Declaration of Havana" in 1962,[95] and Regis Debray's *Revolution in a Revolution.*[96] They can be reduced to the theory that the people of any nation can be organized to defeat the established power if there exists an "insurrectionary center" (*foco insurrectional*). Objective conditions are irrelevant in this *foco* approach. As Debray explained:

> The Cuban revolution . . . [has] made a decisive contribution to . . . Marxism-Leninism: Under certain conditions, the political process is not distinct from the military; both form one organic whole. This organization is the People's Army, whose nucleus is the guerrilla army. The vanguard party can exist in the form of the guerrilla *foco* itself. The guerrilla is the Party in gestation.[97]

Castro carried this theory a step further when he declared: "Every true revolutionary . . . will always come to Marxism! . . . Many, the immense majority of those who today proudly call themselves Marxists-Leninists, arrived at Marxism-Leninism by way of the revolutionary struggle."[98]

Just as the existentialists argue that "existence precedes essence," so Castro argued that revolutionary action precedes ideology for Third World communists. The fact that Castro literally reversed the relationship between objective and subjective factors set him on a collision course with the established communist movement he had only recently joined. Moscow supported all communist movements in Latin America and recognized that while some revolutions might be violent, others, such as those in Guyana, Uruguay, or Chile, could be unarmed. In any event, the Soviet position required that the revolution be built on a developing base of class consciousness that would proceed in stages from national liberation, to socialist construction, to socialism, and, eventually, to communism. Moscow, and therefore the Latin American communists, dismissed "*focoism* as petty bourgeois use of peasants without making them class conscious."[99] The Soviets recognized the Castro-Guevara strategy for what it was—heroic, romantic revolutionism without an ounce of ideological content. To cite only one of many Soviet statements, *Pravda* argued in November 1968:

> Not a single communist party in Latin America denies the Marxist-Leninist proposition on the armed path of revolutionary struggle. But they do reject the thesis about the possibility of causing a revolution in a country artificially, and describe as a departure from Marxism the effort to regard Latin America as something uniform, without taking into account national peculiarities and specific conditions of each country.[100]

The apparent irony of Moscow lecturing Havana on the virtue of national communism only three months after Soviet troops occupied Czechoslovakia is dispelled if we recall that the Soviets consistently supported the national roads position as long as it did not include counterrevolution, and just as consistently warned against attempts to "export" revolution to alien environments.

As early as 1963 Moscow attempted to put the lid on Castro's revolutionary adventurism and briefly succeeded. Che Guevara's efforts to make communist revolution in Latin America were proving embarrassing to Khrushchev in his relations not only with Washington, but also with the established Latin American communist leadership. In May 1963 Castro was summoned to Moscow and signed a joint statement that read in part:

> The PURS [Castro's United Party of the Socialist Revolution] and the CPSU consider that the question of the peaceful or nonpeaceful road toward socialism in one country or another will be definitely decided

by the struggling people themselves, according to the practical correlation of class forces and the degree of resistance of the exploiting classes to the socialist transformation of society.[101]

The theory expressed in this document that "the working out of the concrete forms and methods of the struggle for socialism in each country is the internal affair of the people of each country"[102] was Khrushchev's not-so-subtle way of telling Castro to get out of Latin American revolution.

Although it was Che Guevara, not Castro, who continued to promote armed struggle (until his death in Bolivia in 1966), it was no secret that Che was acting, if not as Castro's surrogate, then at least with his blessing. Why did Fidel Castro persist in his emphasis on violent revolution even to the point of jeopardizing his Soviet support? Draper has argued that it is a matter of identity for Castro. Without his theory of armed struggle to distinguish him, Castro could not "assert himself as an independent force within Latin American Communism."[103] While it is undoubtedly true that Castro's ego would not permit him to be merely a follower in any movement, this does not explain why Fidelismo required armed revolutionary struggle as opposed to some other ideological variation. In order to understand Castro's commitment to violent revolutionary struggle it is necessary to remember why Castro was originally attracted to communism.

Castro became a communist because he was not satisfied with being merely a nationalist or a revolutionary. As a nationalist he would have had to limit his focus to his own small island. As a revolutionary without an ideology he was limited to action in search of a goal. But as a national communist he could pursue his national goal within a universal framework that gave it transcendent meaning. Established in power, Fidel had to face the revolutionist's problem of transforming the urge to destroy into the discipline to build. Revolution is a virtual necessity of Castro's political soul, and once having won his revolution he required a larger stage on which to play out his romantic drama of struggle against overwhelming odds. First Latin America, and later the entire Third World, provided that larger stage. Armed struggle is not just one of Fidel's strategies, it is his *raison d'être*.

Castro's major failure has been his inability to extricate Cuba from the control of a foreign power. Just as prerevolutionary Cuba was dependent on American capital, so postrevolutionary Cuba is dependent on the USSR. The effect is the same, and the history of Castroism has been one of a series of political concessions to Moscow. The Soviets have not hesitated to use Cuba's increasing indebtedness to the USSR to keep Castro in line. Therefore, although he has never explicitly abandoned the path of armed revolution, Castro has had to contain his revolutionary spirit, particularly since the late 1960s when the failing Cuban economy permitted the Soviets to exert strong economic leverage. Castro's last spurt of radicalism was aborted by the dramatic failure of the 1970 sugar harvest, upon which he virtually staked his reputation as a leader. Since then economic planning and management, party organization, foreign policy, and revolutionary strategy have all been brought into conformity with Soviet policy in return for continued Soviet subsidies to Cuba. This taming of Castro in the 1970s has been described by Raul Castro as "the institutionalization of our revolution."[104]

What this meant, of course, was that no matter how one comes to communism, the limits of national communism are prescribed by the USSR to the extent that one is dependent on the Soviet Union for the survival of one's regime. Those limits coincide with Soviet security interests, which, in the case of Cuba, required discontinuing the promotion of armed revolution in Latin America when the interests of the Socialist bloc were best served by détente, and conformity to the Soviet economic and political model.

Castro became a Marxist-Leninist for pragmatic reasons and remains tied to communism for those same reasons. His choice was purely voluntary. But what would happen if he were suddenly to declare, "I am *not* a Marxist-Leninist"? Does his lack of ideological commitment give Castro the freedom to leave the communist movement behind when it no longer serves his needs, or has the element of choice in the relationship been replaced by compulsion? This would not be a compulsion based on the threat of invasion. The experience of Hungary, Czechoslovakia, and Afghanistan is patently inapplicable for geopolitical reasons. The physical proximity of the United States would protect Cuba from the application of the Brezhnev Doctrine. Rather, it would be a compulsion born of Castro's failure to complete the Cuban revolution. What effect would the withdrawal of Soviet economic and military support have on the Castro regime? Is Castro's voluntary road to socialism a one-way street?

Herbert Matthews, whose respect for Castro is unlimited, believes Castro's options to be likewise unlimited. "The dynamism of the Cuban Revolution and the individualism and nationalism of Fidel Castro may lead to surprising changes," wrote Matthews in 1969. "The man who took the Cuban Revolution into Communism could conceivably take it out one of these days."[105] In a similar vein, Theodore Draper argued in 1965 that Castro "established a mass relationship primarily with his person, not with his ideas, and so could change his ideas without changing the relationship."[106] However, this notion that the essence of the Cuban revolution consists in a mystical relationship between Castro and the Cuban people, which may have been true in the early years, conflicted with the harsh realities of Soviet-Cuban relations in the 1970s.

In 1969 Matthews could write, "The fact that the party has no power, in or by itself, makes it fundamentally different from Communist parties in the Soviet and Chinese blocs, and it is different in construction also."[107] Yet in July 1973 Castro himself proclaimed: "In the uncertain times of the 26th of July and in the early years of the revolution, individuals played a decisive role, a role now carried out by the party. Men die, but the party is immortal."[108] The significance of this statement is difficult to exaggerate. Castro had to concede that he was no longer the revolution, that the communist party, not Fidel Castro, would be the vehicle of Cuba's revolutionary transformation. He was, in short, expendable.

In January 1974 Leonid Brezhnev came to Havana to state publicly what everyone already knew.

> Your society has reached a phase of development in which the inevitable and necessary state of breaking off with the old and searching for new ways marks the gradual transition into the phase of systematic, positive construction. The construction of the party, the state, and the economy is being effected with assurance and on the proven basis of socialism.[109]

The operative term in this statement is "systematic." It means depersonalized or institutionalized leadership. For the phrase "proven basis of socialism" one may substitute "the Soviet model." Castro was to remain the *lider maximo* of the Cuban revolution, but the Communist Party of Cuba (PCC) that the Cubans had been compelled to organize in 1965 began to develop the independent existence that it had never had. Radical, personalistic politics began to give way to regularized government, and Castro was the loser in this zero-sum game of political power.

Fidel Castro's revolutionary nationalism led him to Marxism-Leninism, which, in turn, made him a national communist. But as a national communist he does not have unlimited options. He is bound by the well-established parameters of communist behavior, such as the central role of the party, democratic centralism, and public ownership of the means of production. Castro must be judged as a national communist, not as a romantic visionary unfettered by the limits that restrain mortal men. For better or worse, Castro is a member of the socialist bloc, and the fact that he entered of his own volition does not alter the requirements of membership.

Herein lies the significance of Castroism as national communism. Heretofore, the discussion of national communism as national liberation has focused on the attempts of those in the non-Western world who identified with Marxism-Leninism to establish the relevance of communism in that environment. For Mao, Ho, Kim, and the others, national communism was a manifestation of independence from preconceived ideological notions and stale dogma. To a greater or lesser extent each adapted Marxist-Leninist ideology and created new ideology when necessary. Fidel Castro has contributed virtually nothing to communist doctrine or practice. He did not invent guerrilla warfare, the mass line, or peasant-based revolution. Nor was Castro the first member of the socialist bloc to assert leadership of the nonaligned world (both the Chinese and the Yugoslavs were ahead of Castro in that area). And Castro's influence has not been particularly strong in his native Latin environment. The Chilean revolution failed, the Nicaraguan Sandinists are cordial but independent, and Cuban development has not kept pace with that of many noncommunist Latin American economies. Finally, Castro's obvious dependence on Moscow is seen as a sign of weakness and failure by independence-minded, antiimperialist Latin Americans. For Castro national communism has meant a limitation on independent action, not a liberation from foreign control.

The fact that Fidel Castro is a national communist is symbolic of the failure of the Cuban revolution, whereas in the cases previously considered national communism was a sign of the successful transformation of revolutionary movements into national causes. When Mao and Tito employed the national communist appeal it was to lead their movements out of the Soviet orbit, and in this sense national communism was a positive force for national development. But Fidel Castro took his independent revolution into national communism—a move toward dependence, not liberation.

None of this is to suggest that Fidel Castro is a "puppet" of the Kremlin, or that he cannot exercise a leadership role in the nonaligned world. Cuban support for national movements in Africa and the Pesian Gulf region heightens Castro's image as a leader in the struggle against imperialism. The Cubans are not merely surrogates for Soviet troops who might draw a response in kind from the United States, but they do serve Soviet interests. The Cubans have not undertaken any action in the Third World that has not worked to the advantage of the USSR, but neither have they been compelled to do anything that works to the disadvantage of Cuba. In short, there is a coincidence of interest that both Moscow and Havana are willing to exploit. Although many in the West find it difficult to accept Castro's assertion of nonalignment, Havana has been the site of important meetings of nonaligned states, and Castro is a recognized leader of the non-aligned movement.[110] Finally, Fidel has managed to retain a somewhat mystical personal aura in Cuba and throughout the Third World that contributes to his prestige.

Nevertheless, all of these elements of strength and independence exist in spite of, not because of, Castro's communist connections. National communism does not enhance Castro's prestige. It is a burden that Castro must now bear to ensure his political survival. Fidel Castro and the Cuban revolution are unquestionably communist and they have unquestionably survived. The question that remains unanswered is, What would they have been if the *mariage de convenance* had never occurred?

THE SANDINIST VARIATION

In contrast to Castro's ideology at the time of the Cuban revolution, the Marxist orientation of the Nicaraguan Sandinist movement is unquestioned. However, there remains considerable disagreement among sympathizers and critics alike as to the ideological direction the Sandinists will take in pursuit of their revolution. In large measure, the confusion concerning the Sandinist direction reflects the uncertainty of the movement's leadership as to the optimal revolutionary strategy, an uncertainty that has produced contradictory policies and numerous reversals. In early 1982, over two and a half years after the overthrow of the Somoza regime, the Sandinist model had yet to crystallize into a coherent political program. However, a general pattern has developed that suggests that a Sandinist variation of Marxism is emerging and may have significant impact in Latin America. Whether that variation can rightly be labeled national communism remains to be seen.

To put the events that brought the Sandinists to power in July 1979 into perspective, it is necessary to recall that for decades Nicaragua had been under the dictatorship of the Somoza family. The last in that line, Anastasio Somoza Debayle, was so excessive in his greed and political oppression (particularly after the devastating earthquakes in 1972) that by the late 1970s virtually every element of Nicaraguan society supported his overthrow. Furthermore, the Carter administration, with its emphasis on human rights, withdrew traditional American support for the Somoza dictatorship. When American pressure for reform failed to achieve results, President

Carter began to work for Somoza's resignation. The withdrawal of American backing and the disintegration of domestic support made Somoza's downfall inevitable.

At the center of the active opposition to the Somoza regime was a small, Marxist guerrilla organization, the Sandinist National Liberation Front (FSLN). Organized in 1961, and named after a martyred Nicaraguan nationalist, General Augusto César Sandino, the FSLN remained a minor military group until 1978. But with the oncoming collapse of the Somoza dictatorship, the FSLN's guerrilla activities against the hated National Guard galvanized the anti-Somoza forces into a unified movement.

The Sandinists were avowedly Marxist, but after the death in combat of their founder, Carlos Fonseca Amador, in 1976, they split into three factions or tendencies, each promoting a different revolutionary strategy. Those Sandinists who believed in a rural-based guerrilla approach organized as the Prolonged People's War Tendency. Those who subscribed to an urban-based proletarian revolution formed the Proletarian Tendency. Both these factions foresaw a long-term struggle for power against the middle and upper classes and generally opposed cooperation with bourgeois opposition parties. The third faction *(Terceristas)* took the name Insurrectional Tendency and adopted a strategy of cooperation with all anti-Somoza forces in an all-out military insurrection against the dictatorship. Most Sandinists were Terceristas; hence, when the Somoza regime collapsed, the incoming Sandinist leaders were generally conciliatory toward the non-Marxist opposition parties, the middle class business groups, and the Church, all of which had contributed to the revolution. Although the importance of the three tendencies diminished when the Sandinists assumed power, the divisions continued to be recognized in the organization of the Sandinist leadership. A nine-member ruling directorate was established, and three positions on the directorate were allocated to each faction. In general, the former members of the Prolonged People's War and Proletarian tendencies have been less inclined than the Terceristas to support concessions to middle class interests in the reconstruction effort. The Terceristas have been a moderating force within the FSLN and, as yet, there are no outward signs of significant divisions among the Sandinists.[111]

Although there are obvious similarities between the three FSLN tendencies and the Chinese, Soviet, and Cuban revolutionary strategies, there was no overt identification of these tendencies with foreign communist models. It should be noted that a pro-Soviet communist party, the Socialist Party of Nicaragua (PSN), had existed illegally since 1937, totally separate from the Sandinist Party. In 1967, two anti-Soviet splinters, one Maoist, broke off from the PSN, but neither of these had anything to do with the Sandinist tendencies. In short, the FSLN emerged and developed independently of the established communist organization in Nicaragua.

Surprisingly, even Castroism had only minor influence on the political direction of the FSLN. Castro virtually turned his back on Latin American revolution in the 1970s, concentrating instead on support for revolution in sub-Saharan Africa, specifically Angola and Ethiopia. Although the Sandinists admired Castro's accomplishments in Cuba, Castro apparently considered the Sandinist movement to be a nonsocialist national liberation movement of no particular ideological importance.

Once in power, the Sandinist directorate emphasized national unity and cooperation. Official control of the government was turned over to a Junta of National Reconstruction (note the absence of Marxist identification), two of whose five members were representatives of non-FSLN interests. In a further effort to forge unity, a forty-seven-member advisory Council of State, which included representatives of business organizations, was formed in May 1980. The government itself included ministers from diverse political orientations (but excluded communists). FSLN leaders occupied crucial ministries like Interior, Foreign Affairs, and National Defense, but opposition parties were also allocated government posts and a few members of the government were Catholic priests.

Tomas Borge, the surviving founder of the FSLN and interior minister, characterized the political goals of the new government as "a mixed economy, political pluralism and national unity."[112] The ambiguity of this policy presented the Sandinists with a series of political dilemmas. They wanted to introduce socialist economic forms in an underdeveloped system, shattered by civil war, and at the same time to encourage much-needed private investment, both domestic and foreign. They wanted to ensure the preeminent position of the FSLN in the determination of Nicaragua's political direction, and at the same time to provide for the participation of the political opposition in the policy-making process. They wanted to create mass support for the ideological goals of the FSLN, and at the same time to permit the operation of a free press that could criticize FSLN policies. They wanted to guarantee the power of the FSLN over the junta, and at the same time to provide for free, open elections as soon as possible. They wanted to establish the Marxist orientation of their system, and at the same time to project an image of nonalignment in international relations. And they wanted to establish the revolutionary credentials of the FSLN by aiding other national liberation movements (such as that in El Salvador), and at the same time not to alienate the U.S. government upon whose economic assistance the success of the Nicaraguan experiment depends.

FSLN policy was, and remains, patently and consciously amorphous, ambiguous, and ambivalent. The refusal of the FSLN leader to commit their revolution to a specific ideological formula has been at once the greatest strength and the greatest weakness of Nicaraguan development. Thus far, the FSLN has managed not to alienate permanently its non-Marxist collaborators; yet after two and a half years the regime still lacks political and economic direction. Upper, middle, and lower classes alike are becoming increasingly frustrated by the ideological indeterminacy of the FSLN. Those who had hoped for a rapid transformation of the Nicaraguan socioeconomic system, especially for the poor urban and rural masses, have been disappointed by the lack of success in this area, which they believe is attributable to the concessions that have been made to private business interests. On the other hand, the middle and upper class groups, who also supported Somoza's ouster, remain suspicious of the FSLN's ultimate intentions. While they have, for the most part, remained in Nicaragua, the members of the bourgeoisie have hesitated to invest in the future of Nicaragua because they fear eventual confiscation of their property.

The FSLN has had a difficult time allaying the fears and frustrations of all social classes precisely because its policies have been so confusing and contradictory. In the economic sector the difficulties have centered on the regime's attitude toward private property. Although all the holdings of Somoza and his closest associates were confiscated immediately by the junta, the right to private property has been conditionally guaranteed. "The role of the private sector is guaranteed," declared junta and FSLN directorate member Sergio Ramirez Mercado, but on the condition that it is "within the objectives of the revolution."[113] By virtue of the Somoza property seizure alone the government became a major force in the economy, becoming responsible for 100 percent of tobacco production, 45 percent of sugar, 16 percent of cotton, and 20 percent of coffee.[114] Despite this, at the end of 1981, 60 percent of the total economy and 80 percent of production remained in private hands.[115]

The ambiguity of FSLN policy is reflected in the fact that one of the first official acts of the junta nationalized five private banks, but the owners were compensated with interest-bearing government bonds, and the major foreign banks were permitted to operate with minor restrictions. In addition, the development of minerals, forests, and natural resources was placed under government control, but the foreign-owned oil refinery was not confiscated. Even the land taken from Somoza was not distributed among the peasants; rather, the holdings were kept intact, and in some instances, consolidated into larger cooperative enterprises. One candid official was quoted as saying, "It took them [the peasants] a while to understand that they would be peons of the state rather than of a Somoza supporter, but they're now understanding that what counts is production rather than ownership."[116] It would be understandable under such circumstances if the peasants began to lose their earlier enthusiasm for revolution. They had no land before the revolution, and the prospects for acquiring it under the Sandinists are not bright. The government has tried to assure the middle and upper classes that their investments are safe from state control. Roberto Mayorga, the minister of planning, described his view of the economic role of the state just before the takeover. "I don't mean to suggest state capitalism. We know that experience shows that the state is not always an efficient manager; and we want efficient management. The state should not be administering farms and industries."[117] But who should own the farms and industries? That is the question potential investors want answered. Thus far, the Sandinists have been willing to guarantee the security only of private enterprise that is "fulfilling a social function." But the ambiguity of such policy cannot create a healthy investment climate, which is essential to Nicaragua's recovery.

The ambiguity of FSLN policy carries over into the political arena as well. The FSLN directorate has attempted to walk the narrow line between political pluralism and control of "counterrevolutionary" opposition. The inclusive character of the junta, Council of State, and government membership, along with the promise of elections within a year, were reassuring signs of the FSLN's commitment to democratic politics. But increasing criticism of the FSLN's lack of economic success, in these official bodies and among the general population, was met by nondemocratic responses. Elections were postponed until 1985, and the size of the Council of State was increased to guarantee an FSLN majority. In response the non-FSLN junta members resigned and were replaced by more pliant representatives. One of the former junta members, Alfonso Robelo Callejas, became the leader of the opposition parties and subsequently charged that the Sandinists are seeking to push Nicaragua "toward a Communist totalitarian regime."[118]

In March 1981 the junta was reduced to three members—Ramirez, Ortega Saavedra, and Cordova Rivas (the only non-FSLN member). The FSLN so dominated the Council of State that the more moderate members boycotted its meetings. The major business organization in the Council of State, the Superior Council of Private Enterprise

(COSEP), has been particularly vociferous in its criticism of the FSLN's arbitrary economic policies and its unwillingness to consult with the business community. Although COSEP returned to the Council of State in the middle of 1981 in exchange for assurances of cooperation, its leaders were arrested in late 1981 for criticizing the government's economic policies. Yet in November 1981 the government approved a political parties law that preserves the role of organized political opposition. A similarly ambiguous situation prevails for the opposition press. The opposition newspaper, *La Prensa,* has been permitted to publish uncensored, but its operations were suspended on five occasions through 1981 for publication of material judged unacceptable by the FSLN directorate.

The question that arises from these contradictory economic and political tendencies is whether the Sandinist policy of a mixed economy and political pluralism is the product of a sincere commitment, or whether it derives from the necessity not to alienate critical elements of the Nicaraguan population in a time of economic crisis. Is there a Leninist imperative lurking beneath the surface of the Sandinist system, which breaks through in extreme circumstances, or are the Sandinist lapses into arbitrary, one-party control aberrant excesses in tumultuous times? Perhaps, at the time of this writing in early 1982, part of the answer is that the Sandinist leadership is of a mixed mind on the issue.

Faced with an economy devasted by the anti-Somoza civil war, a foreign debt of $1.6 billion that the junta has pledged to honor, increasing oil import costs, a drop in coffee export earnings, suspension of American aid and credits, and problems generated by a burgeoning bureaucracy, the Sandinist experiment in "political pluralism and the private sector" began to unravel. The Sandinist directorate continues to take a pragmatic approach to reconstruction, but some of the more ideological members appear to be "less interested in maintaining a mixed economy and political pluralism than in promoting revolution from a base of popular power."[119] The pragmatic approach is reflected in the comments of FSLN junta member Ortega: "I think definitions are secondary and even demagogic. Our process is clearly of a socialist nature, but we have to respond to our own reality. When we've found an answer to our problems, we'll see what name we give it."[120] FSLN interior minister Borge has observed, "Even if we were Marxist-Leninists, we'd have to be mad to think that socialism is possible here. Nothing will work unless it is economically and politically pluralistic."[121] "To radicalize," declared one junta official, "would mean to admit the failure of our model."[122]

In view of the Sandinist leaders' commitment not to commit

themselves to any predetermined model of development and to respond to changing national conditions, it is crucial to understand the forces, foreign and domestic, that may shape the revolution's direction. In the foreign sphere, undoubtedly the two most important elements will be first, the relationship between the established communist systems, particularly Cuba and the USSR, and Nicaragua; and second, the response of the United States to Nicaraguan developments. Domestically, the critical forces that shape the revolution will certainly be the economic situation and the relationship that the FSLN develops with other social institutions, especially the Catholic Church.

In its relations with foreign socialist systems, the FSLN has been fiercely independent. "We didn't go through all this," a junta member remarked, "to exchange American domination for Soviet domination."[123] Furthermore, the Sandinists have specifically repudiated both the Soviet and the Cuban development models. Minister of Planning Mayorga, in an obvious reference to Soviet economics, declared, "I do not subscribe to the obsession some developing nations have with heavy industry."[124] As for the "Cubanization" of the Nicaraguan revolution, the Sandinists have been particularly sensitive to charges that they are Cuban puppets. Ramirez has pointed out that "it is natural that any young revolution in Latin America should look toward Cuba, but we are building our own revolution."[125] For his part, Castro has specifically advised the Sandinists not to follow the Cuban example. Describing a conversation that a Sandinist delegation to Havana had with Castro, one member recalled, "He told us to avoid a confrontation with the United States, to maintain good relations with the church, to preserve a private sector and not to impose rationing."[126] When Castro visited Nicaragua on the first anniversary of the revolution, he remarked with uncharacteristic humility: "We have humbly come to learn and be influenced. We are sure that the Sandinist revolution will teach us a great deal, that its example will enormously influence the rest of Latin America."[127] Large numbers of Cuban technicians, teachers, doctors, and military advisors have gone to Nicaragua to assist in the development effort. However, there is no evidence to suggest, in the civilian sector at least, a Cubanization process. In fact, there have been reports of anti-Cuban demonstrations in response to antireligious comments by Cuban teachers. The Soviet Union has maintained an extremely low profile in Nicaragua, and Sandinist delegations to Moscow have yet to produce any substantial Soviet aid commitment. The Soviet Union will not, it seems, underwrite another Marxist revolution in Latin America, especially one specifically determined to remain nonaligned.

Then there is the United States. The Nicaraguan revolution was a national liberation struggle against American control through Somoza. Yet the success of that revolution depends on American economic support. The Sandinists have identified themselves as socialists and Marxists, but they have consistently rejected the "communist" label. They realize that the word "communism" carries with it meanings unacceptable in Washington. Nevertheless, the Reagan administration has classified the Sandinists as communists and has made it clear that it has no intention of aiding a communist movement in Latin America.

The problems between Washington and Managua are not, strictly speaking, ideological. The source of the conflict is the Sandinists' connection with Cuba and their joint military support for the leftist revolution in El Salvador. Although the Sandinists are nonaligned, they have declared their support for national liberation movements everywhere.[128] Moreover, the Salvadoran rebels were major supporters of the FSLN in its anti-Somoza campaign. Now that they are in power, many Sandinists feel morally and ideologically obliged to return that support to the Salvadorans. If Nicaragua commits itself openly and actively to the Salvadoran revolution it not only will destroy any chance of receiving aid from the United States, but may also alienate its more moderate supporters in Latin America, such as Venezuela, Costa Rica, Panama, and even Mexico. Without economic aid from the West it will be necessary to impose widespread rationing, which could easily lead to increased popular frustration and unrest, which, in turn, would necessitate more political repression.

The confrontation with the United States has presented the Sandinists with a clear choice—radicalize or moderate. Radicalization would surely create a mass exodus of the middle class, thus curtailing any chance for a mixed economy. It would also force the Sandinists to rely more heavily on Cuban and Soviet aid, which would carry a political price in independence that the Sandinists may be unwilling to pay. On the other hand, moderation in El Salvador would undermine the Sandinists' revolutionary legitimacy in the eyes of the poor masses of Nicaragua and Central America. Can the Sandinists afford to "sell out" their revolution to American capitalism? Can they afford not to?

Owing to the limited Soviet and Cuban response to Nicaraguan economic needs, prospects for the expansion of the public sector are dim. The only hope for economic revival is renewed private domestic investment. But the uncertain political direction of the country creates an environment hostile to long-term investment. Without specific guarantees from the FSLN that private property and investments will be protected from nationalization, the Nicaraguan economy is doomed. The Nicaraguan economy was on the verge of collapse when the Sandinists took over and has hovered there ever since. Not only has there been no improvement, the situation has seriously deteriorated. In short, if there is any domestic economic imperative for the Sandinists, it is to develop the private sector, and that requires accommodations with the non-Marxist opposition. In recent years, the Sandinists have seen both the Soviets and the Chinese make concessions to the private sectors in their own economies. They have witnessed the Polish economic collapse and, closer to home, they have seen the Cuban system economically and politically mortgaged away to the USSR. Castro has as much as admitted that his experiment with communist economics was a mistake. To embark on the Marxist-Leninist "communist" economic course at this juncture would be tantamount to political suicide in Nicaragua.

In addition, there is the religious factor. The people of Nicaragua are deeply religious, and the conservative hierarchy of the Roman Catholic church has played on popular concern that communism would bring atheism and the end of religion in Nicaragua. This is another reason why the Sandinists must be careful to avoid the communist label. The Church supported Somoza's overthrow, and a number of activist leftist priests have participated as members of the Government of National Reconstruction. In general, the Sandinists have been careful not to offend the religious spirit of the masses. In fact, they have tried to identify their revolution with religion. "They have not only decreed religious freedom," comments one observer, "but also sought to identify their construction of a 'new Nicaragua' with the religious concept of the 'new man.' "[129] In response to a rumor that was circulated by the political opposition in 1981 that the Virgin Mary had appeared and told the people to oppose the Sandinist revolution, interior minister Borge told a crowd, "Christ is here. Those who say He is coming want to justify the counter-revolution. Christ has never left the heart of the Nicaraguan people."[130] And Sandinist supporters among the clergy have been preaching that the rebirth of Nicaragua as a nation is an analogue of the resurrection. In this deeply religious environment, it is out of the question for the Sandinists to radicalize their revolution without losing the sympathy of the vast majority of the Nicaraguan people.

Domestically, there is no support for a Marxist-Leninist regime in Nicaragua. There is no class-based spirit behind the Sandinist movement (as there is, for example, in El Salvador), and those upon whom the FSLN depends most—the middle class and the peasants—are the least likely to be mobilized by an ideological appeal. What justification is there, then, for including the Sandinist model as a national communist variation?

The Sandinist model consists of a mixed economy that allows a major role for private enterprise and investment; political pluralism that permits opposition parties, newspapers, and religious groups, as long as they are not overtly counterrevolutionary; a tolerance of religion in the face of its overwhelming popularity; a nonaligned foreign policy that is also antiimperialist and supportive of national liberation; and an explicit rejection of communist (Leninist) politics. Although the revolution was still developing at the time of this writing, the answer to the question of whether this is national communism is a cautious yes.

The Sandinist variation is the Third World equivalent of Euro-communism. As has been argued throughout this book, the refusal to employ the rhetoric of proletarian internationalism, the repudiation of the Leninst label, and the pragmatic concessions to national conditions are all compatible with national communism. What the Sandinists have done, albeit unconsciously, is to integrate the political pluralism and mixed economy of Eurocommunism with the commitment to national liberation and antiimperialism of the Maoist and Castroist traditions. For those in Latin America who wish to develop their systems along socialist lines, the political facts of life are these: strong middle class traditions; deeply religious populations; dependency on the United States. That is the environment that generated the Sandinist variation. Unquestionably, each nation will have to develop its own forms, but the Nicaraguan model, if it survives its own test, is an important development in national communism. To argue that the Sandinist movement is not communist because it does not claim to be, or because it is not part of any bloc or aligned with any communist power, or because it is pragmatic in its Marxism, is to miss the point that the infinite variety of national conditions is capable of spawning an infinite number of variations. The FSLN is a Marxist national liberation party whose goal is the socioeconomic transformation of its society through mass mobilization. That it recognizes its national realities in the process rather than conforming to rigid ideological prescriptions is, as we have seen, the earmark of all truly national communist movements.

NONCOMMUNIST NATIONAL LIBERATION MOVEMENTS

Thus far, we have considered the many facets of national communism as national liberation in an attempt to understand an important aspect of the transformation of Marxism-Leninism. At this point we can conclude that national communism is a form of national development in the Third World that explains not only how these systems arrived at their exploited conditions, but more importantly how they can extricate themselves. Furthermore, we have seen that while national communism is undoubtedly the dominant mode throughout the socialist world, the implications of national communism are not identical for all systems. What all of these systems do have in common is that each of their leaders would echo Castro's 1961 statement, "I am a Marxist-Leninist." What remains is to consider, by way of contrast, those systems that also qualify as national liberation movements and that are apparently "socialist" but are not national communist—in short, those whose leaders would say, "I am not a Marxist-Leninist." It is necessary to understand such movements as African socialism, Arab socialism, and "guided democracy" not only for their own sake, but because by distinguishing them from national communism, by illustrating what national communism is not, we attain a clearer conception of what national communism is.

Throughout this analysis the terms "Marxism-Leninism" and "communism" have been used synonymously. Whether this is correct is debatable. Some would argue that the Soviets have appropriated (or misappropriated) the word communism to mean Lenin's interpretation of Marxism, but that this is not "true communism." Be that as it may, and whatever it is called, there have always been numerous forms of non-Marxist socialism. As we have seen, in his own lifetime Marx competed with other socialists, rather unsuccessfully, to establish his version as the correct one.

Lenin's variations on Marxist themes often represented significant departures from the originals, but Lenin retained the essential commitment to the elimination of private property, public ownership of the means of production, dialectical materialism, and class warfare that qualified him as a Marxist. While these principles by no means exhaust the tenets of Marxism, they are its most essential elements. The merger of Marxism and Leninism may or may not have been "true communism," but it was undeniably a formula for revolutionary success. Yet there continue to be those who subscribe to principles of social equality, anticapitalism, and antiimperialism but who do not accept the Marxist-Leninist principles of class warfare, atheist materialism, or party dictatorship. They are, however, deeply committed to the principles of national independence and development that characterize national liberation movements.

One is tempted to label these noncommunist national liberation movements "national socialism," but that term has an unfortunate connotation that makes it inappropriate although technically accurate. Therefore, the more awkward "noncommunist national liberation movements" will have to suffice as the rubric for this class of systems.

Given the amorphous nature of the category, it is difficult to select representative cases. There are almost as many types as there are systems and leaders, and even within types the variations can be significant. To simplify the picture somewhat, this analysis will focus on three of the movements that have proved most influential, although not necessarily successful: Arab socialism, African socialism, and Sukarno's guided democracy in Indonesia.

Arab Socialism

In 1961 Anwar Al-Sadat, president of Egypt, wrote:

> The Arabs reject Western ideological concepts like capitalism, not because we hate them but because we believe they do not suit the nature, conditions, hopes, needs and requirements of our people. . . . This does not mean that communism, which proved successful in conditions prevailing in other countries, is suitable for successful application in our country. Our people refuse to be limited to this choice between capitalism and communism and believe that the ideological scope in the world extends further than this closed circle.[131]

In these words addressed to then Premier Khrushchev, Sadat was expressing a long-standing aspiration of the Arab people to establish their own political identity in a world dominated by two conflicting ideologies. That identity has proved extremely elusive, but in the search socialism has been offered as a unifying principle that may serve as the vehicle for Arab modernization. This use of the term socialism is not an attempt to copy the ideas of another culture; rather, the emphasis is on *Arab* socialism, and the term is intended to denote not a variation of Marxism, but an alternative to it. In short, the development of Arab socialism must be understood as part of the larger effort to create a modern Arab identity.

Early Arab nationalism, directed first against Turkish rule and later against European control, was essentially a liberal nationalism borrowed from the West. It emphasized liberal values such as individualism and democracy, which were overlaid on an Arabic-speaking, Islamic culture.[132] The problem was that these Western values were at odds with Arabic tradition, and more importantly, with the Islamic religion. Arab nationalism was also unique in that it sought to unite populations living within distinct political jurisdictions that, at the end of World War II, became separate states. Hence, unlike its Western counterparts, Arab nationalism was transnational in its appeal. The loss of Palestine destroyed traditional Arab nationalism because it was seen as the failure of Arab society to stand up to the West, but at the same time a new form of Arab nationalism emerged to replace it that was based not on liberal Western values, but on those of Arab society. Because Arab society is based on a belief in a "unitary organic community,"[133] socialism appeared to be perfectly consistent with these values. Constantine Zurayk, one of the founders of Arab nationalism, believes that socialism became an integral part of the new, postwar Arab nationalism because traditional Arab nationalism had failed to mobilize the Arab people, owing to its lack of emphasis on social reform, and because the socialist bloc supported the Arab position against Israel.[134] In the effort to create this new Arab identity, Arab socialist ideology went through a unique transformation, becoming socialism based on religion.

Although there had been a number of socialist movements in the Arab world, including the Egyptian Socialist Party of the 1920s and the Syrian Ba'athist Socialist Party, founded in 1946, the mainstream of Arab socialism can be traced to the ideas of Egypt's Gamal Abdel Nasser.

When Nasser came to power in 1952 he had no political theory. His was a military coup that overthrew a corrupt monarchy. To the extent that Nasser had any explicit political goals, they consisted in elimination of foreign control, abolition of the feudal agricultural economy, reduction of government control by private financial interests, legal equality, a strong military, and democratic government.[135] Nasser was a pragmatist, uncontrolled by ideology or social theories. His first act of nationalization, for example, the 1956 expropriation of the Suez Canal, was carried out primarily to create a source of revenue to pay for the Aswan Dam project that Nasser believed was essential to Egypt's eventual economic development. It was not an ideological act.[136]

When Nasser did develop his Arab ideology in the realization that every modernizing regime and movement must have a set of principles to legitimate its actions in the eyes of its followers, his brand of socialism was firmly grounded in Islamic principles easily understood by the poorly educated Egyptian masses. The problem was to prove that socialism, rather than being a Western import, was indigenous to Arab society.

One Arab socialist, Abdel Moghny Said, argues that Islam set forth "for the first time, an economic theory of equal opportunities and fair distribution," because the Quran teaches, "Do not exploit;

be charitable; practice unselfishness."[137] The Arab socialists contend that according to the Quran the right to property exists only if it is not used to exploit others. If one does exploit, then the state has the right to take away one's property (nationalization).[138] Further, the Arab socialists argue, the Quran is the first "scientific" theory of socialism because it recognized "the moral aspect of the 'class struggle' in so far as the exploited masses are on one side and the over-rich, the tyrants, and the arrogant are on the other."[139] In brief, the Quran's concern for social justice made it socialist.

Whether or not the teachings common to most of the world's religions that emphasize charity and brotherhood qualify them as socialist, it is clear that no theory that is explicitly atheistic, as is Marxism, can provide a solid foundation for any Arab society. While it is true that not all Arabs are Moslems and not all Moslems are Arabs, there is an intimate relationship between Islam and Arab social philosophy that is incorporated in Arab socialism. As Nasser said, "Marxism-Leninism does not recognize religion; we acknowledge the existence of God and believe in religion."[140]

A second fundamental difference between Marxism and Arab socialism is the latter's rejection of class as the fundamental category of social existence. Marxism-Leninism is a theory of proletarian revolution, whereas Arab socialism is a theory of people's revolution. Nasser believed that all Arab people had a stake in Arab socialism, regardless of their economic position, and that replacing bourgeois dictatorship with proletarian dictatorship would lead to civil war. Nasser's theory was that the interests of the people could not be represented by a single party, but that the state must act in the interest of all the people. Hence, Nasser's Arab Socialist Union was never a party in the traditional sense. This specific rejection of the "vanguard party" did not necessarily set Nasser apart from Marx, but is was a clear departure from Leninism.

Third, although Nasser rejected capitalism on the grounds that it was immoral and not conducive to rapid economic development, Arab socialism accepted the perpetuation of private property. Nasser once said, "We distinguish between exploiting and non-exploiting private ownership. We are opposed only to the former but encourage the latter."[141] Naturally, foreign ownership and control of Egyptian enterprises is, by definition, exploitative, but private enterprise is an important part of traditional Arab culture that had to be recognized. Not only the shopkeeper and the artisan were entitled to private ownership, but the farmer as well. "Marxism-Leninism," Nasser pointed out, "stipulates the nationalization of agricultural land. Our socialism does not. Rather, it believes in private ownership of agricultural land. . . ."[142]

Moreover, Arab socialism rejects the deterministic view of history and posits instead a positive, active role for human beings in the shaping of history. Arab socialism also combines a recognition of the importance of material economic factors to the development of a society with a belief in the importance of "subjective" moral and spiritual factors. Arab socialism is not antimaterialist, but it is not exclusively "objective."[143]

Finally, Arab socialism is a road with no end. Nasser rejected the idea of a final communist stage, which would have conflicted with the Islamic belief in perfection after death, in favor of a continuing process of social improvement. Socialism is not a stage, it is a permanent way of life.

Arab socialism is patently not communism. Both have been employed as theories of national liberation and development, and both have been adapted to national conditions. Arab socialism is an excellent example of Eisenstadt's theory of selective diffusion. Only those parts of socialism that conformed to the cultural traditions of Arab society were diffused, while others, regardless of how essential they were to communist theory, were rejected. Socialism itself was attractive because it conformed to the Arab tradition of communitarianism and social welfare. But Arab socialism is not national communism because adaption to Arab society required the explicit repudiation of Marxism-Leninism.

Despite this selective diffusion effort to make modern socialist doctrine conform to Islamic principles, Arab socialism has not prospered. Nasserism is a "middle of the road" national development strategy that has satisfied neither the left nor the right in the Arab world and has consequently given way to more radical approaches. Arab socialism has always been anti-Zionist, and modern Arab nationalism was generated by the loss of Palestine to Israel. Consequently, the defeat in the 1967 war with Israel was a serious setback for Arab socialist strategy. Many disaffected leftists and supporters of the Arab Palestinian movement attributed that humiliating defeat to Nasserism's failure to mobilize the Arab people against imperialism in the form of Zionism. Moreover, in part as a result of the failure of the military effort, Egyptian economic development based on Arab socialism's moderate strategy was proceeding much more slowly than many leftists were willing to accept.

As a consequence, a "New Arab Left" emerged in 1967 to challenge Nasserism—a New Left that has openly declared its commitment to Marxism-Leninism.[144] At the heart of this New Arab Left is the

Popular Front for the Liberation of Palestine, but it includes numerous radical organizations throughout the Arab world.[145] These organizations are ideologically undogmatic, their common goal being the establishment of a sovereign Palestinian state. They are true national liberation movements in that sense. Although they are committed neither to the USSR nor to China, they are Marxist-Leninist. The major weakness of the New Arab Left thus far has been its lack of any firm territorial base from which it can assert national autonomy and legitimacy, but this is its ultimate goal.

The inability of Nasserism to mobilize the Arab masses can be attributed to its ideological moderation, but this moderation can, in turn, be attributed to the perceived necessity to conform to Islamic tradition. The more radical New Arab Left has been more successful as a national liberation movement, but it has moved further from its traditional Arabic cultural base. If, or when, a Palestinian state is established, the major political question will be whether the Arab Left will maintain an allegiance to Marxism-Leninism, or whether Palestinian and all Arab national development will proceed along a noncommunist path. The determinant factor will undoubtedly be leadership. While it is true that socialism must be adapted to national conditions, we have seen how a committed Marxist-Leninist political elite can use ideology to transform, by force if necessary, a traditional society into a national communist system.

African Socialism

African socialism, like Arab socialism, is an attempt to adapt and diffuse a set of modernizing goals in a traditional society without wholesale borrowing from an alien culture. African socialism, like Arab socialism, is also inextricably tied to anticolonial nationalism in the postwar era. Finally, African socialism, like Arab socialism, explicitly rejects Marxism-Leninism in favor of a form of democratic socialism said to be suitable for African society.

However, unlike Arab socialism, African socialism lacks the common cultural and religious heritage necessary to provide the moral foundations of the movement. Africa does not have a single culture as does the Arab world, nor does it share a common religion like Islam. Therefore, the task of the African socialists has been to convince the diverse populations of Africa first that they share a common heritage, and second that this common heritage has socialist roots. Lacking a Quran to quote, the African socialists have been forced to rely on vague historical evidence to prove that socialism in Africa antedates Marxism, and that there is no inherent conflict between socialism and Africanism.

The need for a unifying ideology was particularly important in Africa in the postcolonial period because the new states of Africa were, for the most part, artificial entities. When the European powers created their African colonies, lines of sovereignty ignored traditional tribal and ethnic boundaries, and no attempt was made to correct this problem in the era of African independence. Each new African state was simply the colony that preceded it; hence, each African state was the victim of cultural, linguistic, and tribal diversity. It is meaningless to speak in terms of African nationalism in this context, because none of the African states was a nation. Rather, Pan-Africanism became the rallying cry of Africa's elites as they attempted to establish a recognizable African identity and a common interest among their people. The two key principles of Pan-Africanism, with which all Africans could presumably identify and around which they could unite, were communitarianism and *négritude*. In the words of the Tanzanian leader Julius Nyerere: "The African is not communistic, he is communitary in his thinking and in his way of living. He is not a member of a commune, some artificial unit of human beings; he is a member of a genuine community or a brotherhood."[146] And Leopold Senghor of Senegal referred to *négritude* as "the common denominator of all Negro Africans."[147] Senghor, who coined the term "African socialism," posited that Africa shared a common culture that emanated from "blackness" and resulted in a unique Negro *Weltanschauung*.[148]

However, as in the Arab case, African socialism could not be Marxist-Leninist because African society is strongly religious and is not class-oriented. Of course, many Africans are Islamic because of the Arabic influences in the north and on the coasts, but Africa's theism is not characterized by a single religion. Sékou Touré of Guinea once remarked, "Nowhere in any African country, and particulary not in Guinea, will you find a single man or women who does not believe in the existence of God. Even if you find someone who tells you that he is a fetishist, or that he hasn't any religion, nevertheless he is a believer."[149] An exaggeration, no doubt, but Touré's point was that any attractiveness that Marxism-Leninism might have held for the African was substantially diminished by its atheism. The same must be said for the class base of Marxism. African socialists refused to think in terms of classes in Africa because the locus of social identification in Africa has always been primarily the tribe, and secondarily the family. Class, determined by one's relationship to the means of production, has no meaning in the preindustrial African environment. Colonial exploitation was seen as a black-white, not a capitalist-proletarian issue, and after independence the truly divisive cultural cleavages within the new nations were tribal. The legitimacy of political leadership was measured not in economic, but in tribal terms. Senghor referred to the bond of tribalism as a "community of hearts,"[150] and Nyerere described the development of African socialism as the organic development of the family structure. "Modern African Socialism can draw from its traditional heritage the recognition of society as an extension of the basic family unit. . . . Our recognition of the family to which we all belong must be extended yet further—beyond the tribe, the community, the nation or even the continent—to embrace the whole society of mankind."[151] This is hardly the stuff of Marxist class warfare. African socialism recognized the tribe as the most serious obstacle to African unity, but the emphasis was on promoting cooperation among tribes. In other words, progress under African socialism was to be the product of cooperation among all Africans, not of conflict between classes.

African socialism has emphasized the importance of a single party as the vehicle of national development. However, these parties were perceived not as the tools of a single class or tribe, but as inclusive mass parties open to all and representing the interests of all. It is impossible to overemphasize the importance of the single mass party in African socialism, but it is equally important to recognize that not all one-party systems are Marxist-Leninist. Communist parties are elite-oriented, exclusive, highly centralized political organizations that do not permit political opposition. African socialist parties such as the Tanzanian African National Union (TANU) under Nyerere are mass-based, inclusive, decentralized organizations within which opposition is tolerated.[152] African socialists believe that the single-party system is essential because only a single party can represent all the people; developing countries require parties that are national in scope; party politics is divisive; party politics tends to exclude qualified persons from power because of their affiliation; parties control representatives who cannot vote as they wish for fear their party will lose power; parties in Africa exacerbate tribal differences, whereas single parties break down tribal loyalties; opposition parties are often manipulated by foreign imperialist forces; partisan politics retards economic development; and Africans are accustomed to a single source of leadership.[153] In short, the single party system is the best suited to African national development.

Along with the single party, the predominant feature of African socialist organization has been centralized state planning. Nationalization of critical resources and capital has been characteristic of African socialism, although by no means to the exclusion of private enterprise. The more radical experiments in socialist economics, such as that in Tanzania, have generally proved unsuccessful. Capital requirements have necessitated continued dependence on private financing, including foreign investment, which has been accepted as a necessary evil of the African development process. In the 1960s Julius Nyerere's plans for Tanzanian self-sufficiency resulted in the sacrifice of economic growth for economic independence. This is a price most African leaders have been unwilling to pay, and even Nyerere eventually modified his position in the 1970s in order to encourage crucial foreign investment in the Tanzanian economy.[154]

There are, to be sure, significant variations within African socialism, but, to the extent that it is possible to generalize, African socialism is a selective adaptation of non-Marxist socialism to African culture— it is not national communism. In the absence of a unifying cause like the Palestinian problem, more radical alternatives have not fared well in the African climate. The only significant exceptions to the rule that communism is not attractive in Africa have been in South Africa and Angola. In both cases, European imperialism has generated a level of extremism that is absent throughout the remainder of the continent. The deep religious roots of African society, the communitarianism and racialism that are contrary to class-based politics, and the development problems that have forced the recognition of the role of the private sector, all join together to make African socialism a non-Marxist program of national liberation and modernization that is a viable alternative to national communism.

African socialism has been more successful than Arab socialism, but that success has created so much variation that it is no longer possible to discuss African socialism in the singular. Just as the development of Eurocommunism has resulted in national variations within that movement, so the emergence of leaders like Nyerere in Tanzania, Senghor in Senegal, and Touré in Guinea makes it necessary to speak of African socialisms, in the plural. If nothing else, this phenomenon demonstrates that no matter how mythical the concept of a nation may be, only a national movement can survive in the Third World, and ideology always gives way to national considerations.

Indonesia: Guided Democracy and
National Communism

"Sukarnoism" is by no means the last of the variations on non-Marxist national liberation, but it is appropriate to conclude this portion of the analysis of national communism as national liberation with the Indonesian case, because that case illustrates how delicate the balance is among the forces of communism, socialism, and nationalism in the colonial world. Heretofore, this book has emphasized successful national communist liberation movements and the unifying effects of the socialist myth in the context of national development; Indonesia is the other side of the coin. Indonesia is an important example of what can happen when both a communist and a noncommunist movement take up the national banner and attempt to coexist in spite of conflicting social programs. In China, Vietnam, and Korea the communists absorbed the nationalist cause; in Cuba the nationalists absorbed the communist cause; in Indonesia the communists and nationalists attempted to absorb each other, and in so doing destroyed themselves.

Indonesian communism originated as an offshoot of European socialism. It was organized and dominated by Dutch émigrés who promoted revolution in Indonesia because they believed that it would contribute to the revolution in Europe by breaking up the Dutch empire. In conformity with Comintern directives, the Indonesian organization became the Communist Party of Indonesia (PKI) in 1921. As a section of Comintern, the PKI officially adopted the strategy of "united front from above," which required that it cooperate with all nationalist movements. Despite some minor differences between the PKI and Comintern over the former's position against land redistribution and its close association with the Pan-Islamic movement, the PKI was a loyal Comintern member.[155]

After an aborted coup attempt in 1926, the PKI was destroyed and from then until 1945 was forced to operate illegally. During this underground period, the PKI became factionalized. Some members remained Moscow loyalists, while others, such as Tan Malaka, argued that the Kremlin was interested in the Indonesian movement only for what it contributed to the Soviet cause. Malaka's argument that Indonesian communism had to be based upon Indonesian conditions, voiced in the 1920s, established a national communist tradition in the PKI that antedated Maoism and Titoism by decades.[156] However, national communism did not represent the mainstream of PKI policy in the intervening period.

The PKI's greatest mistake was its failure to mobilize anti-Japanese resistance when Indonesia was invaded and occupied. Anti-Japanese nationalism was essential to the mobilization efforts of most Asian communist movements, and the PKI's failure to avail itself of the opportunity meant that when the Japanese were defeated, and the PKI was legally reestablished in 1945, it had to take a back seat to the nationalist movement led by Sukarno that had been at the forefront of the national liberation movement. Under its new leader

Dipa Nasuntara Aidit, the PKI joined in a national united front with Sukarno in 1952, and at the same time Aidit began to establish the independence of the PKI from Stalin's monolithic movement. From 1952 onward, the PKI was a national communist organization, and that transformation accounted for a remarkable increase in the size and popularity of the Indonesian party.

Given the overwhelming popularity of the nationalist Sukarno, however, the PKI was forced to support his leadership and moderate its class-oriented position. National unity was the dominant theme of Sukarnoism, and the communists adopted that theme as their own. The PKI's dilemma was that in order to become accepted and increase its power it had to become a national party, but the more national it became the more it lost its identity as a revolutionary movement. The national position had been preempted by Sukarno, but there was no place else for the PKI to go. A radicalization of PKI policy would have isolated the party from the mainstream of public opinion and from Sukarno himself. Sukarno was willing to tolerate a strong communist party as long as it supported his leadership, and that support was very important during the early years of his regime.

For his part, Sukarno expressed a personal preference for non-capitalist economics, antiimperialism, and authoritarianism that eventually was formalized under the rubric of "guided democracy." Guided democracy was formally initiated on 28 October 1956, when Sukarno publicly declared that the earlier decision to permit political parties to operate freely had been a "big mistake," and he intended to eliminate these parties because they were destructive of national unity. Sukarno's plan for guided democracy called for the replacement of parliamentary, party-based politics with a nonpartisan cabinet led by Sukarno and a National Advisory Council that represented key interests in society. By the summer of 1960, when the transition to guided democracy was essentially complete, it was clear that guided democracy was a collection of vague principles that justified Sukarno's personal control over Indonesia. Guided democracy was Sukarnoism.[157]

Sukarno's position was that liberal democracy was inconsistent with the Islamic tradition of Indonesia. Instead, he called for "democracy with leadership," which "does not mean majorocracy. . . ."[158] Sukarno distinguished this new form of democracy, which he referred to as "sociodemocracy," from communist people's democracy on the ground that communism did not guarantee freedom of speech as it pursued freedom from want, but everyone was free to speak under guided democracy.[159] On the other hand, that freedom was not absolute and did not extend to the right to organize opposition. Sukarno left no doubt that in this guided democracy he, as president–supreme commander, was the guide.

The underlying national appeal of guided democracy was very strong. Sukarno argued, correctly, that Indonesians did not identify with liberal parliamentary democracy. What they preferred was social welfare and strong leadership. "Guided democracy," he said, "is a democracy which harmonizes with the personality and the outlook of the Indonesian nation."[160] According to Sukarno the essence of the Indonesian nation was *gotong rojong* (mutual assistance).[161] Although President Sukarno couched *gotong rojong* in terms of the unity of Moslems, nationalists, and communists—the merger of Islam, nationalism, and Marxism into a national ideology—it was clear that what he meant was obedience to the principles of Sukarnoism. Loyalty to Indonesia had become synonymous with loyalty to Sukarno.

The socialist element of Sukarnoism remained vague. He declared himself a socialist, but his definition of socialism was that it "is an effort to achieve happiness for all men . . . justice among men, no exploitation of man by man and all equally happy."[162] "There is," he noted, "religious socialism, there is utopian socialism, there is nihilistic socialism, there is scientific socialism. There is communism. All that falls under the term 'socialism'."[163] Therefore, he included as socialists not only Marx and Lenin, but Fourier, Jaurès, Bakunin, and Mao. Sukarno was not specific as to how socialism would come about, except that he did not believe that it was inevitable. "Socialism," he warned, "cannot fall from heaven like dew during the night."[164] Instead, the state, as the guide under his leadership, would be "the instrument to carry out socialism."[165] Sukarno distinguished between the state's right to guide the economy and the right to control it. Planning and direction were essential, but Sukarno had no wish to establish a state-owned command economy. While the state might limit the use and size of property holdings for the benefit of the nation, property rights remained sacrosanct. Sukarno's major economic effort was in land redistribution, whereby he hoped to give all the people a direct interest in the fate of the Indonesian system. But he specifically rejected collectivization of agriculture as antithetical to the Indonesian culture.

In the final analysis, guided democracy was a socialist program that supported Sukarno's rule in terms of what the Indonesians call *marhaenism*—a combination of populism and socialism. Guided democracy provided Sukarno with his own ideological system in the face of the ever increasing popularity of the PKI. Increasingly, however, the question for both Sukarno and Aidit was this: If Sukarno was indeed a nationalist, revolutionary, antiimperialist socialist and if the PKI was indeed national communist, why did Indonesia need both?

Sukarno was the first to raise this issue of ideological redundancy, at the end of 1961. He equated Marxism with *marhaenism* (*marhaen* means poor man), and suggested that since PKI ideology was communism of the Indonesian variety, and since *marhaenism* is Indonesian Marxism with which he could identify, then he, Sukarno, was really the leader of Indonesian communism.[166] In view of Sukarno's unchallengeable political position, Aidit was willing to accept this interpretation, especially as it seemed to suggest a larger role for the PKI in the Sukarno regime.

Therefore, by the early 1960s a mutual dependence had developed between the nationally oriented communist party and the Marxist-oriented nationalist leader. The PKI had adopted a gradualist strategy that involved following Sukarno on all issues in the hope of continuously increasing its power until, one day, it could assume leadership of Indonesia. Sukarno's willingness to recognize Aidit's legitimacy undoubtedly encouraged the PKI dream. As Sukarno became more militantly antiimperialist, he become more isolated from the USSR and the more moderate Afro-Asian bloc. Inevitably, Sukarno moved closer to Mao, with whom he shared an unalterable opposition to East-West rapprochement. In its attempt to stay with Sukarnoism, the PKI even went so far as to shift its allegiance to China in the emergent Sino-Soviet rift, thereby guaranteeing itself a larger role in Indonesian foreign policy making. By 1965, Sukarno and Aidit were in so close a partnership that it was evident to everyone that it would be only a matter of months before the PKI had a full share of power. The completion of the merger between national communism and guided democracy would have given Sukarno the added strength of an organized political party at his disposal (something he had never managed to develop on his own), and would have given the PKI the strength of Sukarno's charismatic personality to bring it to full power.

The end, when it came, was sudden. What appeared to be an unbeatable combination of Sukarnoism and communism collapsed on 1 October 1965. While there is no consensus on how or why this happened, it appears that the military, which had become very strong under Sukarno, was very concerned over the radicalization of Sukarno and the prospect of PKI leadership. Some have suggested that in the wake of reports that Sukarno had become seriously if not fatally ill, Aidit became impatient and decided to eliminate the military obstacle to PKI control by assassinating the general staff. On the other hand, others have noted that Aidit's gradualist strategy was working and there was no reason for him to carry out a coup against an ailing Sukarno or move against the military leadership at that point.

Whatever the explanation, the attempted coup and the assassination of six generals in the early morning hours of 1 October 1965 resulted in swift retribution against the PKI from the military under General Suharto. Rumors that China had supported the coup resulted in retaliation against the sizable Chinese population of Indonesia as well. Communists were arrested and killed and party organizations were forcibly disbanded throughout the country. Aidit was executed, the PKI destroyed. Whether or not Sukarno would have become an open communist, his association with Aidit lost him the support of the military, and with Sukarno's position in question the PKI became totally vulnerable.

Sukarno's own role in the affair remains a mystery. Although he denied complicity in the assassination of the military leaders, he continued to support the communists through early 1966. In view of the fact that the new military leadership laid the blame for the coup on the PKI, General Suharto relieved President Sukarno of all power on 12 March 1967, criticizing him for having supported the PKI but stopping short of accusing him of complicity in the assassination plot.[167]

The significance of these events for this analysis of national communism has little to do with Sukarno's involvement or the reasons for the coup. Rather, the Indonesian case teaches that although communism must be national to be successful, the nationalization of communism does not inevitably lead to success. And, while the line between national communist and non-Marxist socialist national liberation movements is not always distinct, the difference may be crucial. While socialist nationalism may be acceptable because of its national appeal, national communism may not be in spite of its national appeal. In Cuba, Castro made the successful transition to national communism from revolutionary nationalism; in Indonesia Sukarno failed to make that same transition. In both instances it is clear that communism could not have survived without being nationalized. Castroism is now a form of national communism, but Sukarnoism is dead because the delicate balance between national and communist impulses could not be maintained in the Indonesian political culture.

CONCLUSION

Third World socialist movements, Marxist or not, are national movements. Third World national movements are socialist movements, Marxist or not. These identities have been established beyond doubt. The inspiration of national communism as national liberation is antiimperialism. Every national communist movement in the colonial world has embraced the goal of eliminating foreign economic and political intervention. The ideological foundation for revolutionary movements in the Third World is the marriage of radical economic transformation with the universal mobilizing myth of antiimperialism.

Antiimperialism is a myth not because it is based on false premises, but because it has taken on symbolic meaning that transcends the facts. The West, or more recently the North (particularly the United States), is imperialist by definition, not by deed. This is not to say that Western capitalist nations have not engaged in exploitative behavior in the Third World, but that regardless of what the West does it will be labeled imperialist because revolutionary nationalists, communist or not, need imperialism. In fact, as the Chinese appraisal of the USSR and the Vietnamese view of China illustrate, it is no longer necessary to be capitalist in order to be accused of imperialism. An imperialist is simply the national enemy of a national liberation movement. Antiimperialism is, therefore, inspired by nationalism, not Marxist-Leninist ideology. Antiforeignism, not anticapitalism, is the true source of antiimperialism, and national communism is one form of that antiimperialism in the Third World.

The emergence of national communism as national liberation was, as has been argued here, not the result of the evolution of Leninism in a colonial environment. To use the Darwinian analogy, although apes and humans are closely related, apes do not give birth to humans in some environments and apes in others. Apes and humans are distinct evolutionary tracks with a common source. Leninism and Maoism are "biologically" related by their common source in Marxism, but Leninism did not give birth to Maoism. Indeed, Leninism and Maoism are forms of national communism, but all communism has been national communism, from Marx to the present. Western and Third World national conditions differ markedly, and each environment has produced its own national communist variant.

The indigenization of communism is patently a matter of survival. Nationalization nurtures communism; it does not destroy communism. The view that the nationalization of communism manifests the weakness of Marxism-Leninism and the decline of communism is predicated on the false premise that nationalism and internationalism are incompatible principles.[168] National and communist goals are not, and never have been, mutually exclusive. It makes as little sense to argue that Maoism and Castroism are not "real" communism because they are national movements as to argue that Marxism and Leninism are not "real" communism because they were adapted to specific national situations. Even in the case of the Nicaraguan Sandinist movement, where national conditions have, thus far, necessitated the very renunciation of the "communist" label, the essential merger of Marxist socioeconomic revolution and antiimperialism has occurred. The position that national liberation movements cannot be truly communist, in the Marxist-Leninist sense, is Europocentric at best and intellectually dishonest at worst. Certainly, not all national liberation movements are national communist, but national communism as national liberation is a distinct, legitimate, noncontradictory, and consistent category of Marxism.

SUGGESTIONS FOR FURTHER READING

Aguilar, Luis, ed. *Marxism in Latin America.* rev. ed. Philadelphia: Temple University Press, 1978.

Dominguez, Jorge. *Cuba: Order and Revolution.* Cambridge: The Belknap Press of the Harvard University Press, 1978.

Draper, Theodore. *Castroism: Theory and Practice.* New York: Praeger Publishers, 1965.

Eisenstadt, S. N., and Azmon, Yael, eds. *Socialism and Tradition.* Jerusalem: Van Leer Jerusalem Foundation, 1975.

Johnson, Chalmers. *Peasant Nationalism and Communist Power: The Emergence of Revolutionary China, 1937–1945.* Stanford: Stanford University Press, 1962.

Lacoutre, Jean. *Ho Chi Minh: A Political Biography.* New York: Vintage Books, 1968.

Matthews, Herbert. *Fidel Castro.* New York: Simon and Schuster, 1969.

Ottaway, David and Marina. *Afrocommunism.* New York: Africana Publishing Company, 1981.

Palmier, Leslie. *Communists in Indonesia: Power Pursued in Vain.* New York: Anchor Books, 1972.

Pike, Douglas. *History of Vietnamese Communism, 1925–1976.* Stanford: Hoover Institution Press, 1978.

Said, Abdel. *Arab Socialism.* New York: Harper and Row Publishers, Inc., 1972.

Scalapino, Robert, and Lee, Chong-Sik. *Communism in Korea.* Berkeley: University of California Press, 1972.

Schram, Stuart. *The Political Thought of Mao Tse-Tung.* rev. ed. New York: Praeger Publishers, 1969.

Townsend, James. *Politics in China.* 2nd ed. Boston: Little, Brown and Company, 1980.

6
Prospects for
National Communism

Communism is and always has been national communism. Every international communist organization from the Communist League to Comecon has been characterized by national differences. Every communist party has formulated policies and practices in conformity with national conditions. But to contend that all communism is national implies that there is an elemental meaning to the term "communism" that is subject to national variation. The problem has always been to establish the content of communism *in abstracto,* without reference to the interpretation of a particular communist party.

At the very least, communism is a system of self- and other identification. A communist is someone or some institution that labels itself communist and is so labeled by others. The very fact that some people choose to identify themselves as Marxist-Leninist suggests that there is at least a perceived set of Marxist-Leninist characteristics to which they wish to conform. That these communist characteristics may not in fact exist cannot abrogate the belief that they do, and that belief alone is enough to establish a self-fulfilling identity of interest among those identified as Marxist-Leninists. However, as has been the case in Nicaragua, there may be political reasons why a movement that is communist may not wish to label itself as such. Therefore, it is necessary to go beyond self- and other identification and look at the actual behavior of recognized communist movements.

Decades of practice have established certain tenets of Marxism-Leninism that are not immutable but are commonly accepted. Among these are the existence of a single ruling vanguard party that identifies itself as Marxist-Leninist and that does not permit political competition from noncommunist parties; the rejection of private property—defined as property used to exploit labor—as a principle of economic organization (communist systems may make pragmatic concessions to property rights, but they reject private property in theory); a dialectical view of historical development that is premised on class warfare; an antiindividualist social philosophy; and antiimperialism as the cornerstone of foreign policy. No one of these characteristics alone defines communism, but taken together they constitute a syndrome of Marxist-Leninist behavior. Emphasis on these elements varies from movement to movement. For example, Sandinists are more pluralist than Maoists, and the Poles have made greater concessions to private property than the Soviets. However, one cannot conclude on the basis of the variations that one system is more or less communist than another. A system must accept these principles to be communist, but it must be reemphasized that these characteristics are not components of a universal a priori ideology but the distillation of practice that has become principle.

National variation on these themes is neither aberration nor heresy. National communism is the norm of Marxism-Leninism. The perversion of communism results not from the nationalization of ideology and practice, but from the proclivity of some national communists to attempt to universalize their national models. Stalin, Mao, and Castro each adapted Marxism to national conditions, and in so doing practiced national communism. But then each attempted to transform his national variation into a communist model, and in so doing practiced communist national chauvinism. Hence, the struggle among communists is not among national communist ideologies, but between communist systems that attempt to use communism to increase their national influence and those that seek merely to maintain their national autonomy. The single unalterable characteristic of national communism is that it is national and, therefore, not exportable.

The ability of a communist party to universalize its experience has been a function of the power of the nation it rules and the determination of its leaders to impose their will on others. Unquestionably, the Soviet party under Stalin has thus far been the most able and determined communist party, and thus the most successful at transplanting its model into alien soil. Stalin, in other words, came closest to creating a monolithic communist system based on the principles of Marxism-Leninism as they developed under Soviet conditions. The ability of a national communist party to resist the imposition of doctrine or practice by a more powerful, chauvinist party is a function of numerous factors, including the degree of domestic support enjoyed by the national communist party, which is, in turn, dependent on such factors as the party's role in the national independence struggle and its willingess to include other national forces in the development process; support from foreign sources, communist and capitalist alike; and the importance of the particular nation in the USSR's calculation of its security interest. The limits of national communism have been in constant flux, varying from time to time and place to place. No particular variation is unacceptable per se. Its acceptability depends on which nation practices it, which nations support it, how threatening the Soviets perceive it to be, and what the Soviets are able to do about it.

The limits of national communism will undoubtedly be broader in the 1980s and beyond than they were in Stalin's time, or even in Brezhnev's, because a strong Soviet Union will be a more tolerant one and national communism is more pervasive than ever. But, as long as power differentials exist among communist states and national interests vary, attempts to maintain a unified movement based on a set of principles derived from one nation's needs will persist. Although the post-Stalin Soviet leadership has never denied the right of a Marxist-Leninist party to develop its own national variations (short of counterrevolution), neither has the USSR denied itself the right to attempt to influence the direction of those variations. In short, both the tendency to nationalize and the countertendency to universalize will persist and conflict for the foreseeable future. What, we must speculate, are the ramifications of this fact?

First, we must understand that national communism does not signal the decline and fall of Marxism-Leninism. On the contrary, the persistence of national variation is a sign of the continued dynamism and vitality of communism. Only those who erroneously believe that communism is supposed to be a monolithic, cosmopolitan ideology transcending all national distinctions will interpret national communist trends as indications of the ebb of communism. The root of this error is the tendency in the West to equate Soviet communism with communism in general. Those who are heartened by China's challenge to Soviet hegemony, who exalt in the disintegration of the East European bloc, and who support every assertion of independence from Soviet control, regardless of how repressive the national communist regime may be, do so in the belief that each of these developments represents a setback for communism. Generally, those in the West who encourage and support national communism do so not because they believe that all communists should have equal rights, but because they believe that national communism is a prelude to anticommunism. They hold that if Romania, for example, can be weaned from its dependence on the USSR by offers of Western consumer goods and technology, it will be free to assert its national programs, the Soviet Union will lose an ally, and the communist bloc will eventually lose a member. In other words, national communism is the first stage of counterrevolution.

The idea that when a communist nation reduces Soviet control it becomes in the process less communist is predicated on the false assumption that no nation in the Soviet bloc would pursue a Marxist-Leninist path unless it were forced to do so. While no one can say for certain whether Poland or Czechoslovakia would conform to the Soviet model if the USSR were not there to ensure it, the point is moot because the USSR is an inescapable, permanent political fact. But there are numerous nations that are communist as a matter of choice, not coercion, and that have prospered as national communist states. And even those systems where communism was originally imposed but where Soviet influence has been minimized have shown no inclination to depart from the Marxist path. Vigorous national movements within the communist world may pose a challenge to Soviet power, but they promote the development of communism nevertheless. While Soviet power is communist power, communist power is not always Soviet power.

Second, we have seen that national roads are not contrary to post-Stalin Soviet policy, as long as they do not become roads out of the communist world. The fact that a communist nation rejects the Soviet model may not make those in the Kremlin happy, but it is not necessarily a defeat for the USSR. The Soviet leadership has established a "firebreak," between legitimate national variations and counterrevolution within its own alliance system, that cannot be crossed without activating the Brezhnev Doctrine. However, even within the Soviet bloc the Marxist-Leninist parameters of party control and adherence to military alliance are quite broad. Beyond the Soviet security network there are virtually no limits on national communism. The Brezhnev Doctrine has not been applied to Albania, China, Yugoslavia, Kampuchea, or Cuba, all of which have departed from the Soviet model, because Moscow has no wish to revive the rigid conformity of Comintern or Cominform. From the Kremlin's point of view, what other communist systems do in pursuit of national development is their business, as long as it does not threaten Soviet security, which is not synonymous with a Soviet hegemony over *all* Marxist states.

Rather than condemn another system's interpretation of Marxism-Leninism and assert the superiority of one's own version, the tendency in recent years has been to argue that one's antagonists are not communists at all. The Sino-Soviet rift, for example, began as a conflict between two exponents of Marxism-Leninism, but each party has now taken the position that the other is no longer communist. Brezhnev has gone so far as to offer to normalize relations with China on the basis of the principles of "peaceful coexistence," which as every Marxist-Leninist knows are the principles that guide the state-to-state relations of the USSR and capitalist-imperialist nations. For its part, the Chinese leadership has issued calls to the Soviet proletariat to rise up and overthrow the Soviet "revisionist renegade clique." The effect of all this is to render the conflict truly national.

Third, the myth that national communism is synonymous with liberalism must be discarded. Because postwar national communism has generally been anti-Soviet and because the Soviet Union is generally identified as a repressive, dictatorial, totalitarian regime, national communism has been equated with political and economic reform, democratization, and freedom, However, as we have seen, communism of all types, including Soviet communism, has always been national, and China, Vietnam, Kampuchea, Korea, and Romania are not liberal in comparison to the USSR. If the Soviet Union is made the standard of Marxism-Leninism, then some communist systems will be more liberal and others less so. But at this point it should be clear that there is no such standard, and all that can be said is that, owing to different national traditions and current conditions, some communist systems are more liberal than others. In any case, the level of national sentiment expressed by a communist state is not an indicator of its liberalism. Why should we identify nationalism as liberalism when a communist state refuses to conform to Soviet policy but not when a noncommunist state such as France or Israel refuses to conform to American policy? Anti-Soviet behavior in the name of national communism is no more or less liberal than anti-American behavior in the name of national liberation or national sovereignty. It is the content of a policy, not its target, that makes it liberal. Throughout this analysis it has been evident that national conflicts among communists have usually originated not over the content of a particular policy, but over who had the right to make that policy. Some controversial policies, like the Czech Action Program of 1968, were unquestionably liberal, but others, like Romanian resistance to Comecon integration, are not. Disagreements over policy content are secondary to questions of national integrity, which constitute the essence of national communism.

The prospect for liberalism as a strain of national communism is that dual trends will persist. In those systems where some level of democracy has been part of the national tradition, such as Poland, Czechoslovakia, and Hungary, liberalization will remain an element of national communism. Reforms such as independent labor movements, a freer press, increased political participation by noncommunist groups, freedom to travel, and even competitive elections will be on the agendas of these East European national communists. But it is these very same systems that constitute the heart of the Soviet defensive network in Europe. Therefore, liberalization will continue to be perceived as a potential threat to Soviet interests and the prospects for liberalization in this region will remain marginal.

In the Third World, where liberal democratic traditions are weak or nonexistent, national communists are unlikely to exhibit liberal tendencies. Experiments with "democracy walls" in Beijing by the post-Mao leadership were quickly abandoned and were probably intended more to impress Western audiences than to change Chinese political practice. No evidence of liberalism has yet emerged in Indochina or Korea. The political character of a national communist regime reflects the national political culture in which it is embedded, and the selective diffusion of Marxism-Leninism in traditionally authoritarian societies will invariably favor the nondemocratic elements of the Marxist tradition.

Since the regions where communism is most likely to be attractive are those that are least likely to have had a liberal democratic tradition, and those regions where liberalism is most likely to be attractive are those where the Soviet Union is least likely to permit it, the prospects for liberal national communism are dim.

In summary, national communism is not communism in decline; it is not Soviet power in decline; it is not the liberalization of communism. Most importantly, it is not a change in the nature of communism, but a continuation of communism's traditional pattern. However, the fact that national communism has always existed does not mean that its character will not change. Throughout this study two persistent patterns have emerged: (1) communist systems have, with rare exceptions, been established in conditions created by the upheaval of world war in a contiguous geographical zone; and (2) communist regimes have generally coalesced around the personality of a charismatic leader. These patterns are likely to change, and as they do, communism will become increasingly more national in character.

With regard to the first pattern, the relationship between communism and world war in a contiguous zone, it is unlikely that communism can expand in the same way in a nuclear age. If there is another world war, the prospects for mobilizing against an invading foreign power, filling a political vacuum left by a defeated occupation force, or overthrowing a regime bankrupted by extended war efforts will be very limited. Similarly, the continued contiguous spread of communism has inherent limits. Except for Cuba (and Nicaragua, if it is indeed communist), all communist states border on other communist states, and the Soviet Union has been the geographical if not the ideological heart of the communist zone. Future communist expansion, particularly in Europe, the Middle East, the Pacific region, and Latin America, may be perceived as a direct threat to vital Western security interests—a perception that will make the potential costs of communist revolution much higher than in the past. Cuba, the only self-identified communist system established in the absence of world war and outside the communist zone, may be the pattern for the future, or the exception that proves the rule. More than two decades have passed since the Cuban revolution, and the only subsequent deviation from the traditional pattern, Nicaragua, has, thus far, persistently refused to label itself communist. All of this is not to say that there will never be another communist revolution, but it does appear that the conditions under which communism has traditionally prospered have substantially changed.

Because the prospects of being swept into power by world war or external forces are exceedingly small, future communist revolutions will have to be even more national than before. But national revolutionary leaders in the Third World are increasingly recognizing the disadvantages of becoming embroiled in intrabloc and interbloc conflicts, and the advantages of nonalignment. In other words, while communists must be national to suceed, nationalists do not have to be communists. In fact, as the Sandinist case illustrates, the communist label is becoming a liability for national liberationists. In an era when Vietnam invades Kampuchea, China invades Vietnam, and the Soviet Union invades Afghanistan, antiimperialism has taken on an entirely new meaning in the Third World that transcends ideology. On balance, the prospects for communism are dramatically reduced in an era when world war must be discounted, the ability to export revolution is constrained, and communist states are regularly invading other communist states.

With regard to the second phenomenon, the relationship between personalistic leadership and communism, significant changes have already begun and are likely to continue. Successful national communism has traditionally depended upon personalistic, if not charismatic, rule, because Marxism-Leninism has had to be interpreted and applied by strong national leaders who understood and reflected the value systems of the traditional cultures that produced them. The personal legitimacy of these national prophets of communist ideology legitimated Marxism-Leninism where it was not imposed by force of arms. The charismatic national leader bridged the gap between national tradition and ideology. In order to claim the right to interpret Marxist-Leninist principles, each of these national leaders had to be elevated to the level of Marx and Lenin. But this elevation to godlike omniscience has not changed the fact that each has been mortal, and as each dies his personal movement must be institutionalized in the party. This dismantling of the personality cult of communist leadership is a difficult but essential process if the revolution is to outlive the revolutionary, and it has significant consequences for the future of national communism.

Contrary to the expectations of some that the deaths of Mao, Ho, and Tito would result in the collapse of their national movements, their personal power has been quite successfully institutionalized. In the past, many, including Stalin, believed that a communist movement could be denationalized by the removal of a powerful national leader. But the fact is that national sentiment is an inalienable element of communism, and though a charismatic leader is often the vehicle of that sentiment, he is not its source. The charismatic leader is essential to establish the connection in the popular mind between national tradition and communist ideology, but he is not essential to the long-term survival of national communism. The institutionalization of national communism gives it a stability and permanence that it can never attain under personalistic leadership. Institutionalized national communism is less volatile, less dynamic, and less personal, but it is no less national. Maoism was Chinese communism, but Chinese communism is not necessarily Maoism. Similarly, Titoism was one form that Yugoslavian communism could take and Hoism was a form of Vietnamese communism, but each was only one form among numerous possibilities consistent with their national cultures. In short, though some sinification of Marxism was inevitable, Maoism was not. In fact, as communism becomes depersonalized, it is likely to reflect a broader range of national values than it can under a charismatic leader.

What is likely to result from the passing of the overpowering figures is more "national" national communism: national communism that is the product of collective experience rather than of a single individual's interpretation of that experience. By virtue of the fact that postcharismatic national communism is less idiosyncratic, it is likely to have broader appeal. In addition, the transfer of power from one generation to the next is less destabilizing in systems that are not identified with a single personality.

The nationalization of communism will also affect how future communist revolutions will be received in the communist world. Specifically, the nationalization of communism means that the communist powers no longer view Marxist-Leninist revolutions or post-revolutionary transformations as necessarily positive developments. The idea that either the USSR or China supports *all* communist revolution is a myth born of the confusion between the power of a particular communist state and the dynamism of communism in general. Although it is unlikely that Moscow or Beijing would openly repudiate the revolutionary efforts of a self-proclaimed Marxist-Leninist movement, either's enthusiasm for any revolution oriented toward the other would undoubtedly be reserved.

Support for any revolutionary movement by one of the communist powers requires careful analysis of potential risks and benefits. Quite simply, it may be more in a communist power's national interest to deal with a noncommunist, nonaligned state than with a communist state aligned with a national adversary. The fact that Soviet-French relations, for example, were generally better in the 1970s than Soviet-Chinese or even Soviet-Romanian relations must certainly have some influence on Soviet calculations as to how beneficial a communist victory in France would be to Soviet interests and how far Moscow would be willing to go to bring such a victory about.

Successful communist revolutions, as Indochinese experience confirms, require substantial support from communist powers, but these powers may calculate that state-to-state relations may be less costly than party-to-party obligations, and that the risks involved in promoting communist revolution may outweigh the benefits. Does the Soviet Union, for instance, need any more Albanias, Chinas, Kampucheas, or Romanias? Does China need any more Vietnams? Thus, the likelihood that the Soviet Union or China will lend massive support to communist national liberation movements in the future is not very great. However, Cuba, with very little to lose and much to gain by asserting its influence in the Third World, can be expected to continue to lend primarily military support to national liberation movements. Castro's personal prestige, now that he has been brought to heel within the Soviet bloc, depends on his ability to project the image of the leader of the antiimperialist, "nonaligned" movement. The fact that Cuba is a small former colony without great-power potential could make the universalization of the Castroist model less threatening and more acceptable to Third World leaders. The major drawback of Castroism remains the fact that it has largely failed and Cuba is heavily influenced by Soviet policy. Thus, while Castro is likely to continue to cultivate an image of independence and assert leadership in the national liberation movement, it is unlikely that he will have significant impact.

Communism has survived because it has been national, and its continued survival depends on how successfully it can maintain this national impulse under changing conditions. The real question is not whether communism will survive but how long the myth of communism as an immutable universal ideology that transcends national distinctions will persist. That form of communism never existed, and those who view national communism as a transformation of Marxism-Leninism are wrong. The myth of monolithic communism has been perpetrated by Marxists who have tried to use communist ideology as a means to extend their own nations' power, as well as by anticommunists who have tried to use the threat of communism to enhance the power of their nations. That myth will become increasingly less tenable with the growing realization that communism has been, is, and always will be national communism.

SUGGESTIONS FOR FURTHER READING

Kaplan, Morton, ed. *The Many Faces of Communism.* New York: Free Press, 1978.
Rakowska-Harmstone, Teresa, ed. *Perspectives for Change in Communist Societies.* Boulder, Colo.: Westview Press, 1979.
Wesson, Robert. *The Aging of Communism.* New York: Praeger Publishers, 1980.
Ulam, Adam. *The Unfinished Revolution: Marxism and Communism in the Modern World.* rev. ed. Boulder, Colo.: Westview Press, 1979.

Notes

NOTES TO CHAPTER 1

1. Milovan Djilas, *The New Class* (New York: Praeger Publishers, 1957), p. 181.

2. Ibid., p. 174.

3. Ibid., p. 190.

4. Zbigniew Brzezinski, *The Soviet Bloc: Unity and Conflict* (Cambridge: Harvard University Press, 1960), p. 62.

5. Thomas T. Hammond, "The Origins of National Communism," *The Virginia Quarterly Review* 34 (Spring 1958): 277–78.

6. Peter F. Sugar, "External and Domestic Roots of Eastern European Nationalism," in *Nationalism in Eastern Europe,* ed. Peter F. Sugar and Ivo J. Lederer (Seattle: University of Washington Press, 1969), p. 4.

7. Switzerland and Belgium are examples of multilingual states; and the United States, Canada, and England are examples of different nations using the same language.

8. K. R. Minogue, *Nationalism* (Baltimore: Penguin Books, 1967), p. 120.

9. Ibid., p. 124.

10. Ibid., p. 25.

11. Scholarly opinion is virtually unanimous that nationalism assumed its modern form after the French Revolution. See, for example, Hans Kohn, *The Idea of Nationalism: A Study of Its Origins and Background* (New York: Macmillan Company, 1944); Louis L. Snyder, *The Meaning of Nationalism* (New Brunswick, N.J.: Rutgers University Press, 1954); Elie Kedourie, *Nationalism* (London: Hutchinson & Co. Ltd., 1960); and Minogue, *Nationalism.*

12. Kohn, *Idea of Nationalism,* p. 4.

13. Minogue, *Nationalism,* p. 134.

14. Carlton Hayes, *Nationalism: A Religion* (New York: Macmillan Company, 1960).

15. Kohn, *Idea of Nationalism,* p. 16.

16. For a more complete consideration of the relationship between nationalism and liberalism, see Minogue, *Nationalism*, pp. 133–38.

17. Snyder, *Meaning of Nationalism*, p. 11.

18. Ibid., pp. 16–17.

19. Kohn, *Idea of Nationalism*, p. 16.

20. Ibid., p. 15.

21. Minogue, *Nationalism*, p. 147.

22. John H. Kautsky, "Comparative Communism Versus Comparative Politics," *Studies in Comparative Communism* 6 (Spring–Summer 1973): 135–170. See also his *Communism and the Politics of Development* (New York: John Wiley, 1968) and *The Political Consequences of Modernization* (New York: John Wiley, 1972).

23. Kautsky, "Comparative Communism," p. 141.

24. Ibid., p. 147.

25. Richard Lowenthal, "Development vs. Utopia in Communist Policy," in *Change in Communist Systems*, ed. Chalmers Johnson (Stanford: Stanford University Press, 1970), pp. 33–116.

26. Ibid., pp. 48–49.

27. Emile Ader, *Communism: Contemporary and Classic* (Woodbury, N.Y.: Barron's Educational Series, Inc., 1970), pp. 18–23.

28. Chalmers Johnson, "Comparing Communist Nations," in *Change in Communist Systems*, ed. Chalmers Johnson (Stanford: Stanford University Press, 1970), pp. 27–28.

29. Richard C. Gripp, *The Political System of Communism* (New York: Dodd, Mead & Company, 1973), p. 16.

30. Kautsky, "Comparative Communism," p. 156n.

31. Minogue, *Nationalism*, p. 155.

32. Frances Hill, "Nationalist Millenarians and Millenarian Nationalists," *American Behavioral Scientist* 16 (November–December 1972): 275.

33. Minogue, *Nationalism*, p. 32.

Notes to Chapter 2

1. Milovan Djilas, *The New Class* (New York: Praeger Publishers, 1957), p. 190.

2. See, for example, Bertrand Russell, *Freedom Versus Organization, 1814–1914* (New York: W. W. Norton & Company, Inc., 1934), p. 213; Elliot Goodman, *The Soviet Design for a World State* (New York: Columbia University Press, 1960), pp. 1–25; Joseph Petrus, "Marx and Engels on the National Question," *Journal of Politics* 33 (August 1971): 797–825; and V. G. Kiernan, "On the Development of a Marxist Approach to Nationalism," *Science and Society* 34 (Spring 1970): 92–98.

3. Max Nomad, "Marx and Bakunin," *The Hound and Horn,* April–June 1933, p. 388; and Bertram Wolfe, *Marxism: One Hundred Years in the Life of a Doctrine* (New York: Dial Press, 1965), p. 40.

4. Goodman, *Soviet Design*, p. 20.

5. Karl Marx and Friedrich Engels, "Preface to the Russian Edition of 1882 of the *Manifesto of the Communist Party,"* in *The Marx-Engels Reader,* ed. Robert Tucker (New York: W. W. Norton & Company, Inc., 1972), p. 333.

6. Ibid., p. 334. Actually this preface was in Engels's handwriting, but it was corrected by Marx and signed by both on 21 January 1882, in London. (Paul Blackstock and Bert Hoselitz, eds., *The Russian Menace to Europe* [Glencoe, Ill.: Free Press, 1952], p. 282.) This statement is also in sharp contrast to Engels's rebuke of the Russian revolutionary Peter Tkachev in 1875 for suggesting that Russia's primitive land system provided a satisfactory revolutionary base. See Friedrich Engels, "Russia and the Social Revolution," in Blackstock and Hoselitz, *Russian Menace,* pp. 203–15.

7. Accounts of the formation and development of the First International may be found in Jacques Freymond and Niklos Molnar, "The Rise and Fall of the First International," in *The Revolutionary Internationals, 1864–1943,* ed. Milorad Drachkovitch (Stanford: Stanford University Press, 1966), pp. 3–35; G.D.H. Cole, *A History of Socialist Thought,* vol. 2: *Socialist Thought: Marxism and Anarchism, 1850–1890* (London: Macmillan and Co. Ltd., 1954), Chapters 6, 7; and Wolfe, *Marxism,* Chapter 14.

8. Letter from Marx to Engels, 4 November 1864, in *Marxist Library,* vol. 29: *Selected Correspondence, 1846–1895: Karl Marx and Friedrich Engels,* trans. Donna Torr (New York: International Publishers, 1942), p. 161 (hereafter cited as *Selected Correspondence*).

9. Ibid., p. 162.

10. Letter from Marx to Engels, 4 November 1864, in Marx and Engels, *Selected Correspondence,* p. 163. It is not at all surprising that Engels responded with the greatest admiration for his friend's political acumen in the IWMA affair, commenting that it "must have been a real sleight of hand." By way of absolving Marx, Engels concluded, "But it is all to the good that we are once more in contact with people who are at least the representatives of their class." (Freymond and Molnar, "First International," p. 26.)

11. Karl Marx, "Inaugural Address of the Working Men's International Association," in Tucker, *Marx-Engels Reader,* pp. 379–80.

12. Karl Marx and Friedrich Engels, *Selected Correspondence,* ed. S. W. Ryazanskaya, 3rd ed. (Moscow: Progress Publishers, 1975), p. 139.

13. As a brief sampling: French socialists were often referred to as *crapauds* (toads) and chauvinists. The dark-complexioned German socialist leader Lassalle was called "the little brown Jew" and even "the Jewish nigger." The anarchist Bakunin was accused by Marx of being a Russian agent who had informed on Polish revolutionaries even after the facts proved otherwise. Scandinavian nationalism came under attack for promoting the "old Nordic nationality," which expressed itself, according to Marx, "in brutality towards women, chronic drunkenness, and teary sentimentality alternating with berserk fury." Some Slavic nations were considered to be "ruins of people," and there was a strong anti-Semitic tinge to many of Marx's earlier references to Jews.

In fairness, however, it should be noted that everyone in the Marx family had a nickname and Karl's was "Moor," a reference to his dark complexion. Therefore it may be assumed that these epithets were not always pejorative.

14. James Guillaume, *Karl Marx: Pangermaniste* (Paris: Librairie Armand Colin, 1915), p. iii.

15. Tucker, *Marx-Engels Reader,* p. 350.

16. Solomon Bloom, *The World of Nations: A Study of the National Implications in the Work of Karl Marx* (New York: Columbia University Press, 1941), p. 194.

17. Ibid.

18. Ibid., p. 195.

19. Russell, *Freedom Versus Organization,* p. 215.

20. Bloom, *World of Nations,* p. 204.

21. Ibid., p. 211.

22. Petrus, "National Question," p. 811.

23. Ibid., p. 809.

24. Tucker, *Marx-Engels Reader,* p. 344.

25. Ibid., p. 390.

26. Bloom, *World of Nations,* p. 207.

27. For the details of what Bertram Wolfe called Marx's "skillful and remorseless intrigue" in this affair, see Franz Mehring, *Karl Marx* (New York: Covici, Friede, 1935), p. 233; and Gustav Mayer, *Friedrich Engels, A Biography,* 2 vols. (New York: A. A. Knopf, 1936), 2: 2.

28. Cole, *Marxism and Anarchism,* p. 163.

29. Letter from Friedrich Engels to Friedrich Sorge, 12 (and 17) September 1874, in Marx and Engels, *Selected Correspondence,* pp. 329–30.

30. Ibid., p. 330. This was the last chance for Marx, as the Second International was organized in 1889, six years after his death.

31. The willingness of the leadership of the IWMA (including Marx) to compromise on questions of national integrity within its ranks is illustrated by a series of events that involved the Belgian section of the International in 1865. According to the minutes of the first Belgian meeting, a representative of the London headquarters of the International informed the Belgians that membership cards would be issued by him in the name of the General Council. This meant that the Belgians would be forced to join the International directly, rather than as the Belgian section of the IWMA. The Belgians protested to the General Council, arguing that "Belgian workers must form an independent group and not submit to decisions of any other section. . . . The Belgian section had to take its place alongside the other national sections with its own program and statutes, it own administration—in short, its complete rights." The London Committee, of which Marx was a leading member, granted the Belgians approval to organize independently. (Freymond and Molnar, "First International," pp. 3–35.) The similarity between the Belgian statement and those made by Eastern European national communists a century later is striking.

32. Karl Marx, "Hungary and Panslavism," in Blackstock and Hoselitz, *Russian Menace,* p. 63.

33. Ibid.

34. Ibid., p. 65.

35. Karl Marx, "Poland's European Mission," in Blackstock and Hoselitz, *Russian Menace,* p. 108.

36. Bloom, *World of Nations,* pp. 36–39.

37. Ibid., p. 34.

38. Karl Marx, "The British Rule in India," *New York Daily Tribune,* 25 June 1853, cited in *Karl Marx on Colonialism and Modernization,* ed. Shlomo Avineri (New York: Doubleday & Company, Inc., 1968), pp. 76–82.

39. Marx, "British Rule in India," in Avineri, *Marx on Colonialism,* p. 89.

40. In a letter to Engels, dated 14 June 1853, Marx postulated that it was the "Mohammedans who first established the principle of 'no property in land' through the whole of Asia." (Avineri, *Marx on Colonialism,* p. 432.)

41. In the Preface to *A Contribution to the Critique of Political Economy,* in *Karl Marx: Selected Writings,* ed. David McLellan (Oxford: Oxford University Press, 1977), pp. 388–91.

42. Avineri, *Marx on Colonialism,* pp. 4–5.

43. Marx, "British Rule in India," in Avineri, *Marx on Colonialism,* p. 88.

44. Ibid., p. 89.

45. Ibid. Marx's motive for writing this is somewhat questionable in view of certain comments he made in a letter to Engels concerning the editorial policies of the *Daily Tribune* under Horace Greeley and Charles Dana. Marx asserted that "under the guise of Sismondian philanthropic socialistic anti-industrialism they represent the protectionists, i.e., the industrial bourgeoisie of America." The *Tribune*'s attacks on English colonialism seemed misdirected to Marx; hence, he decided to describe the English efforts as revolutionary. He confided to Engels that this would "be very shocking to them [Greeley and Dana]." (Letter from Karl Marx to Friedrich Engels, 14 June 1853, in Marx and Engels, *Selected Correspondence,* pp. 68–71.)

46. See Engels's response to Tkachev in Blackstock and Hoselitz, *Russian Menace,* p. 205.

47. Avineri, *Marx on Colonialism,* p. 131.

48. Marx and Engels, *Selected Correspondence,* p. 399.

49. Ibid.

50. In 1879 Vollmar wrote: "The assumption of a simultaneous victory of socialism in all cultured countries is abolutely ruled out. . . ." He concluded that the "isolated socialist state" was "not the only possibility" but "the greatest probability." Quoted in Goodman, *Soviet Design,* p. 4.

51. Ibid., p. 10.

52. It might also be argued that this same authoritarian tendency accounted for the eventual dissolution of all the subsequent Internationals as well.

53. Tucker, *Marx-Engels Reader,* p. 351.

Notes to Chapter 3

1. Stephen Garrett, "On Dealing with National Communism: The Lessons of Yugoslavia," *The Western Political Quarterly* 26 (September 1973): 529.

2. Charles C. Herod, *The Nation in the History of Marxian Thought* (The Hague: Martinus Nijhoff, 1976), p. 52.

3. Ibid., pp. 52–53.

4. Ibid., p. 24.

5. The Bund, organized in 1897, was an amalgamation of numerous Jewish socialist organizations in Russia devoted to improving economic conditions among Jewish workers.

6. Richard Pipes, *The Formation of the Soviet Union: Communism and Nationalism, 1917–1923* (Cambridge: Harvard University Press, 1954), p. 28.

7. Cited in ibid., p. 33.

8. V. I. Lenin, *Collected Works* (Moscow: Progress Publishers, 1964), 20: 19–51.

9. Pipes, *Formation of the Soviet Union*, p. 35.

10. Branko Lazitch and Milorad Drachkovitch, *Lenin and the Comintern*, vol. 1 (Stanford: Hoover Institution Press, 1972), p. 365.

11. Joseph Stalin, *Marxism and the National and Colonial Question* (New York: International Publishers, 1935), p. 8. Pipes observed that this translation is not accurate and translates it as "a historically evolved, stable community arising on the foundation of a common language." (Pipes, *Formation of the Soviet Union*, pp. 37–38.)

12. Lenin, *Collected Works*, 22: 146.

13. Lenin, *Collected Works*, 20: 45–46.

14. Ibid., p. 400.

15. Ibid.

16. Ibid., p. 29.

17. Ibid., p. 35.

18. Ibid., p. 33.

19. Ibid., p. 32.

20. Ibid., p. 403.

21. Bertram Wolfe, *Three Who Made a Revolution* (Boston: Beacon Press, 1948), p. 580.

22. Lenin, *Collected Works*, 22: 325.

23. The secessionists included the Ukraine, Belorussia, Bessarabia, Crimea, Azerbaidzhan, Armenia, and Georgia.

24. J. V. Stalin, *Sochineniia*, vol. 4 (Moscow, 1946), pp. 31–32.

25. Cited in Pipes, *Formation of the Soviet Union*, p. 111.

26. Ibid.

27. L. Trotsky, *Between Red and White* (London: Communist Party of Great Britain, 1922), p. 86.

28. Cited in Pipes, *Formation of the Soviet Union*, p. 111.

29. Ibid., p. 112.

30. J. V. Stalin, *Collected Works*, vol. 3 (Moscow: Foreign Languages Publishing House, 1955), pp. 32–33.

31. Cited in Pipes, *Formation of the Soviet Union*, p. 245.

32. For example, he supported Germany in the Franco-Prussian War.

33. Cited in Julius Braunthal, *History of the International,* vol. 2 (New York: Praeger Publishers, 1967), p. 48.

34. Braunthal, *History of the International,* p. 49.

35. For the complete text of the "Twenty-One Points" see Braunthal, *History of the International,* pp. 537–42.

36. Ibid., p. 542.

37. Lazitch, *Lenin and the Comintern,* p. 67.

38. G. Zinoviev, "Vistas of the Proletarian Revolution," *The Communist International* 1 (May, 1919): 39–44.

39. Demetrio Boersner, *The Bolsheviks and the National and Colonial Question* (Geneva: Libraire E. Droz, 1957), p. 12.

40. Ibid., p. 96.

41. Ibid., p. 121.

42. Cited in Pipes, *Formation of the Soviet Union,* pp. 261–62.

43. Boersner, *The Bolsheviks and the National Question,* p. 123.

44. By that time Stalin was General Secretary of the Russian Communist Party.

45. M. N. Roy, *Memoirs* (Bombay: Allied Publishers, 1964), p. 346.

46. Cited in Lazitch, *Lenin and the Comintern,* p. 388.

47. Ibid.

48. Ibid., p. 387.

49. Ibid., p. 395.

50. Ibid., p. 396.

51. Ibid.

52. Lenin, *Collected Works,* 20: 405.

53. Braunthal, *History of the International,* p. 541.

54. Stalin, *Marxism and the National Question,* p. 103.

55. Ibid., p. 106.

56. Ibid., p. 150.

57. Ibid., p. 168.

58. See, for example, Moshe Lewin, *Lenin's Last Struggle,* trans. A. M. Sheridan Smith (New York: Pantheon Books, 1968).

59. Cited in ibid., p. 148.

60. Cited in ibid., p. 52.

61. Cited in ibid., p. 53.

62. Cited in Pipes, *Formation of the Soviet Union,* p. 283.

63. Cited in Lewin, *Lenin's Last Struggle,* p. 84.

64. Cited in ibid., p. 99.

65. Cited in ibid., p. 101.

66. Cited in ibid., p. 102.

67. Ibid., p. 103.

68. Robert Wesson, *The Russian Dilemma* (New Brunswick, N.J.: Rutgers University Press, 1974), p. 15.

69. Ibid., p. 79.

70. Stalin, *Marxism and the National Question,* p. 147.

71. Robert Tucker, *Stalin as Revolutionary: 1879–1929* (New York: W. W. Norton & Company, Inc., 1973).

72. Cited in ibid., p. 310.
73. Cited in ibid., p. 371.
74. Ibid., p. 394.
75. Stalin, *Marxism and the National Question*, p. 78.
76. Cited in Tucker, *Stalin*, p. 379.
77. Ibid., p. 383.
78. Cited in ibid., p. 384.
79. Cited in ibid., p. 387.
80. Lenin, *Collected Works*, 22: 346.
81. Lenin, *Collected Works*, 19: 175.

NOTES TO CHAPTER 4

1. For a brief description of Cominform, see Witold Sworakowski, ed., *World Communism: A Handbook, 1918–1965* (Stanford: Hoover Institution Press, 1973), pp. 76–78.
2. Ibid., p. 507.
3. *Political Report of the Central Committee of the Communist Party of Yugoslavia*, Report to the Fifth Congress of the KPJ, by Josip Broz Tito (Belgrade, 1948), p. 117.
4. Dennison Rusinow, *The Yugoslav Experiment: 1948–1974* (Berkeley: University of California Press, 1977), p. 22.
5. Hoxha of Albania, while independent of Moscow, was dependent on Tito and is excluded for that reason.
6. This correspondence was subsequently made public by the Yugoslavs and has been published as *The Soviet-Yugoslav Controversy, 1948–58: A Documentary Record*, ed. Robert Hugo Bass (New York: Prospect Books, 1959). Stalin's 27 March letter referred to "answers of March 18 and 20." This indicates that Stalin wrote to Tito before the advisers were withdrawn. The original letter, if it existed, and Tito's response of 18 March have not yet been made public. The official documentary record published by the Yugoslavs begins with Tito's 20 March letter. There is undoubtedly a self-serving element to this editorial decision, but it is impossible to infer the content of the alleged earlier letters. Certainly, they could not have differed substantially in tone or content from those available.
7. Although the Soviet letters were officially signed "CC of the CPSU" they unquestionably expressed Stalin's position.
8. *Soviet-Yugoslav Controversy*, p. 9.
9. Ibid., p. 10. Trotsky, of course, was expelled from the USSR and eventually assassinated by Stalin's agents in 1940.
10. Ibid., p. 12.
11. Ibid.
12. Cited in Vladimir Dedijer, *Tito* (New York: Simon & Schuster, 1953), p. 338.
13. Ibid., p. 316.
14. Ibid.

15. Ibid., p. 320.

16. Kardelj was so shaken by the confrontation that he signed the document on the line reserved for Molotov by mistake and had to return the following day to sign a redrawn copy in the correct place.

17. Cited in Dedijer, *Tito,* p. 342.

18. Cited in ibid., p. 328.

19. Rusinow, *Yugoslav Experiment,* p. 33.

20. Ibid., p. 52.

21. Cited in ibid., p. 50.

22. Cited in ibid., p. 52.

23. *Soviet-Yugoslav Controversy,* p. 15.

24. Ibid., p. 41.

25. Ibid., p. 45.

26. For a complete discussion of this relationship, see John C. Campbell, *Tito's Separate Road: America and Yugoslavia in World Politics* (New York: Harper & Row Publishers, Inc., 1967), pp. 14–29.

27. Milovan Djilas, *The Unperfect Society: Beyond the New Class* (New York: Harcourt, Brace & World, Inc., 1969), p. 187.

28. Ibid., p. 185.

29. Milovan Djilas, *Conversations with Stalin* (New York: Harcourt, Brace & World, Inc., 1962), p. 129.

30. Ghita Ionescu, *The Breakup of the Soviet Empire in Eastern Europe* (London: Penguin Books, 1965), pp. 26–27.

31. W. Gomulka, "United We Are Strong," *Nowe Drogi* 1 (January–February 1947): 12.

32. Ibid.

33. Nicholas Bethell, *Gomulka: His Poland His Communism* (London: Penguin Books, 1972), p. 142.

34. Cited in ibid., p. 148.

35. Many victims of the purges were Jewish, and the Stalinist campaign had taken on a definite anti-Semitic air climaxed by the alleged "Doctor's Plot" against Stalin in 1953.

36. Cited in Francois Fejto, *A History of the People's Democracies: Eastern Europe Since Stalin,* trans. Daniel Weissbort (New York: Praeger Publishers, 1971), p. 8.

37. Nissan Oren, *Revolution Administered: Agrarianism and Communism in Bulgaria* (Baltimore: Johns Hopkins University Press, 1973), p. 108.

38. Ibid.

39. Fejto, *History of People's Democracies,* p. 20.

40. *Soviet-Yugoslav Controversy,* p. 57.

41. "Announcement of the Dissolution of the Information Bureau of the Communist and Workers Parties," *Current Digest of the Soviet Press (CDSP)* 8 (30 May 1956): 6.

42. Ibid.

43. "Declaration on Relations Between the Yugoslav League of Communists and the Communist Party of the Soviet Union," in *National Communism and Popular Revolt in Eastern Europe: A Selection of Documents*

on Events in Poland and Hungary, February–November 1956, ed. Paul Zinner (New York: Columbia University Press, 1956), p. 13.

44. Zinner, *National Communism and Popular Revolt*, p. 107.

45. All quotations attributed to Ochab are from his address to a party conference on 6 April 1956 in Zinner, *National Communism and Popular Revolt*, pp. 81–82.

46. "Bulletin on the Poznan Incidents," *Trybuna Ludu*, 29 June 1956, in Zinner, *National Communism and Popular Revolt*, pp. 145–86.

47. Ibid.

48. Zinner, *National Communism and Popular Revolt*, pp. 143–44.

49. Bethell, *Gomulka*, pp. 197–99.

50. Ibid., p. 210.

51. Ibid., p. 212.

52. Ibid., p. 210.

53. "Address by Wladyslaw Gomulka Before the Central Committee of the Polish United Workers Party, October 20, 1956," in Zinner, *National Communism and Popular Revolt*, p. 208.

54. Ibid., pp. 226–27.

55. "Address by the First Secretary of the Polish United Workers Party, Gomulka, Before a National Conference of Party Activists, November 4, 1956," in Zinner, *National Communism and Popular Revolt*, p. 292.

56. Ibid., p. 301.

57. "Letter from Imre Nagy to the Central Committee of the Hungarian Workers Party Seeking Reinstatement," in Zinner, *National Communism and Popular Revolt*, p. 387.

58. "Communique on Talks Held Between Representatives of the Yugoslav League of Communists and the Hungarian Workers Party," in Zinner, *National Communism and Popular Revolt*, pp. 399–401.

59. Ferenc Vali, *Rift and Revolt in Hungary: Nationalism Versus Communism* (Cambridge: Harvard University Press, 1961), p. 276.

60. "Proclamation by Imre Nagy on the Restoration of a Multi-Party System and a Coalition Government," in Zinner, *National Communism and Popular Revolt*, p. 454.

61. "Address by Imre Nagy, Chairman of the Council of Ministers, October 31, 1956," in Zinner, *National Communism and Popular Revolt*, p. 459.

62. "Telegram from . . . Nagy, to the Secretary General of the United Nations," in Zinner, *National Communism and Popular Revolt*, p. 463.

63. "Radio Address to the Nation by Imre Nagy Proclaiming the Neutrality of Hungary," in Zinner, *National Communism and Popular Revolt*, p. 464.

64. "The Formation of a New Party: Radio Address to the Nation by Janos Kadar . . . ," in Zinner, *National Communism and Popular Revolt*, p. 466.

65. "Statement by Imre Nagy Announcing an Attack by Soviet Forces on the Hungarian Government," in Zinner, *National Communism and Popular Revolt*, p. 472.

66. "Formation of the Hungarian Revolutionary Worker-Peasant Government," in Zinner, *National Communism and Popular Revolt,* p. 473.

67. "Address by . . . Tito, Before a Meeting of League Members, November 11, 1956," in Zinner, *National Communism and Popular Revolt,* p. 529.

68. "To Consolidate Further the Forces of Socialism on the Basis of Marxist-Leninist Principles," *Pravda,* 23 November 1956, in Zinner, *National Communism and Popular Revolt,* p. 543.

69. Ibid., p. 544.

70. Translated in *CDSP* 9 (1 January 1958): 5.

71. Ibid.

72. Ibid.

73. Ibid., pp. 5–6.

74. Cited in H. Gordon Skilling, *Czechoslovakia's Interrupted Revolution* (Princeton: Princeton University Press, 1976), p. 159.

75. Ibid., p. 169.

76. Ibid., p. 166.

77. Ibid., p. 624.

78. "Czechoslovak Communist Party Action Programme," in *Eastern Europe Since Stalin,* ed. Jonathan Steele (Newton Abbot, England: David & Charles, 1974), p. 162.

79. Ibid., p. 163.

80. Ibid.

81. Translated in *Reprints from the Soviet Press* 6 (17 May 1968): 3–27.

82. Ibid.

83. Cited in Skilling, *Interrupted Revolution,* p. 663.

84. Ibid., p. 670.

85. *Pravda,* 21 August 1968, p. 1; translated in *CDSP* 20 (11 September 1968): 3.

86. Ibid.

87. *Pravda,* 14 August 1968, pp. 3–4; translated in *CDSP* 20 (4 September 1968): 3–5.

88. Ibid., p. 3.

89. Ibid.

90. Ibid.

91. Ibid., p. 4.

92. Ibid.

93. *Pravda,* 18 August 1968, p. 4; translated in *CDSP* 20 (4 September 1968): 10–11.

94. Ibid., p. 10.

95. *Pravda,* 20 August 1968, p. 4; translated in *CDSP* 20 (4 September 1968): 13–14.

96. Ibid., p. 13.

97. Ibid.

98. Ibid., p. 14. The reference is to an organization of Sudeten Germans headquartered in West Germany.

99. *Pravda,* 26 September 1968, p. 4; translated in *CDSP* 20 (16 October 1968): 10–12.

100. *Pravda,* 13 November 1968, pp. 1–2; translated in *CDSP* 20 (4 December 1968): 4.

101. *CDSP* 20 (16 October 1968): 10.

102. Ibid., p. 11.

103. Ibid., p. 12.

104. *CDSP* 20 (4 December 1968): 4.

105. Trond Gilberg, "Ceausescu's Romania," *Problems of Communism* 23 (July-August 1974): 29–30.

106. For a complete account of this maneuver see Stephen Fischer-Galati, *Twentieth Century Romania* (New York: Columbia University Press, 1970), pp. 166–67.

107. For a discussion of the economic aspects of this plan and its effects on Romania see John Montias, *Economic Development in Communist Romania* (Cambridge: M.I.T. Press, 1967), pp. 205–30.

108. Cited in Montias, *Economic Development,* p. 216.

109. Fischer-Galati, *Romania,* p. 178.

110. In Steele, *Eastern Europe,* pp. 125–26.

111. Ibid.

112. Cited in George Schöpflin, "Rumanian Nationalism," *Survey* 20 (Spring-Summer 1974): 92.

113. Schöpflin, "Rumanian Nationalism," p. 113.

114. Cited in ibid., p. 119.

115. This theory is put forth in Montias, *Economic Development,* p. 205.

116. Aurel Braun, *Romanian Foreign Policy Since 1965* (New York: Praeger Publishers, 1978), pp. 24–25.

117. Ibid., p. 173.

118. Cited in ibid., p. 17.

119. *New York Times,* 31 August 1980, p. 16.

120. Ibid.

121. *Izvestia,* 5 April 1981; translated in *Radio Liberty Research Bulletin (RLRB)* 146/81 (6 April 1981): 3.

122. *Pravda,* 15 July 1981, p. 5; translated in *CDSP* 33 (26 August 1981): 6–7.

123. *RLRB* 373/81 (19 September 1981): 1–2.

124. Ibid., p. 2.

125. *Pravda,* 13 October 1981, p. 4; translated in *CDSP* 33 (11 November 1981): 8.

126. *New York Times,* 13 December 1981, p. 8.

127. Ionescu, *Breakup,* p. 130.

128. Santiago Carillo, *Eurocommunism and the State* (Westport, Conn.: Lawrence Hill & Co., 1978).

129. Ibid., p. 154.

130. Ibid., p. 19.

131. *New York Times,* 1 July 1976, p. 12.

132. For a discussion of this decision, see Eusabio Mujal-Leon, "The

PCE [Communist Party of Spain] in Spanish Politics," *Problems of Communism* 27 (July-August 1978): 15–37.

133. Richard Lowenthal, "Moscow and the 'Eurocommunists,'" *Problems of Communism* 27 (July-August 1978): 47.

134. Jean-Francois Revel, *The Totalitarian Temptation,* trans. David Hapgood (New York: Penguin Books, 1978), p. 311.

135. *New York Times,* 1 July 1976, p. 12.

136. Ibid.

137. Ibid.

138. Cited in Franco Ferrarotti, "The Italian Communist Party and Eurocommunism," in *The Many Faces of Communism,* ed. Morton Kaplan (New York: Free Press, 1978), p. 60.

139. *New York Times,* 1 July 1976, p. 12.

140. Ibid.

NOTES TO CHAPTER 5

1. John Kautsky, *Political Change in Underdeveloped Countries* (New York: John Wiley and Sons, Inc., 1962), p. 69.

2. Ibid., p. 37.

3. S. N. Eisenstadt, "The Patterns of Incorporation of Different Dimensions of Socialist Tradition," in *Socialism and Tradition,* ed. S. N. Eisenstadt and Yael Azmon (Jerusalem: Van Leer Jerusalem Foundation, 1975), pp. 221–27.

4. Ibid., p. 223.

5. Ibid., p. 224.

6. Chalmers A. Johnson, *Peasant Nationalism and Communist Power: The Emergence of Revolutionary China, 1937–1945* (Stanford, California: Stanford University Press, 1962).

7. Although the Japanese entered Manchuria in 1931, the outbreak of full-scale hostilities between Chinese and Japanese forces did not begin until 1937.

8. Johnson, *Peasant Nationalism,* p. 4.

9. Ibid., p. 7.

10. Chalmers Johnson, "Peasant Nationalism Revisited: The Biography of a Book," *China Quarterly* 71 (September 1977): 766–85.

11. See, for example, Benjamin Schwarz's review of Johnson's book in *China Quarterly* 15 (July 1963): 166–71; Stuart Schram, *Mao Tse-tung* (London: Penguin Books, 1966), p. 203n; and Donald Gillin, "'Peasant Nationalism' in the History of Chinese Communism," *Journal of Asian Studies* 23 (February 1964): 268–89.

12. Schram, *Mao Tse-tung,* p. 203n.

13. Gillin, "History of Chinese Communism," p. 277.

14. Johnson, *Peasant Nationalism,* p. 27.

15. Ibid.

16. Ibid., p. 29.

17. Ibid., p. 28.

18. Ibid., p. 177.

19. For a general review of Sun's ideas, see Harold Hinton, *An Introduction to Chinese Politics,* 2nd ed. (New York: Holt, Rinehart and Winston/ Praeger, 1977), p. 19.

20. Mao Zedong, "A Study of Physical Education," *Hsin Ch'ing-Nien* (April 1917), translated in Stuart Schram, *The Political Thought of Mao Tse-tung,* rev. ed. (New York: Praeger Publishers, 1969), pp. 152–53.

21. For pertinent excerpts of this report see Schram, *Political Thought of Mao,* pp. 250–59.

22. Cited in Stuart Schram, ed., *Mao Tse-tung Unrehearsed* (London: Penguin Books, 1974), p. 271.

23. Schram, *Mao Tse-tung,* p. 86.

24. Schram, *Political Thought of Mao,* p. 30.

25. Cited in ibid., p. 172.

26. Cited in Richard Starr, "Marxism and the Political Legacy of Mao Tse-tung," *International Journal* 32 (Winter 1976–77): 155.

27. Mao Zedong, *On New Democracy* (Peking: Foreign Languages Press, 1954).

28. Winberg Chai, *The Foreign Relations of the People's Republic of China* (New York: Capricorn Books, 1972), p. 21.

29. Mao Zedong, *On New Democracy,* p. 56.

30. Ibid., p. 58.

31. Ibid., pp. 54–55.

32. Ibid., p. 24.

33. Ibid.

34. Ibid., pp. 24–25.

35. Ibid., p. 27.

36. Ibid., p. 80.

37. Ibid., p. 82.

38. Ibid., p. 81.

39. Mao did theorize at some length on the problem of contradictions in socialist society. However, his distinctions between antagonistic and nonantagonistic contradictions were not original, having been introduced by Lenin and developed by several Soviet theoreticians. See Arthur A. Cohen, *The Communism of Mao Tse-tung* (Chicago: University of Chicago Press, 1963), pp. 139ff.

40. James Townsend, *Politics in China,* 2nd ed. (Boston: Little, Brown and Company, 1980), p. 76.

41. Mark Selden, ed., *The People's Republic of China: A Documentary History of Revolutionary Change* (New York: Monthly Review Press, 1979), p. 16.

42. Mao Zedong, "Some Questions Concerning Methods of Leadership," *Selected Readings from the Works of Mao Tse-tung* (Peking: Foreign Languages Press, 1971), p. 290.

43. For a general discussion of the Great Leap Forward see Hinton, *Introduction to Chinese Politics,* pp. 37–55.

44. Mao's admissions of culpability were made in his speech at the Lushan Conference, 23 July 1959. Pertinent sections are translated in Selden, *People's Republic,* pp. 480–82.

45. Schram, *Political Thought of Mao,* p. 60.

46. Michel Oksenberg, "Mao's Policy Commitments, 1921–1976," *Problems of Communism* 25 (November-December 1976): 2.

47. Ibid., p. 24.

48. *Facts on File,* 41, 2120 (3 July 1981): 450.

49. *Keesings Contemporary Archives,* 27 (1981): 30948.

50. Lucien Bianco, "'Fu-Chiang' and Red Fervor," *Problems of Communism* 23 (September-October 1974): 2–9.

51. For a discussion of the Sino-Soviet conflict see Harold Hinton, *The Sino-Soviet Confrontation: Implications for the Future* (New York: Crane, Russak and Company, Inc., 1976); Donald Zagoria, *The Sino-Soviet Conflict, 1956–1961* (Princeton: Princeton University Press, 1962); and William Griffith, *The Sino-Soviet Rift* (Cambridge, Mass.: M.I.T. Press, 1964).

52. Evidence of demaoization has accelerated with each passing year since Mao's death. In the summer of 1980 the Chinese leadership began a campaign to remove Mao's pictures from public places in its continuing efforts to dismantle the Mao personality cult.

53. Chalmers Johnson, "Building a Communist Nation in China," in *The Communist Revolution in Asia: Tactics, Goals, and Achievements,* ed. Robert Scalapino, 2nd ed. (Englewood Cliffs, N. J.: Prentice-Hall, Inc., 1969), p. 80.

54. Robert Scalapino, "Communism in Asia: Toward a Comparative Analysis," in Scalapino, *Communist Revolution,* p. 46.

55. "Chairman Mao Zedong's Statement Calling upon the People of the World to Unite. . . ," *Peking Review,* no. 33 (16 August 1963): 7.

56. Ho Chi Minh, "The Path Which Led Me to Leninism," *L'Echo du Vietnam,* July 1960, cited in Jean Lacoutre, *Ho Chi Minh: A Political Biography* (New York: Vintage Books, 1968), p. 31.

57. Ibid.

58. Lacoutre, *Ho Chi Minh,* p. 75.

59. Ibid.

60. Ibid.

61. Le Duan, "All United to Build the Unified Socialist Fatherland of Vietnam," *Hoc Tap,* July 1976, p. 28, cited in William Turley, "Vietnam Since Reunification," *Problems of Communism* 26 (March-April 1977): 36.

62. *Hoc Tap,* September 1966, cited in John Donnell and Melvin Gurtov, "North Vietnam," in Scalapino, *Communist Revolution,* p. 159.

63. There is considerable disagreement as to the true identity of Kim Il Sung. Whether he is the popular bandit-hero who operated against the Japanese or someone who merely adopted the name is open to question.

64. Robert Scalapino and Chong-Sik Lee, *Communism in Korea* (Berkeley, Calif.: University of California Press, 1972).

65. Chong-Sik Lee, "Stalinism in the East: Communism in North Korea," in Scalapino, *Communist Revolution,* p. 121.

66. Kim Il Sung, *Selected Works,* vol. 1 (Pyongyang: Foreign Languages Publishing House, 1963), pp. 315–16.

67. Ibid., p. 326.

68. Kim Il Sung, "The Present Situation and the Task Confronting Our Party," *The Pyongyang Times,* no. 41, 13 October 1966, p. 12.

69. Herbert Matthews, *Revolution in Cuba: An Essay in Understanding* (New York: Charles Scribner's Sons, 1975), p. 231.

70. Ibid.

71. Andrew Suarez, *Cuba: Castroism and Communism, 1959–1966* (Cambridge, Mass.: M.I.T. Press, 1967), pp. 140–42.

72. Suarez contends that the role of the communist party in a system is the crucial criterion of whether a regime is Marxist-Leninist. Hence, since the communist party did not rule Cuba in 1966 when he wrote his book, Suarez continued to contend that Castroism was not communism. (Suarez, *Castroism and Communism,* pp. 237–41.)

73. Theodore Draper, *Castroism: Theory and Practice* (New York: Praeger Publishers, 1965), p. 49.

74. Herbert Matthews, *Fidel Castro* (New York: Simon & Schuster, 1969), p. 351.

75. Fidel Castro, "History Will Absolve Me," in *Revolutionary Struggle, 1947–1958; Volume I of the Selected Works of Fidel Castro,* ed. Roland Bonachea and Nelson Valdes (Cambridge, Mass.: M.I.T. Press, 1972), p. 171.

76. Suarez, *Castroism and Communism,* p. 32.

77. Cited in Draper, *Castroism,* p. 59.

78. W. Raymond Duncan, "Nationalism in Cuban Politics," in *Cuba, Castro, and Revolution,* ed. Jaime Suchlicki (Coral Gables, Fla.: University of Miami Press, 1972), p. 39.

79. Nita Raus Manitzas, "Cuban Ideology and Nationhood: Their Meaning in the Americas," in *Revolutionary Cuba in the World Arena,* ed. Martin Weinstein (Philadelphia: Institute for the Study of Human Issues, 1979), p. 153.

80. Draper, *Castroism,* p. 49.

81. Ibid.

82. Matthews, *Revolution in Cuba,* p. 227.

83. Ibid.

84. Ibid., pp. 228–29.

85. Ibid., pp. 227–30.

86. Ibid., p. 237.

87. Matthews, *Fidel Castro,* p. 329.

88. Cited in ibid., p. 328.

89. Draper, *Castroism,* p. 51.

90. Ibid., p. 56.

91. Matthews, *Fidel Castro,* p. 326.

92. Cited in ibid., p. 343.

93. For a complete discussion of these elements see Draper, *Castroism,* pp. 52–54, 130–33.

94. Che Guevara, *Guerrilla Warfare* (New York: Vintage Books, 1961).

95. In Martin Kenner and James Petras, eds., *Fidel Castro Speaks* (New York: Grove Press, Inc., 1969).

96. Regis Debray, *Revolution in a Revolution?* (London: Penguin Books, 1968).

97. Ibid., p. 90.

98. *Granma,* 19 March 1967, cited in William Ratliff, *Castroism and Communism in Latin America, 1959–1976* (Washington, D.C.: American Enterprise Institute, 1976), p. 33.

99. Ratliff, *Castroism and Communism,* p. 93.

100. *Pravda,* 20 November 1968; translated in *CDSP* 20 (11 December 1968): 21.

101. Cited in Draper, *Castroism,* p. 43.

102. Ibid.

103. Ibid., p. 48.

104. *Granma,* 8 September 1974, p. 3, cited in Edward Gonzalez, "Castro and Cuba's New Orthodoxy," *Problems of Communism* 25 (January-February, 1976): 5.

105. Matthews, *Fidel Castro,* pp. 318–19.

106. Draper, *Castroism,* p. 127.

107. Matthews, *Fidel Castro,* p. 321.

108. *Granma,* 5 August 1973, p. 5, cited in Gonzalez, "Cuba's New Orthodoxy," p. 5.

109. *Granma,* 10 February 1974, p. 4, cited in Gonzalez, "Cuba's New Orthodoxy," p. 13.

110. Nonalignment has many meanings. In its broadest sense it means not being allied with any of the military blocs and being neutral in the East-West competition. Within the socialist world, it can mean not being aligned with either the USSR or China in their continuing conflict. Cuba would not seem to qualify under either meaning.

111. William M. LeoGrande, "The Revolution in Nicaragua: Another Cuba?" *Foreign Affairs* 58 (Fall 1979): 28–50.

112. *New York Times,* 16 August 1981, IV, p. 2.

113. Ibid., 1 June 1981, p. 2.

114. Ibid., 23 July 1980, p. 2.

115. Ibid., 30 November 1981, p. 3.

116. Ibid., 23 July 1980, p. 2.

117. Ibid., 10 July 1979, p. 3.

118. Ibid., 26 January 1981, p. 4.

119. Ibid., 23 August 1981, p. 20.

120. Ibid., 31 January 1980, p. 3.

121. Ibid., 30 November 1981, p. 3.

122. Ibid., 9 March 1981, p. 2.

123. Ibid., 9 July 1980, p. 10.

124. Ibid., 10 July 1979, p. 3.

125. Ibid., 3 January 1980, p. 3.

126. Ibid., 9 July 1980, p. 10.

127. Ibid., 20 July 1980, p. 13.

128. Ibid., 7 September 1979, p. 3.

129. Ibid., 29 May 1981, p. 2.

130. Ibid.

131. Anwar Al-Sadat, *The Egyptian Economic and Political Review,* May-June 1961, pp. 27–28.

132. Tareq Ismael, *The Arab Left* (Syracuse, New York: Syracuse University Press, 1976), p. 10.

133. Ibid., p. 17.

134. Ibid., p. 12.

135. Abdel Said, *Arab Socialism* (New York: Harper & Row Publishers, Inc., 1972), p. 64.

136. Ibid., p. 65.

137. Ibid., p. 24.

138. Ibid., p. 28.

139. Ibid., p. 24.

140. Cited in ibid., p. 76.

141. Ibid.

142. Ibid.

143. Ibid., p. 69.

144. Ismael, *Arab Left,* p. 109.

145. Ibid.

146. Cited in Bede Onuoha, *The Elements of African Socialism* (London: Andre Deutsch, 1965), p. 34.

147. Leopold Senghor, *On African Socialism* (London: Pall Mall Press, 1964), p. vi.

148. Ibid., p. 74.

149. Cited in Fritz Schatten, *Communism in Africa* (New York: Praeger Publishers, 1966), pp. 328–29.

150. Cited in Onuoha, *African Socialism,* p. 41.

151. Cited in Onuoha, *African Socialism,* p. 40.

152. In 1977 TANU was merged with the Afro-Schirazi Party of Zanzibar. Since then Nyerere's party has been known as the Party of the Revolution (CCM).

153. Onuoha, *African Socialism,* pp. 62–66.

154. Naomi Chazan, "Myths and Realities in African Socialism," in Eisenstadt, *Socialism and Tradition,* pp. 141–68.

155. For a complete discussion of early PKI history see Leslie Palmier, *Communists in Indonesia: Power Pursued in Vain* (New York: Anchor Books, 1972).

156. Ibid., p. 105.

157. For a discussion of Sukarno's formulation of guided democracy see Jeanne Mintz, *Mohammed, Marx and Marhaen: The Roots of Indonesian Socialism* (New York: Praeger Publishers, 1965), pp. 157–64.

158. From a speech delivered in May 1953, cited in ibid., p. 165.

159. Cited in ibid., p. 168.

160. Ibid., p. 171.

161. Ibid., p. 184.

162. Ibid., p. 188.

163. Ibid.

164. Ibid., p. 190.

165. Ibid., p. 191.

166. Palmier, *Communists in Indonesia,* pp. 210–11.

167. For a full account of this episode see Antonie C. A. Drake, *In the Spirit of the Red Banteng* (The Hague: Mouton, 1973), pp. 433–35; and Rex Mortimer, *Indonesian Communism Under Sukarno* (Ithaca, N.Y.: Cornell University Press, 1974), pp. 364–99.

168. See, for example, Richard Lowenthal, *World Communism: The Disintegration of a Secular Faith* (New York: Oxford University Press, 1966).

Abbreviations

CCM	Party of the Revolution (Tanzania)
CCP	Chinese Communist Party
CDSP	*Current Digest of the Soviet Press*
CMEA Comecon	} Council for Mutual Economic Assistance
Cominform	Communist Information Bureau
Comintern	Third Communist International
COSEP	Superior Council of Private Enterprise (Nicaragua)
CPSU	Communist Party of the Soviet Union
CPY	Yugoslavian Communist Party
DRK	Democratic Republic of Korea
FSLN	Sandinist National Liberation Front
GATT	General Agreement on Trade and Tariffs
GDR	German Democratic Republic
IWMA	International Workingmen's Association
KMT	Guomindang
KPJ	Communist Party of Yugoslavia
KWP	Korean Workers' Party
MFN	Most Favored Nation
NEP	New Economic Policy
OPEC	Organization of Petroleum Exporting Countries
PCC	Communist Party of Cuba
PCE	Communist Party of Spain
PKI	Communist Party of Indonesia
PSN	Socialist Party of Nicaragua
PSP	Popular Socialist Party
PURS	United Party of the Socialist Revolution
PUWP	Polish United Workers' Party
RKP	Russian Communist Party
RSDLP	Russian Social Democratic Labor Party
RSFSR	Russian Soviet Federated Socialist Republic
SSR	Soviet Socialist Republic
TANU	Tanzanian African National Union
WTO	Warsaw Treaty Organization

Index